BRINGING UP A
HANDICAPPED CHILD

Based on hard-earned experience, this book provides
insight, humour, and useful practical information, showing
how one family has coped.

BRINGING UP A MENTALLY HANDICAPPED CHILD

It's not all tears!

by

LIZ THOMPSON

THORSONS

Wellingborough, Northamptonshire
·
Rochester, Vermont

First published 1986

© LIZ THOMPSON 1986

British Library Cataloguing in Publication Data

Thompson, Liz
  Bringing up a mentally handicapped child,
  1. Mentally handicapped children — Care and
  treatment
  I. Title
  362.3'088054   HV891

ISBN 0-7225-1253-8

Printed and bound in Great Britain

DEDICATION

This book is dedicated to James – for being there and providing the motivation.

My most grateful thanks to:

Alan Leighton, for having sufficient faith in me to have picked up the phone and asked me to do the book;

John Hart, for providing me with a room so I could write the book and retain my sanity!

Monica and Sheila for helping me with typing the final draft and thus possibly saving me from having sleepless nights!

Gladys, for helping me to marshal my thoughts in the beginning;

Bob, the caretaker at Goldie Leigh, for his unfailing help and good humour;

and, of course, all the parents I have talked to who allowed me to intrude into their lives and the professionals who allowed me to pick their brains.

Last, but not least, Neville and the boys for putting up with more chaos than usual while I made my deadline.

God love all of you.

CONTENTS

FOREWORD

The arrival of a new baby in most families is a time for considerable excitement and rejoicing. But nearly all parents question 'is the baby all right?' Unfortunately, at birth, it is not always possible to diagnose mental handicap and, even if it is, the baby's eventual intellectual and physical development will remain unknown.

The breaking of the news to parents that their child is mentally handicapped has, understandably, a shattering effect. There is disappointment and uncertainty and the question 'how will I cope?' is followed by intense periods of gloom and despair.

This book, with its positive and unsentimental approach to unique problems, will be an immense encouragement to every parent with a handicapped child. Furthermore, it provides considerable information for such parents — particularly the type of services which should be available to all. In addition, it is the story of one family's unique experience — giving insights into the personal depth of a very special human experience. I hope it will be widely read, for I am convinced it will be of value and practical assistance to many.

BRIAN RIX CBE, MA, DU
Secretary-General
MENCAP

INTRODUCTION

Almost every type of handicap you can think of now has its own specialist organization and literature to help parents to deal with that handicap. What I am aiming to demonstrate with this 'non-text book' is that a mentally-handicapped child can allow a family to lead an almost normal life (and, after all, what is normal?) and that a family can help a mentally-handicapped child to do the same.

If you are a parent or a carer you have probably decided that a mentally-handicapped child has needs and rights and you are engaged, hopefully, in establishing that neither is neglected. I have tried to cover, in the following chapters, the areas where parents and carers will have to be most vigilant in obtaining the best services for the child or adult in their care. The MENCAP Stamina Papers contained in the book are the *minimum* standards we should be requesting. Many of you will find that your local services will fall well below the required standards. The Papers cover subjects concerning ante-natal care, birth to five years, school, adult training centres, residential care (including the required services for a child or adult still at home) and the elderly mentally handicapped. I hope, when you have read them and realized that there is nothing unreasonable therein if we are to give the mentally handicapped the advantages that they are unable to seek out for themselves, you will agree that pleas of poverty by those in power who hold the purse strings are unacceptable and must not be tolerated. We are surrounded by groups of so-called normal people who are protesting and demonstrating for what they consider to be their rights. Who will speak up for our mentally-handicapped children and adults if we don't? There are many adults who have no training centre to go to; in some areas local authorities are excluding people from centres on the grounds of lack of transport, thus throwing further burdens upon parents who have either got to keep their 'adult children' at home or face taking them to the centre themselves. Every day for thirty years? Remember, many mentally-handicapped adults never reach a point of being able to travel by public transport. I do earnestly believe that the parents of young mentally-handicapped children should start now to get it right for the future.

It can be very tough indeed caring for a mentally-handicapped person and he or she will draw from you patience, unselfishness, consideration and tolerance in quantities you never dreamed you possessed. There is no easy way to come to terms with having a child who does not conform to what society considers to be 'normal'. All parents make plans for their children, however much they know that their children will end up going their own sweet way and it is devastating to have a child who not only frustrates those plans and ambitions for them almost from the moment of his or her birth but who will not even become independent of the family in the foreseeable future. It is a daunting prospect and they are courageous parents who do not, at some time (or maybe frequently), quail at the task stretching before them across the years. In my own case, James being the eldest of four boys so close in age, I tried to take each day as it came and didn't think too much about what lay ahead. Neville and I had no idea what James's potential might be (we still haven't — we still expect and get a lot from him) so each example of progress was greatly valued. When he walked, it was great, when he fed himself it was great and when he was toilet trained it was ultra-great! In case you think I'm making a big deal out of toilet training, we did have four in nappies at one time and one less was very welcome!

Mothers have a tendency, not unnaturally, to ask paediatricians: 'What will my handicapped baby do — how much will he progress?' What a loaded question that is. It's a bit like asking, at the moment of his birth, whether your normal son will get nine O-Levels! I look forward to the day when consultants will tell parents that mentally-handicapped children like theirs have walked or talked or both, and really emphasize the positive side without falsely raising the parents' hopes, rather than casting them into the depths of gloom by the grim prognostications of which they are all too fond.

I have always tried not to worry about things which I cannot alter; the trap can be in not being aware of the things you can alter. Attitudes can be altered and, as public awareness grows, so also I hope will the realization that the standards parents are seeking for their mentally-handicapped children and adults are no more than a humane and caring society should provide and provide with generosity and goodwill.

For obvious reasons this book is very much slanted towards the mentally-handicapped child at home with his or her family, and it would seem that with the current policy of care in the community, more families are going to be closely concerned with their handicapped children, whether they are at home or in a local establishment of some kind. I am sure that no one, except possibly those who have made their homes there, will regret the passing of the large subnormality hospitals. I am writing from my own experience of keeping my handicapped child at home and my main concern is to show that you can do this and stay sane. Whether or not you can keep your normal children at home (and into adulthood) and stay sane is another ball game entirely!

I have not, I hope, treated the subject too flippantly. In a 'laugh or cry' situation I have always thought it better to laugh and I hope most of you will agree with me. To illustrate this point briefly, when I was reading part of this introduction aloud one evening James was apparently listening: 'You've forgotten something,' he said. 'Oh,' I said, in some surprise. 'What's that?' 'I'm a very heavy drinker,' said James, with a most lamentable degree of satisfaction! I would hasten to inform you that his 'heavy drinking' consists of two cans of supermarket lager each evening and one visit to the pub at Sunday lunchtime. Big deal! Not really excessive for a young man of twenty-seven but how easy it would be to keep him forever a child.

I assure you that in no way do I wish to belittle the job that parents and carers are doing in looking after a handicapped child. I have always been very conscious that our 'yoke is easy' and our 'burthen light' (to quote from the Old Testament) and I duly give grateful thanks for that. Neville and I are ever mindful of the fact that many of our friends and acquaintances have children who are obsessive, hyperactive and repetitive — all characteristics which James lacks, and we are well aware of the amount of love and dedication which those parents extend to their mentally-handicapped offspring.

I would like to conclude by delving, just for a moment, into the realms of philosophy. There isn't much of it in the following pages as I have tried to concentrate on the practical, but I must make the following points. Many handicapped babies (both physically and mentally) are, as a result of medical 'progress', doomed from the womb. In addition to those babies who will never be allowed to be born there are many others who, as a result of the same progress and technology, create a question of whether or not they should be kept alive. In the past large numbers of severely malformed babies would not have survived their birth or would have lived, at the most, for a few hours — maybe minutes. The debate continues on the right of the handicapped baby to live and as, I hope, by virtue of the fact that I am writing this book, it will be clear which side of the debate I am on, I can do no better than to quote from a paper written by Professor Joan Bicknell, Professor of the Psychiatry of Mental Handicap at St George's Medical School, Tooting. She says:

> The decisions that surround the giving or witholding of treatment to a handicapped baby, are similar to those that surround the decision to switch off the life-support machine and to help on the elderly demented sick individual to a peaceful end.
>
> There are four people or groups of individuals who contribute to this decision-making process for the handicapped new-born baby. The parents, the doctors and society will view this decision each from different standpoints. The fourth and most important person in this whole affair is the one who cannot speak and cannot decide, the child himself.
>
> Doctors have always had a key role to play in these difficult decisions. Society expects doctors to become skilled in weighing up the pros and cons in every matter concerning illness, whether it be a simple matter of one drug or another for

a relatively simple illness or the more profound complex decisions about the prolongation of life in someone, for example, who is terminally ill. Most, if not all, doctors, on qualification, sign either the Hippocratic Oath or the Declaration of Geneva. The latter states: 'I will maintain the utmost respect for human life from the time of conception.'

Society has looked upon the doctor as the final arbiter when the decision is difficult and indeed many parents at times of such stress and sadness want to remove themselves from decision making and rely on the doctor and his so-called 'greater wisdom' that our society has traditionally accorded him. Given this great responsibility, doctors become used to acting 'in good faith' and making the best decisions that are possible having taken every aspect of the problem into account. In the last few years there has been a shift from this view by society that the doctor is omnipotent to the view that the sick person should be more equally involved in decision making. For the aware adult this should create no difficulty, but the equivalent for the new-born child is not, in my view, automatically the parent.

The majority of people would feel that the parent has a major role to play in the decision about whether a severely handicapped offspring should live or should be encouraged to die. However, all of us would look askance if we were saying the same thing about a new-born baby who had no handicap at all. Such a child would be rapidly taken into the care of the state and the parents regarded as wicked or perhaps mentally ill. What then is the difference between the so-called normal child and the child with a severe handicap? The fact that they are both human beings with the potential for life is obscured by nebulous ideas about quality of life, damage to the existing family and possibly life span. I feel that the similarities between the handicapped child and the normal child are far greater than these differences. It is hard to predict at birth what is the potential of a handicapped child and what his capacity for happiness is going to be. It seems dangerous, therefore, to prophesy a particular quality of life and then allow a child to die or live on such intangible evidence. Such arbitrary dividing lines are those that will creep into arguments about euthanasia and lead to value judgements about the importance of one individual as opposed to another. Already these arbitrary judgements are being made about the abortion of a handicapped foetus. If we allow this to happen, concerning the handicapped new-born, then the next step is that we will condone the 'letting die' of the mentally-handicapped child or adult because we judge that his lifestyle is not in some way satisfactory or good enough. The parental decision to allow their handicapped new-born to die must be coloured by the inadequacy of the services that we provide, as well as a feeling for the quality of life itself. The services for mentally-handicapped children and adults are far from good in this country and an organization such as MENCAP dedicates its very existence to the improvement of these services. It seems a wholly unsatisfactory short-cut to the solution of this problem if we allow children to die because the services are insufficiently developed. 'It may be morally better to press for improved social services than to bury the problem,' is Ian Kennedy's viewpoint (*The Times*, 8 September, 1981). If parents do not have the ultimate right to decide whether a child should live or not they should retain the right to decide whether they can look after the child or not, and our services for handicapped children should be so good that an alternative home system should be readily available and of such a standard that the parents find this alternative easier to accept than the death of the child.

What of society? Other societies in recent history have indulged in value judgements about the importance of various groups of human beings with disastrous results. Let us hope that we in England will never start on the slippery slope to the annihilation of the handicapped, the incompetent, the inadequate and the dependent, but rather let us together build a society that cares for those who need extra support whatever their problems, so that each human being is valued and cherished as a member of society. Our voluntary organizations often lead the statutory bodies in this development of services and attitudes. While the doctor is seen to be making the ultimate decision, it is not his own decision but the result of his own upbringing, education, personal beliefs and value judgement, many of these heavily influenced by the society that he has experienced. None of us can stand back and condone or criticize the decision made by one individual about another and neither can we hide behind the belief that it is his specialized medical training that was the only influence on the decision making. The many shades of public opinion crystallize into the decision made by that one person as consciously or unconsciously he has been influenced by the world in which he has lived, by the services that have or have not been developed and by his own experiences of the way in which society supports or rejects dependent members. All of us share in the burden of guilt which must follow when a handicapped baby is allowed to die because of the poverty of lifestyle that society will afford.

The baby himself is the most important member of this decision-making process and yet cannot, by definition, join in. For me, his right to live is unqualified. Some will live with current technology available and others will die because of the life-limiting nature of their handicap, however we intervene. For those who live we have a far less dramatic but much longer lasting challenge to provide a lifestyle that justifies his living.

I am profoundly grateful to Professor Bicknell for allowing me to use her words which put the case so much better than mine would. I should like, however, to add just a few comments of my own — and they are very personal to me. I do truly believe that there is a Higher Authority to whom we are all ultimately answerable and that that Higher Authority has the final say in any question of living or dying. We have a duty to care for the poor, the disabled, the starving and I have always thought that we will be judged — by those who will read about us in their history books as well as by God — by our actions towards these fellow human beings, whether we are in a position of power or just an ordinary person. Let us not be found wanting — whoever and wherever we are.

1

PREGNANCY AND BIRTH

A few years ago, when my son James was about ten years old, my husband Neville was manning a stall for Greenwich Society (MENCAP) at the lovely Trinity Hospital which overlooks the river Thames at Greenwich. During the course of the afternoon, Neville happened to catch James 'with his fingers in the till', so to speak. 'Hey,' he said, 'what do you think you're doing?' James gazed back at him innocently, with the 10p clutched in his sticky fist. 'It's for the handicapped,' he said, with devastating logic and went off to spend the money to which he considered he was entitled, leaving his dad speechless!

I am starting with what I think is a very funny story because I am anxious that people should not put aside this book feeling weighed down with depression and thinking that, yes, to have a handicapped child must indeed be the worst thing that could happen to you. It's not.

Let's go back to the beginning. My beginning. This took place at Leigh-on-Sea in Essex, where I was born, the third child in a family which would later be four. I have an older sister and brother and a younger sister. We lived very orderly and sedate lives, all going to the local convent schools, until 1939 when we moved, with Granny who by then lived with us, to Ilford, Essex. Nearer to London — 1939 can't have been the best time to choose to do that! (We all survived the war, ending up with a few less ceilings and windows but, thank God, all the personnel intact.) In 1940 my elder sister, Pamela, and I were sent, with the Ursuline High School which we attended, to Devizes in Wiltshire. We became evacuees. Now I am a mother myself I view the whole business of sending one's children away like that with absolute horror. I suppose the possible alternative of keeping them in London and risk them being bombed was even more horrific. It was a terrible choice for a family to have to make at that time. However, Devizes proved to be very educational for both my sister and myself. It was our first experience of country life and I still remember going to the farm at the end of the road to buy milk, virtually straight from the cow, a bring-your-own-jug set-up. Incidentally, I also got Undulant Fever from drinking untreated milk, but that is another story!

Devizes gave me my first glimpse of mental handicap. The lady next door to 'Auntie' and 'Uncle' Abrahams (lovely generous people) had a son called Stanley. We sometimes saw Stanley in the garden and very often peeping out from behind the net curtains. I never saw Stanley out with his mother or father and I don't remember anyone ever putting a name to Stanley's condition, but I think, looking back, he must have had Down's Syndrome. So I suppose it was implanted in my mind at the age of seven that a handicapped person should not be allowed to be seen. I dread to think what sort of life that boy must have had. Man. Stanley was quite grown-up when we went to Devizes. This, of course, was in the bad old days when handicapped children were locked away and looked upon as objects of shame. My parents' generation (and they weren't much older than Stanley) was not without fault in this attitude. I recently talked to a mother whose own 'Christian' father told her that her child was handicapped because of the sins of her (the child's) father. In this day and age! I don't remember having any other experience of mental handicap until we came back to London. I actually thought country people had a more prosaic attitude to it anyway, but maybe that is one of the few times that Down's people are at a disadvantage — they can't seem to be looked upon as 'simple' in the way that I have always understood country people saw their backward children.

When Pamela and I returned to London twenty months after we left, I then had to contend with the young man who lived quite near to us. This young man, Peter, was liberated. He was allowed out. To go where he liked and talk to whom he liked. Great for those days and great for Peter. Terrible for me! My fear of this harmless young man (who, by the way, was not a Down's Syndrome person) was completely prompted by ignorance. We were all ignorant in those days, but I do hope that not everyone was as frightened as I was by Peter. I remember hearing that a great friend of my parents was standing at the bus stop one day (so the story goes) in the pouring rain. Peter strolled up to Fred, who'd been waiting ages for a bus, 'Nice day,' he said affably, with his friendly grin. Fred was, hopefully, ashamed of his instinctive response to this piece of gross inaccuracy! But that is exactly what a large number of mentally-handicapped people are like. Full of uninhibited friendliness. Unfortunately we didn't talk about such things in those days. I kept all my fears to myself and even if I had attempted to discuss it at the meal table — where all our family discussions took place — nobody would have known how to put my childish fears at rest because nobody knew anything at all about the subject. Looking back, there were a couple of oddities in my own family. My grandmother, for instance, was 'unable to rear boys', we were told. My mother had a brother, Charles, who died quite young. Why? Mother's eldest sister had a daughter who had a lump on her spine when she was born; it was operated upon and Eileen was called 'slow' for the rest of her life. I would dearly love to know a little more about these things, but will have to wait until we meet up again, I suppose.

I was brought up in a fairly religious household and by that I mean that we went to Mass on Sundays, confession every fortnight, observed fasting and abstinence when necessary and the Holy Days of Obligation. Nobody, at that time, ever seemed to suggest that you went out of the house and put your religion into practice. Oh, there were various groups within the Church to which one could belong, who helped the poor families of the parish, but I do think that the Church (or my Church, at any rate) has improved its image as far as going out into the highways and byways is concerned — we are exhorted far more frequently from the pulpit these days to involve ourselves with some sort of voluntary work. I know a lot of people feel that there should be no need for voluntary organizations and that the state should be able to provide for all the needs of the handicapped and the elderly, etc., but 'caring' is an activity which extends far beyond what even a solicitous state can provide. It is also an integral part of many people's nature to render service to those less fortunate than themselves and to illustrate this I would recommend you have a look at the Gateway Clubs. They couldn't function without their young volunteers and I stress the word 'young'. We have some super kids helping in our clubs, which demonstrates that the whole subject of mental handicap is so much more out in the open now. Thinking back to my own schooldays I have absolutely no idea whether any of my friends had handicapped relatives because such things were ignored. Nobody wanted to know.

I got through school without too much disgrace and even less distinction! It was at this time that, looking back, I have to realize what a very exceptional person my father was. When I got a job, in the July I left school, I informed my future employers that I would be available to take up my post in the first week in September and then proceeded to have six weeks' holiday, a period I shall never forget. It was the summer of 1951 when the Festival of Britain was on. A whole group of us were in the same situation (presumably with similarly long-suffering parents) and my lovely dad just let me go ahead and have this last carefree six weeks without a murmur of disapprobation. I think it was also a sign of those times that we knew we were all going to get jobs, no question about that, and we were quite content to spend a penniless few weeks before taking on the ultimate cloak of adulthood. Or so it seems to me.

Five uneventful years pass by (well — uneventful in terms of my subject!) and then I went on a fateful summer holiday with my great friend Mary to Jersey, in the Channel Islands. Two days before we were due to come home I ran into a young man with whom I had worked at the insurance company where I was a shorthand typist. I had typed a few letters for him during the fairly short time he was there and we always found something to chat about. After he left I occasionally ran into him in the City but when I saw him in Jersey our paths hadn't crossed for some considerable time. I must tell you, here and now, that John was on holiday with half a dozen or so other young men from his Old Boys' rugby club. The last two days of Mary's and my holiday got quite hectic! On the last evening I found myself in the company of one Dudley (they never used their given names, for some unknown reason) and as we enjoyed each other's company greatly I wasn't too surprised when he contacted me a few days after we had all gone home. That was the beginning — Neville (Dudley) and I have now been married for 28 years and John (who is, of course, Lou to his friends) and Mary have been married for slightly less. Isn't life funny?

I had to leave Ilford, of course, when I got married, as Neville is a South Londoner. I wonder what today's feminists would make of that! We lived for five months in a flat while our house was being finished then moved to Mottingham in south-east London, where we have been ever since. My family, at least my mother, father, brother and younger sister, were in Australia (in fact Mum, Dad and Monica had gone out there to visit my brother Mike, who'd been there for several years), and my older sister, Pam, was married and still living in the environs of Ilford. I had a very emotional moment that first Christmas without my family (and no disrespect to Neville). I was six months pregnant and rather easily upset, as is the wont of pregnant ladies. The BBC — with a total lack of consideration for people in my condition and situation — put on a record of Kenneth McKellar singing 'Oh, How I'm Longing for My Ain Folk'. Well, I'm sure you can guess the rest; floods of tears and a heartfelt wish that they hadn't gone away. I also felt rather guilty as my mother had said to me, when their sailing time had been notified: 'Don't you dare get pregnant before we go!' Obviously my pregnancy was the result of Murphy's Law and nothing to do with Neville.

If everyone felt the way I did during my first pregnancy it surprises me that anyone, let alone me, ever has more than one baby. I felt ill for the whole of the nine months and I do truly believe that this had nothing whatsoever to do with James's (as he was to be) handicap. Ante-natal care in those days was brief but as thorough as they knew how and it was never, for me, an ordeal to go to the ante-natal clinic at the British Hospital for Mothers and Babies in Woolwich (or 'Ma's and Ba's', as it was known locally). We were all in the smiling care of a very nice lady called Sister Garland (with whom I renewed my acquaintance just last summer at the last Founder's Day before the hospital was closed — she didn't remember me!). All we had was a stab in the earlobe by the 'blood lady' every month, a specimen of urine at each visit and a 'test-tube' full of blood a couple of times during the whole period. No question then of aborting unwanted handicapped babies. Our family would have been the poorer if there had been that facility and if I had been the sort of person to take advantage of it.

I have to confess that I needed all the tuition I could get on the baby front. I must have been one of the most ignorant mothers to have passed through the doors of that hospital. I suppose I knew which end to put the nappy on but that was about all. Neville wasn't much better — in fact he was, of course, much worse. Girls often have a chance to practise on neighbours' babies, whereas boys wouldn't want to anyway. Actually, it was my younger sister, Monica, who wheeled out the baby neighbours, not me. I really didn't want to know.

Ante-natal care has changed terrifically now, of course. A phrase you never heard 'in my day' (and actually I don't think it's been around more than a couple of years anyway) was 'pre-conceptual nutrition'. I suspect that this is just another name for healthy living and eating but if it is going to be treated seriously it should be taught in secondary schools. I feel extremely sorry for teachers of home economics who would dearly love to instruct their pupils on the advantages of a healthy diet but know that they are battling against the ever-rising tide of convenience foods. Even my own kids howl 'hippy food' if I give them lentils! They also profess (well, not Mike) to hate wholemeal bread so I allow them one white loaf a week — between them, that is, not one each. That's what I call compromise. Lentils can be sneaked into casseroles quite easily but peas and beans tend to show up more. I've never forgotten when Peter, as a very small boy indeed, picked up a kidney bean from his plate, peered at it in a mystified manner and said, 'What's this thing full of mashed potato?' I still laugh — can you imagine trying to get someone to do the job of filling something that size with mashed potato? I do think that you can do a certain amount by way of encouraging them not to smoke or drink (or at least drink in moderation — a glass of wine occasionally hurts no one, normally) but, of course, as in everything else, they will be swept along with the crowd (unless they are the leaders) and on the whole you can really only trust that their hopefully stable home life and own good sense will see them through. If they are fortunate enough to have the former I really believe that it counts for a lot.

I visited the local ante-natal department of the Greenwich District Hospital to see what went on these days and was blinded by science! Let me tell you a little of what is available now to pregnant mums. First, blood tests for rhesus factors, anti-bodies, VD (syphilis only), rubella and a full blood count. May I just say, before going on, that where a mother has had, for instance, a rubella baby and is known to be at risk, it is enormously reassuring if the hospital doesn't lose her notes or the blood-test results. This sort of thing can make pregnant mothers very unhappy indeed and I am afraid it is not unknown. At sixteen weeks the AFP (alpha-fetoprotein) is measured, and if this is raised a further blood test is done. If the AFP level is still raised, amniocentesis is offered to the mother, as a raised AFP indicates, among other things, the presence of spina bifida. Abnormal haemoglobins such as sickle cell are looked for, along with other unusual conditions in ethnic groups. Tests are made for hepatitis on anyone with a history of jaundice, also people with tattoos. Anyone with major heart problems in the family will be followed up and the baby will have a cardiac scan at Guy's Hospital at the end of the pregnancy if the consultant feels it is necessary. Blood pressure is taken at every visit, the prospective mum is checked for oedema and the correct growth of baby. Urine examinations will show any infections, toxaemia (now called pre-eclampsia) and raised sugar levels.

At sixteen to eighteen weeks a routine scan is done which Mums find quite fun as it gives them a picture of their baby. The scan will pick up accuracy of dates, and any major abnormalities (hydrocephalus, severe spina bifida, any missed spontaneous abortions in the case of a mother who feels pregnant). The scan will also, of course, confirm the pregnancy and check for twins. Placenta position may also be observed and little details of the baby — the mothers are asked, of course, if they would like to know the sex of their baby!

As far as amniocentesis testing for Down's Syndrome is concerned, the minimum age in Greenwich used to be thirty-seven but is now thirty-five. It is to be hoped that the mother of thirty-seven I heard about, who was refused amniocentesis on the grounds that there was no history of mental handicap in the family, was an isolated example. She subsequently had a Down's baby. Most people must know by now that the risk of having a Down's Syndrome baby increases with your age. Incidentally, I look at my handicapped son and find it difficult to reconcile the word 'risk', but that is something personal. For those who are unaware of exactly what amniocentesis is, let me explain. A needle is inserted into the abdomen (at about twelve to sixteen weeks into the pregnancy) and fluid is removed from around the baby (the amniotic fluid, as it is called). This is then tested and the mother will be told whether or not she is expecting a Down's Syndrome baby. In the case of my last child who was due to be born shortly before my thirty-ninth birthday, abortion was out of the question so I refused the test. Actually, this incident led to a beautiful moment with one of my children. Discovering I was pregnant at this ripe old age I was written up for amniocentesis (Dr Morris should have known better, but I suppose couldn't make decisions for me), and I thought to myself, 'Well, in the interests of medical science I'll have that.' Then I found out what they did. 'No way,' I thought to myself, and declined their offer with thanks. As I mentioned before, there really was no point, if you'll pardon the pun. However, having refused the test and being very aware of the risk, I thought maybe I ought to mention the possibilities to the boys. I was walking down the road one day with David (I was about seven months pregnant and he was coming up to nine-and-a-half) and I said to him, quite casually, 'You know, David, this baby could be handicapped.' He thought about it for a minute, then said, 'Do you mean like James?' I said, 'Yes', and he replied, 'Well, it wouldn't matter, would it?' I still get a warm glow from the memory of that conversation. He said exactly what I felt. We had done it once and we could do it again if necessary. The worst part was not knowing about children like James — we were now experts. Who better to do it? I would be less than honest if I pretended anything but enormous relief that Peter, when he was born, was normal in every way!

MENCAP have a series of papers called 'Stamina' in which they provide checklists of the things which local societies and parents should be looking for in the way of services for the mentally handicapped. In Stamina Paper No. 5 they recommend the following:

Before birth
All women should have access to the full range of ante-natal services.

Check:
1   That these services include screening programmes for women who are suspected of being at risk of having a handicapped child, e.g. rubella immunization, cmv (cytomegalovirus) screening, amniocentesis, genetic counselling and ante-natal and obstetric services which are appropriately equipped and staffed to monitor foetal growth and to take appropriate action.

Greenwich carry out all the ante-natal tests recommended except cmv. How are things in your area?

To resume my story, after this dreary nine months I went into labour on the 1st April, 1958 (James was born ten months after I was married — why wait to find out how much you don't know!) and I was admitted to hospital on that morning. It really wasn't a particularly arduous labour. Even on the afternoon of the second day I was still walking around and I well remember my Auntie Edna (people of my generation always had an Auntie Edna and this one was very special) coming to see me. She was an old friend of my mother's who had known me since 'before I was born' and she walked round with me, rubbing my back when I stopped to have a contraction. Easily the worst part of that labour was the rectal examinations which a particular lady doctor kept giving me. It seemed like three hundred but was probably only three. In the end I gave up being brave about it and just wept. They do these things to you when you are at a very low ebb. It seems that it was something to do with James facing the wrong way. I'm sure I don't have to tell you that he turned himself round as he was being born and emerged, in textbook fashion, at about 11 p.m. that night. I have been devoutly grateful ever since that he wasn't born on the 1st. A sick joke that would have been.

Yes, my first question to the staff nurse who delivered him was, 'Is he all right?' and the staff nurse's reply was, 'Of. course he is,' and we should all have lived happily ever after.

2

POST-NATAL CARE AND DIAGNOSIS

Life on the maternity ward proceeded normally, I suppose. Being my first experience I had no idea what to expect, then when James was about a week old (I was in hospital for twelve days altogether), Neville came to see us one evening, and I caught him looking at the baby in a very odd way. 'Why are you looking at him like that?' I asked. 'I just thought he looked a bit odd,' Neville said. I reacted as any new mum would. 'What do you mean, "a bit odd"?' 'Well,' said my husband, 'I thought he looked a bit mongol.' 'Right,' I said, 'I'll get this sorted out.' To this day I do not know why I didn't dismiss it as rubbish. It had never crossed my mind for one single instant that there might be anything wrong with James and, with hindsight, I think the Almighty was letting the hospital off the hook.

That evening, after visiting was over, I wandered out into the corridor and waylaid the Junior Night Sister. 'I've got something on my mind,' I said. She gave me a big, bright smile. 'Well, you'd better get it off then, hadn't you?' she said. 'Is my baby a mongol?' I asked her. I have never seen a smile leave anybody's face so quickly in all my life. 'I've heard something — you'd better see Sister Spink,' she said and I was taken to see the Senior Night Sister. I was alone in her office, I remember (my mind was beginning to go into reverse by now) and all I could think was, 'Thy will be done,' over and over again. Acceptance was a very important part of our faith; whatever came you got on with it, prayed for help and got it.

To this day I can't remember a single word that Miss Spink said to me, but she arranged for me to see Dr David Morris who had a clinic at the hospital the next day. Then

gave me a sleeping pill and that was that. The next day I
went to see Dr Morris, who asked me, 'Would you be very
distressed if you had a handicapped child?' I suppose he
didn't know what to say, either. Nobody knew what to say.
I did tell him that, 'We have to accept these things,' and, in
my opinion, to his everlasting credit he didn't give me any
alternative. I have heard that some consultants will actually
say to a mother, 'Do you want to take the baby home?'

When I got back to the ward one of the other mothers,
with whom I had become quite friendly, must have guessed
that there was something wrong — probably from my grey
face (she wouldn't have known that it was cold as well). 'Is
the baby all right, Liz?' she asked and I, like a fool, said,
'Yes,' as brightly as I could manage. Nothing more was said
and I may have missed a golden opportunity to 'open up'
to a sympathetic listener. Years and years later I met this
lady at a French class we both attended and, despite the fact
that I was able to tell her her daughter's age and name (the
one she had at the time we were both in Ma's and Ba's) she
didn't remember me at all! What a put down! Perhaps if
she'd known that James was handicapped and been
involved in the trauma she might have remembered. I do
know that when I reminded her of our previous
acquaintance she was totally and completely disinterested! I
was in no danger of getting a swelled head that day!

Looking back, the worst thing about the last few days in
hospital was everybody who knew about it pretending that
there was nothing wrong. We bathed the baby and fed the
baby and all the time no mention was made either of his
handicap or my state of mind. I used to cry after lights out.
The night my sleeping pill was stopped I queried it and was
told, 'We don't want you to get used to them.' Oh, to be
the sort that has hysterics!

I am afraid that there has not been a great deal of change
in this respect even after all these years. Of course, a great
many mentally-handicapped babies just cannot be
diagnosed at birth. Margaret and Tony (two of the many
people I talked to and whom you will meet as we progress)
have had two mentally-handicapped children (out of four),
each of whom appeared normal when they were born.
Margaret, in fact, had great difficulty in persuading anyone
to take her worries seriously. Neil, her second child (Susan,

the first was perfectly all right) was nearly eighteen months old before a paediatrician told Margaret that he was 'a funny little chap' and recommended tests and X-rays. The results of these tests were an opinion that Neil wasn't functioning at his correct level (which Margaret already knew, of course), and a letter was given to her for an appointment at Great Ormond Street Hospital, London. The doctor at that hospital confirmed that Neil was mentally handicapped, no reason was offered and no counselling given except to advise Margaret to have another child. This made Margaret 'very cross' and she told the doctor, in no uncertain terms, that she didn't know what to do with the handicapped child she'd got, to say nothing of Susan! Margaret and Tony asked what would happen if they had another child, and lots of investigation was done with the result that Margaret was told that the chances of having another handicapped child were 'infinitesimal'. Lisa was born when Neil was just over four. For six months Lisa appeared to be the perfect baby except that she passed extraordinarily large motions, and at no time was anyone ever able to give Margaret any successful help or advice about this problem, which eventually righted itself.

Sandra, on the other hand, had an albino baby born to her in King's College Hospital, London. She should have had the baby in a local hospital, St Nicholas in Plumstead, south-east London, but when Sandra was taken in for bed rest and went into labour prematurely, she was moved to King's as St Nick's didn't have the facilities for coping with such a premature baby. The baby was due in January and born at the end of October (the previous one, of course!). Despite this, Elizabeth weighed four pounds twelve ounces and was twelve inches long. Nothing was said about the baby's condition straight away and Sandra and her husband were told together that the baby was what is known as 'albino' (the baby at this time being about a week old). The young parents were not unduly worried by the fact of the condition and the doctor encouraged them by telling them that albino children usually have a very high IQ. No one at that time said anything about mental handicap but Elizabeth didn't walk until she was five. The doctors at King's ultimately expressed surprise that she walked at all. If there was any lack of responses Sandra was not told about it. It is difficult to understand why the so-called experts are so unwilling to listen to mothers' worries. This applies to health visitors as much as doctors (but not all of them, of course — before I'm inundated with cross letters!). Doreen and Jack's younger child, Colin, was given sun-ray treatment at the age of twenty months which Doreen associated with the fact that he wasn't standing yet. Colin was terrified by the treatment and Doreen was told by the clinic that if he didn't walk by the time he was two, they would make further investigations.

In the case of Doreen and Don, they had been married for eleven years before Doreen became pregnant with Kathrine and they had undergone all the usual tests. Doreen started the baby, would you believe, when they moved house! Doreen remembered that at the very beginning of her pregnancy she was very sick and 'it was brilliant green'. As she didn't have this experience with Michael, the next baby, she has often wondered if it was at all significant. This 'brilliant green' matter was only vomited the first time; in fact Doreen was sick for about five or six months. At about seven months she had an X-ray and says that now she would ask a lot more questions. We (Doreen, Don and I, who are all of an age) agreed that we have got 'older and bolder' where the medical profession is concerned! Doreen was admitted into Farnborough Hospital, Farnborough, Kent, with raised blood pressure two weeks before the baby was due and it was decided that an induction should be performed. On the day it was due to be done Doreen read in the paper that a very close friend had been drowned, and the induction was postponed for a couple of days to allow Doreen to recover. (Doreen and Don were trying to remember where Don was at the time and quite a lot of hilarity was caused by Doreen saying to Don, 'At least you weren't at a MENCAP meeting!') Further hilarity was caused when, in answer to Doreen saying she had something over her mouth during labour I suggested that it was the doctor's hand! Actually, it turned out to be the good old gas and air, which gives you something to hang on to and puff into but doesn't do much else. Oh — it made Doreen tiddly! She tried to climb off the bed. Kathrine was six pounds twelve ounces when she was born and was very long and thin. She had straight stiff legs and clenched fists. Doreen didn't attach any significance to this; nothing was said by the staff, but she felt at the time that the baby was 'not right'. She would have liked to feed Kathrine, but it was very difficult and the nurses were not very patient (rushed off their feet perhaps — let's be charitable), so she had to resort to the bottle. For the baby, of course. Before Doreen left hospital with the baby, a heart murmur had been found and they wanted to follow this up. Doreen and Don are now convinced that the heart murmur, such as it was, provided the excuse the hospital needed for bringing Kathrine back to the out-patients department, without telling Doreen and Don of their suspicions. They took Kathrine back to Farnborough Hospital every three months, saw a different doctor each time and every doctor asked Doreen if she had had a good delivery. They can't believe, now, that it wasn't written down *somewhere* about Doreen's delivery. What do they have notes for, anyway, if they have to ask the same questions every time you go? Kathrine smiled for the first time at six months and it occurred to me that that is a terribly long time to wait for your baby's first smile. Doreen had kept in touch with another mother from Farnborough Hospital who had had a baby the day after Doreen had Kathrine and this friendship emphasized the difference in progress between the two babies. Both mums knew that there was something wrong but didn't talk about it. Doreen feels she probably didn't want to talk about Kathrine's poor progress until she had had some sort of diagnosis.

When Kathrine was nine months old, Doreen took her to the welfare clinic (Don happened to be with her that day). The very elderly (and in Doreen's opinion, useless) doctor looked consideringly at Kathrine and said to Doreen, 'Would you say your baby was spastic?' Doreen describes this as being 'rather a shock'. When I asked her and Don what they said, Don laughed and said, 'We were probably very pleasant!' and we all agreed that we had been brought up not to make a scene. Mustn't make other people feel uncomfortable. Especially doctors. This particular doctor made an appointment for Doreen and Don to take Kathrine to see a paediatrician at Farnborough Hospital who examined her and said, 'No, she is not a spastic.' No other diagnosis was offered. Or asked. All this time they were still taking Katherine to the out-patients department for the heart murmur but they decided not to pursue the paediatric side. When Kathrine was aged about fifteen months, Doreen had to take her to the GP because she had a cold (she had had a runny nose since the day she was born). The GP had never said anything about Kathrine's condition or progress and on this occasion there was a locum in attendance. He did, of course, what locums often seem to do best — he let the cat out of the bag. Actually, I suppose it is unfair to blame the locum. If a GP hasn't the courage to tell parents about their child's true condition the least he can do is mention it in the notes. Anyway, this locum made passing reference to Kathrine's cerebral palsy and was very taken aback to see how shocked Doreen and Don looked and said, 'You have been told, haven't you?' They hadn't, of course, and the inference is that there was a letter on file from Farnborough Hospital telling the GP about Kathrine's condition. So, after fifteen months Doreen and Don now had a firm diagnosis, by accident, of their child's handicap.

Celia also has a child, Paul, with cerebral palsy. She was only twenty when he was born and had already ended the relationship with the baby's father, who was an Italian. The father never saw Paul and the relationship took place in Italy, Celia coming back to England to have the baby. She had a 'very nice' pregnancy (a phrase which made us both laugh — a lot of laughing went on during these interviews!) and Celia never had a day's sickness, lucky girl. She did, however, fall over a couple of times and 'this rotten dog bit me', a complaint which had all my sympathy. Paul was born by Caesarean section; it was a late decision which was made owing to the water being discoloured when it broke. A monitoring instrument had been inserted to discover the baby's condition and he was found to be in distress, hence the decision to operate. The baby was born and Celia said his life was 'stop-start stop-start' and after two days he got going properly. The baby was born with a gangrenous arm and Celia was given no explanation as to what caused the gangrene. The baby's arm was amputated when he was two weeks old and, as it touched a personal nerve of mine, this upset me far more than the baby's cerebral palsy. Celia remembers reading in the papers at that time of other babies having a similar experience. This was 1973. She also said that if the baby had been born half-an-hour earlier he would have been perfect — but he would still have lost the arm. Celia asked if the gangrene had been caused by the cord being wrapped around the baby's arm but was told 'No'.

Everything else about Paul seemed to Celia to be quite normal. He was feeding well and was very responsive. He stayed in hospital for six weeks and after she brought him home Celia continued to take him to the out-patients department in Lewisham Hospital, South London, for progress check-ups. She saw nothing unusual in this and while she knew it was nothing to do with the arm, she assumed that because he had been in the hospital for six weeks, they were just keeping an eye on him. Nothing was said to Celia as to why she was being asked to take the baby to the out-patients clinic. No mention was made of brain damage and when Paul was nine months old Celia, concerned about his progress, asked her GP if he could tell her what was the matter with Paul. The GP couldn't give her a diagnosis, but gave her a letter to Great Ormond Street Hospital, London, where they told Celia straightaway what was wrong with her baby. Paul was, by this time, nearly a year old and Celia said it came as 'quite a shock'. (The medical profession — or parts of it — does seem to excel at inflicting 'shocks' on the parents of handicapped children.) I also found it very interesting to observe how many of the families I spoke to didn't recognize the handicap in their baby because it was (in a number of cases) their first child and they were, to put it mildly, inexperienced. This would have been my own case exactly with James if Neville had not lived for a number of years near to a Down's Syndrome young man.

In the case of Ann, things were somewhat different. Julie was perfectly normal when she was born. When the baby was six weeks old Ann took her to the clinic and the baby was given an injection which should have been given at three months. There were no bad reactions to this injection, but two weeks after the second 'triple', Julie started having convulsions and couldn't suck. Ann took her straight round to her doctor who said that there was nothing wrong with Julie. Ann phoned later in the day, the baby being no better, and the doctor said if she wasn't satisfied she had better take the baby to the Brook Hospital, which of course Ann did. The Brook didn't seem to think there was a lot wrong, but nonetheless did keep Julie in for observation. The hospital said it would be 'the lesser of two evils' for them to keep Julie. Whatever did they mean? The next day Julie seemed very vague and was not smiling at all and the day after that the police called at Ann's house to tell her that the baby was in a deep coma and she should go straight to the hospital — in fact they took her. At the hospital Ann was told that the baby had encephalitis and if she didn't emerge from the coma in a week she would be severely brain-damaged. Julie was in the coma for ten weeks. At the end of that time Ann was told that the baby was only functioning on a quarter of her brain and that she had cerebral palsy. Nobody has ever acknowledged that the injections might have had anything to do with Julie's illness, but Anne vaguely recalls that there were one or two incidents of this nature in 1971 when Julie was born.

Joan and Jim had two daughters, out of four, with an unrecognizable and unnamed handicap. Penny, now thirty-three and the first daughter, was born in England when Joan herself was twenty-five. Everything was quite straightforward — the ante-natal care was a bit primitive in those days and Joan doesn't remember having any particular tests. When Penny was born she was very small, five pounds and three ounces, and Joan said that when she eventually got to eighteen pounds, 'she stuck there for ages and ages'. Nobody showed any concern over the inability of the baby to put on even an adequate amount of weight. She was a good feeder and Joan feels now that it was odd that Penny didn't gain weight. When she was a year old, Joan and Jim went to India (Jim worked for the Commonwealth Relations Office) and before embarking on the trip Joan asked her clinic doctor what the medical care was like and whether he considered Penny was fit to go; Jim had also expressed concern. The doctor referred them to St Helier Hospital who said, 'This baby is too fat!' Joan admits that Penny, while weighing so little, did appear to be well covered. No objection was made as regards the trip and off the family toddled to India.

While they were out there Penny got diarrhoea — not entirely unexpectedly — but Joan was really concerned about this as Penny, though now two-and-a-half, still weighed less than twenty pounds and Joan felt she couldn't stand any weight loss. She was advised to go back to England and she, Penny and Carolyn, who had been born in the October, returned in January of 1955. Jim had to finish his tour of duty, but the British High Commission arranged for Joan to take Penny to Guy's Hospital, London, and Penny was duly admitted there for tests. The results were very inconclusive and no advice was offered to Joan. In fact, Joan had to keep on ringing Guy's to get the results of the tests as, 'they left me high and dry,' she said. Penny was walking by the time she was there (not toilet trained) and when Joan asked the doctor at the clinic about the backwardness the doctor expressed the opinion that she would probably grow out of it! Making a jump now (because we will meet Penny again later on) to when Joan's third daughter, Cathy, was born, Joan told me that when she saw Cathy she immediately thought that history was about to repeat itself. Jim was of the same opinion and they were both absolutely right, only this time, of course, they had had their own previous experience to guide them.

I do think that parents who have a Down's Syndrome child have an advantage in being able to recognize and, hopefully, come to terms with their baby's handicap. The problem here *is* rejection, it seems. Though not in the case of Rhoda, a very interesting mum I met and who was a 'traveller' until her Down's Syndrome son, Edward, was old enough to go to school. Rhoda's family, up to and including her own generation, had never married and never gone to school. They travelled in caravans between Hertfordshire and Kent because her mother came from Hertfordshire and her father from Kent. She was quite mystified, incidentally, as to how they originally met as it appears that travellers tend to keep to their areas! Only one person in Rhoda's family had married. She told me that one of her sisters married 'one of your kind of people'. The description shook me somewhat — we were spoken of as if Rhoda looked upon non-travellers as foreigners. She plainly wasn't surprised that the marriage didn't last. Rhoda, now living alone in a council flat with Edward and John (six years old and very normal) struck me as a most caring mother. After all, she had given up the way of life of the whole family in order to do what was best for her handicapped child. She doted on Edward and had done a great deal of work with him in helping him to speak (she herself was unable to read or write).

Edward was born in hospital in Welwyn Garden City, Hertfordshire, and Rhoda had had absolutely no ante-natal care whatsoever. She put up with the morning sickness and bought *Rennies* indigestion tablets for the heartburn. Nobody commented on the baby when he was born, but when he was about three days old, the doctor explained to Rhoda that the baby was handicapped. However, he put it so obscurely that Rhoda didn't understand what he was talking about and she got it into her head that they were telling her that her baby was going to die. Rhoda was alone at this time, nobody having thought to tell her and her husband together. (She referred to 'husbands' and 'wives' all through the interview, despite the lack of 'ceremony'.) When her husband came to visit her, Rhoda told him that there was something wrong with the baby but she couldn't understand what and John went to the doctor immediately to find out what was going on. When John learned the truth, he and Rhoda's sister, Priscalla, thought that Rhoda was in far too distressed a state to take the truth straightaway and decided to wait until she was calmer. Rhoda, by the way, was seventeen at the time. When she brought Edward out of hospital at seven days old, her sister asked her if she wanted to know what was wrong with the baby, Rhoda said 'Yes' and Priscalla told her. It seems that Rhoda's imaginings had been far worse than the Down's Syndrome the baby actually had.

I do wonder if there is some sort of euphoria which can blank out a mother's (or father's) ability to see a handicap in a newly-born baby. Most of the mothers of Down's Syndrome babies I talked to had not spotted it straight-away, and often someone else in the family — either a husband or mother — had been the first to suspect. Not so with Pauline. She had Keith at home and was very happy with the care, particularly that of the student midwife who, when the furore started later, made a point of coming back and seeing how the family was getting on. No mean task for a student. Keith's birth was quite straightforward and Pauline queried, when she saw the baby, whether he might

possibly have Down's Syndrome. The midwife told her that
the baby would probably look different the next day (!), but
at Pauline's insistence called in the GP. By the time the
doctor arrived Pauline's husband was present. Pauline
pointed out that Keith's eyes looked 'mongol' and when
the doctor examined him she also told Pauline and Edward
that the baby 'might look different tomorrow'. She said
Keith had slight oedema, which made him look strange, and
she asked Pauline if she had been a nurse. (I have been
asked that question if I have displayed a little knowledge
about my own 'workings' and it has the effect of making
me extraordinarily angry!) The doctor gave Pauline a letter
for Guy's Hospital, London, where they said that Keith was
a 'typical Down's Syndrome child' and she was asked if she
was going to keep him. Pauline told them quite
emphatically (and Pauline can be very emphatic indeed!)
that she was going to keep him and they told her to take
Keith home and treat him normally. 'He won't think,' the
doctor said. 'He'll learn everything parrot fashion.' I must
say Pauline and I had a hearty laugh over this, thinking
about all the awful things our respective Down's Syndrome
sons had done, without copying anything or anybody!
Certainly nobody ever showed James how to eat a
cyclamen.

Elsie and Jim's fourth child, Mark, was also born at home.
Elsie was thirty-eight when she had him and she had no
tests or screening — this was in 1967. The delivery was
quite straightforward, as had been her pregnancy, and Elsie
had no reason to fear that anything was wrong until, shortly
after Mark was born, she sensed 'panic among the staff'.
The staff consisted of the midwife, the student midwife and
the doctor (Elsie's GP did midwifery). I expressed some
surprise at the presence of the male doctor as I had not seen
one for any of my five deliveries. Well, it's women's work,
isn't it? Sorry male midwives, it's just how I happen to feel
about it. Anyway, during the few minutes after Mark's birth
the midwife 'fiddled about with the baby' and the doctor
went downstairs. Elsie remembers looking at Mark and
thinking, 'Well, he looks all there.' Elsie asked the midwife
if anything was the matter and was told that there was not,
to lie still and the midwife would come and see to her in a
minute. The doctor then came back upstairs with Jim

whom, it transpired, he had told about the baby's condition in quite a forthright manner. The doctor then told Elsie, whose immediate reaction was, 'Will you please take it away.' The doctor pointed out to her that it was very difficult to find somewhere for the baby as quickly as that and Elsie was 'very, very upset'. This episode does make me wonder how many home-confined mothers of handicapped babies would have left them in hospital if the circumstances had been different. Elsie and Jim's older daughter, Hilary, was at home from school unwell at the time of Mark's birth and she came upstairs and said, 'Don't cry, Mummy, please don't cry — he's not going to die,' and Elsie was lying in bed thinking maybe it would be better if he did. Hilary, of course, had not been told about the Down's Syndrome. In spite of not wanting to keep the baby, Elsie still wanted to feed him herself. The midwife advised against this as Down's babies could have problems and also, Elsie said, the midwife was 'completely against' Elsie keeping the baby. She advised Elsie to put him away because 'he would spoil your lovely family'! What Down's Syndrome baby needs a midwife like that, I ask myself. When Elsie's health visitor made her home visit she picked Mark up out of his cradle, cuddled him and said to Elsie, 'I don't know how you knew — he's absolutely beautiful,' and was very nice and supportive. I guess this may have been a turning-point for Elsie. After about eight days her GP brought a paediatrician from Queen Mary's Hospital to examine the baby and she told Elsie, 'I don't have to tell you that you have a very healthy mongol baby.' By this time Elsie had got over the feeling of wanting to put Mark into care, a feeling probably helped along by the doctor telling her that it would be very difficult to find a place which she would accept as suitable for her baby. Elsie agreed that it would have taken the wind out of her sails more than somewhat if, after the first week, the GP had come in and said, 'I've found a place.'

Chris and Bill had no idea, when he was born, that Paul was a Down's Syndrome baby. Chris, even though she was forty-five when Paul was born, was unaware of the particular risks of having a baby at that age. He was born in 1966 and she had no tests other than the normal blood, urine and blood-pressure tests. Paul's birth was quite uneventful (in a manner of speaking) and when, immediately afterwards, the nurse offered to let Bill come in and see Chris, she declined with thanks as she was being stitched at the time. We agreed that one did not look one's best in that situation! Bill saw the baby and told Chris that he thought there was something wrong with Paul's eyes and when Chris told one of the staff about this it seems that the decision was probably made then to tell Bill and Chris about Paul. Bill was told on his own first, then Chris was sent for. The paediatrician said to her, 'I understand you think there is something wrong with your son — what do you think is wrong with him?' Chris was disconcerted by his approach and said, 'Well, I think he's spastic or something,' and the paediatrician said, 'Well, he's mongol,' Chris cried and Bill was shattered. One of Bill's colleagues at work advised him not to bring the baby home as someone in his family had had a bad experience with a Down's child. Bill passed this piece of gratuitous advice on to Chris, whose reaction was the down-to-earth common sense you would expect from her. She said, 'Look, Bill, if he'd been normal he'd have been a helpless baby, so I suggest we take him home, do everything we can for him and see what happens.' Chris spent the rest of her stay in hospital in the bed-rest ward, helping the staff and timing the new mums' pains, etc., and coped with her own emotions without counselling or advice from anyone. Bill presumably spent the time at home doing the same. I think that the dads have a very hard time on these occasions. They are supposed to cope with work in what must be just as (or almost) difficult circumstances as the mums. So Bill and Chris got on with it.

It was not entirely surprising that Doff and John didn't recognize the fact that Gavin was a Down's baby because he is so very like his mum! It never ceases to fascinate me how many Down's children resemble their parents. No reason why they shouldn't, as far as I know. They must be carrying all the family genes as well as that tell-tale little chromosome, but nonetheless the family likeness always takes me by surprise. Doff (her older sister couldn't say 'Doris' — so it's been Doff ever since!) was due to have the baby at home but as he appeared to be a breech presentation it was decided to take her into St Nicholas in

Plumstead. The birth was straightforward, as had been her pregnancy, but before leaving the hospital (it was a forty-eight-hour confinement) an appointment was made for Doff to see the paediatrician. Doff assumed that this was due to the baby being a breech birth but no explanation was given and, again, none asked. At the first interview with the paediatrician (and Doff was on her own on this occasion — why did the hospital not suggest that John should be with her if there was a possibility that they were to be told of Gavin's handicap, or even if there wasn't?), he asked her, 'How do you find your baby?' With commendable restraint Doff said he was rather sleepy and the doctor, after looking at Gavin's hands, told Doff that he thought she might find him a bit slow to develop. The midwife, during the following days, made a comment on 'these babies ...' and Doff began to dwell in a very worried manner on the interview with the paediatrician. John managed to be with Doff for the second appointment (still nobody had suggested that he should be there), and on this occasion the same doctor looked at the notes and said, 'Oh yes, suspicion of Mongol.' Doff and John were both devastated. Gavin was, by this time, three months old. The doctor redeemed himself a trifle (after the somewhat brutal opening remark) by talking to Doff and John for about an hour and Doff remembers that he was very helpful and compassionate. He also suggested a follow-up with Professor Polani at Guy's and they thus embarked on the long hospital trail so familiar to mothers and fathers of handicapped children.

Sue Stevens (and I mention her surname for a reason) was thirty when she had Christopher. Normal enough age for having a baby. The reason I mention her last name is that she and her husband run the Bexley (Kent) branch of the Down's Children's Association. I went to talk to her to find out what the association is doing (there isn't a branch in Greenwich yet) and spent the interview also in the company of the charming Christopher, aged two. More about the association later — I'd like to tell you about Sue and Mike.

 Sue had threatened to miscarry but didn't attach any importance to it as she had a history of this. She already had Ian and Richard and it had happened each time with them.

She was all right after four months and booked into 'Ma's and Ba's' for her confinement. She had her ante-natal care at the doctor's and there was no need to treat her as an 'at risk' mother as far as her age was concerned. In fact, Sue asked her doctor if she should have tests for Down's, but the doctor laughed and said that she had a one-in-a-million chance of having a Down's baby. We agreed that she ought to go back to her doctor and point out to him that she was a woman in a million! She was obviously very worried about this all through her pregnancy and used to phone her husband up at work, in tears, saying that she was sure that she was carrying a Down's baby. During the course of our chat she mentioned that a friend of hers had had a Down's baby with spina bifida — the test for the spina bifida had been negative as it was what is known as spina bifida occulta. The mother of this baby was only eighteen.

When Christopher was born, the cord was wound three times around his neck (the midwife said she thought he had been skipping with it!) and when the staff gave the baby oxygen, Sue was convinced he was dying. Mike was with Sue and the midwife reassured them both that the baby would be all right. He wouldn't feed when Sue tried, and he didn't grip her finger, which she found disturbing. She thought he was brain-damaged. The midwife kept leaving the room for long periods of time which Mike and Sue found strange; Sue was then taken to the ward and a doctor came and told her that the baby had a cleft palate (but no harelip) which, Sue realizes, is why he didn't suck. Sue asked what else was wrong with the baby and the doctor said, 'Oh, don't worry about anything like that,' (like what?) and told Sue that she was to be moved to another ward nearer to the special care unit. Later on, before Mike had gone home, one of the midwives came in with Christopher and, while Mike was on the telephone to Sue's mum, she asked where he was. Sue told her and she said, 'Oh, it doesn't matter,' put the baby in Sue's arms and said, 'What do you think is different about him from the others?' Sue said 'silly things' like the baby was hairy and had a receding chin and the midwife said, 'Anything else?' and Sue replied, 'I don't know why you're bothering with all this because he's a mongol, isn't he?' and the midwife said, 'I haven't got to tell you now, have I?' and that was how it was left, with

Sue having to tell her husband. A cup of tea was offered. Ten minutes later, Sue and Mike had to break the news to their respective parents as visiting time had arrived. After the families had all expressed surprise and stated that there was 'nothing like that on our side', the conversation became very superficial and everyone admired Christopher and acted as though nothing had happened. All frightfully British.

Linda's case was quite different. She had had (and been cured of) cancer of the cervix. This, however, had played havoc with her menstrual cycle and when she had her first appointment at the ante-natal clinic she was fifteen weeks pregnant — having thought that she wouldn't and couldn't be pregnant. She had already got five children and the letter for her sterilization came the day after her pregnancy was confirmed. Linda then indulged in what her eldest daughter called 'mass hysteria on her own'! We'll leave the rest to your imagination. She was offered amniocentesis at the hospital but as this wouldn't have taken place until after Linda was sixteen weeks pregnant and as she wouldn't consider an abortion anyway, the test was not done.

Linda's husband was not of the same mind, didn't want another child and would have been prepared for Linda to have had a termination, but agreed to abide by Linda's decision. (Linda said that when she talks about this now in the presence of the baby, she feels she should cover her ears, even though she is only three months old!) Linda had what her specialist called a 'boringly normal' pregnancy, but remembers that she felt unwell the whole of the time — something which she has noticed with other mothers of children with handicaps and also something which I remember myself with James. Having said that, though, I felt ill with all mine except the last, so I really don't think that any real significance can be attached to this. It may be, of course, that research has been done on illness in pregnancy where the result is a handicapped baby, but I haven't come across it. Linda's baby, Stephanie as she was to be, was very quiet *in utero* and Linda wasn't aware of any movement until the twenty-fifth week. Linda had several scans to make sure that everything was all right and the staff were inclined to say that she was closing her mind to the baby's movements because she didn't want it but they also told her that she was carrying a very big baby and Linda is more inclined to the theory that the baby didn't have room to move.

It had been decided to do a Caesarean Section for Linda because she had no cervix and this was arranged for the 8th January. However, as is so often the case, the baby thought otherwise and decided to come on Christmas Day. 'The best laid plans of mice and men ...'. Even though she was over three weeks premature, Stephanie weighed seven pounds one ounce, so at full term she would probably have been very heavy. Linda had a sterilization straightaway so there were no more worries on that score.

Robin, Linda's husband, noticed something wrong with the baby and when the surgeon commented on his 'lovely girl', Robin asked him if the baby was OK and the surgeon said Stephanie was perfect. Linda, at that time, had not seen the baby, of course.

The next day Linda changed the baby's nappy and was concerned at how she looked but couldn't exactly define what she thought. When Linda's mother came to visit, Linda was aware of a sharp intake of breath (as she put it), but nothing was said.

Stephanie then contracted jaundice and was taken to Lewisham Hospital in South London, which Linda disliked so much that the next day she asked if she could go back to Greenwich, where the baby had been born. One of the doctors at Lewisham asked Linda if she had been told what was wrong with the baby and Linda said, 'She's got jaundice,' the doctor then said, 'No, not that. Have you been told what's wrong with her?' Linda told him she didn't know what he was talking about and after a quick staff meeting in the corner of the ward, the curtains were pulled around Linda's bed and the doctor said, 'Well, she's Down's isn't she?' and Linda burst into tears. This all happened in a large ward and Linda was on her own. She eventually got back to Greenwich Hospital, where they were saying only that Stephanie *might* be Down's. Linda seems to have derived some comfort from this. She found the staff, with one exception, very supportive at Greenwich and though she never saw a social worker at the hospital speaks very highly of the paediatrician who looked after her and Stephanie.

One of the doctors did say — when Linda had a sudden feeling that she couldn't cope — that perhaps they should have said something to her, but they didn't like 'dropping these things on people'. The picture does emerge, it seems to me, of hospital staff desperately hoping that the parents will spot the handicap for themselves and absolve the staff from the unenviable task of having to tell them. Everybody concerned at Greenwich now took the trouble to explain to Linda all about Stephanie's features and how they could be related to Down's Syndrome, and were generally as informative as they could be.

Like so many Down's babies, Stephanie was a very sleepy baby and difficult to feed. Linda was convinced that if they would let her have Stephanie in the ward with her (she was in special care and being tube-fed when she didn't wake up) she would be able to feed her. There was no doubt that Stephanie responded to her mother and, after a certain amount of argument, the doctor gave Linda twenty-four hours to get the baby to feed. Needless to say Linda was quite right and fed the baby, inasmuch as the baby was ever going to feed at all at that time, and after six days Linda, the doctor and the nurses had a chat, during which it was decided that it would be a good idea to top the baby up with a bottle. Gradually, therefore, as time went by Linda stopped feeding Stephanie herself and put her entirely on the bottle. I can remember James being sleepy like that and taking practically all his clothes off to see if the cold would wake him up! Poor little thing! When I think of it now I cringe.

During the remainder of her stay at Greenwich Hospital the staff continued to do everything they could to provide Linda and Robin with all the information they needed about the baby. At no time did the paediatrician suggest that Linda might not want to keep Stephanie; she obviously agreed with another of her colleagues that Linda and Robin were very caring parents and would give Stephanie all the love they had given their other children. When someone at the hospital suggested that perhaps Linda and Robin might like to get in touch with the Down's Children's Association, Robin told them that he had already done so. It would be interesting to know how many 'new fathers' acted so promptly in contacting one of the help agencies.

To sum up, it does seem that the main lack is that of education — education of practically everybody. More understanding of the task in hand needs to be applied by both medical staff and parents when it comes to breaking the news — that constant thorn in everybody's side. Parents, understandably I suppose, are very hard on the people who have to do this difficult task and, not so very long ago, while showing the film 'James is Our Brother' to a group of young wives, I sat at the back of the hall and embarked upon a silent exercise. I tried to put myself in the place of a doctor who had to go, now, and tell a mother and father that their child was handicapped. I honestly concentrated very hard in trying to imagine what I would be thinking and what I would be planning to say and when I had thought it all through (with difficulty) I can tell you, with my hand on my heart, that the palms of my hands were all sweaty.

My exercise indicated clearly to me that these people have a job to do of which no one in the world would rob them. We tend to think that a white coat is the ultimate protection, but it isn't. If a consultant seems brusque or abrupt on occasions, I am sure that it is because the situation is 'getting to him', as my boys would term it. After all, these people are intelligent enough to be able to put themselves in the parent's position (as I put myself in theirs) and, if they have any imagination at all, it must surely come home to them what a terrible moment it is and they, the doctors, must be the ones who will bear the brunt of the parents' distress and disappointment. Not nice at all.

Having extended my sympathy to the chap (or 'chapess') who has to do it, I would say that the medical profession seems to be very slow in giving their students any advice or guidance in this area. Or, if they are, it hasn't started filtering through yet. If I was called upon to say anything upon this touchy subject, I think my only contribution would be to advise them to take off their white coats (their protective clothing), pick up our babies, cuddle them and sit on our side of the table, with us. Let's have it informal. Get out of the consulting-room atmosphere into a sitting-room situation. Get the tea cups out and if we all want to have a good cry make sure that we can have it without feeling that we are letting ourselves and our country down.

It is a traumatic time for parents — and a mother in particular (after all, she is generally the one who is going to have to look after this baby that's about to be condemned for life); she doesn't want to have to think about how she is behaving and the doctor shouldn't be worried about that either. It is not the time to stand on one's dignity.

Stamina Paper No. 5 suggests the following:

After birth
Basically there are two ways in which parents are likely to be told that their child is not normal: during the first few days after birth, if it is a condition that can be recognized then; or in not-so-easy stages as the child misses milestones and falls further and further behind during the early months or years. Generally, it is recommended that parents should be told of the diagnosis as soon as it is certain. In the past, there has been considerable controversy about when parents should be told — largely, we feel, because not enough attention has been paid to how they should be told. What should be said or done will depend on many things. It may not be possible for the doctor to give an accurate diagnosis; it is often a case of waiting to see — even for the specialists. But it is certainly possible to explain this to the parents, as well as the whole procedure of assessment, and to offer advice and support in coping with developmental delay.

We believe that the doctors, nurses and other professionals involved must have sufficient knowledge, training and experience to handle the situation with skill and understanding.

Check:
2 That if it is reasonably certain that there is evidence of handicap both parents are told, whenever possible, together.
3 That it should not be left to one parent to inform the other unless this is a specific request.
4 That in the very early days there should be someone from MENCAP for the parents to confide in and talk to — preferably another parent.
5 That the family doctor is informed as soon as possible

because he may be approached by other members of the family for information and advice.

6 That every care is given to follow up and provide emotional support, as parents begin to comprehend the diagnosis and experience a 'sense of loss'.

7 That the parents are referred to the District Handicap Team.

More about the District Handicap Team later. It will be obvious to most parents that most of the aforementioned is missing altogether, but it is hoped that the local societies and professional people will be pressing for all these points as being in the best interests of those parents who have the initially dismal experience of giving birth to a mentally-handicapped child. More should be done in the way of 'public relations'. We are always going to have mental handicap — the more that is known about it the less people are going to fear the unknown. Doctors have got to stop saying, 'He'll never be any good — put him away,' or words to that effect. In actual fact, with the current trend towards care in the community, there aren't going to be places for parents to 'put' their unwanted handicapped children. I think a great deal can be contributed by parents themselves. People like those I've mentioned in this chapter. None of the people I know well has any inhibitions about taking their handicapped son or daughter out and about with them — quite the reverse. All our handicapped children can be ambassadors for 'the cause' and we can turn them into *good* ambassadors. Indeed, we not only can but we must if we are to improve their lot in life.

3

COMING TO TERMS

Looking back, the day Neville and I brought James home from the hospital was most odd. I suppose, with subsequent babies, you have to have other people around, but on this occasion there was just the three of us. Neville, me and this tiny scrap of humanity. We wheeled his pram into the kitchen, laid him in it and stood back to admire the effect. He at once began to yell and Neville and I looked at each other in consternation. What now? Well, in the event of not knowing what else to do I fed him and all was well! In fact I breast-fed James for three months and he was quite difficult to get going. Actually I couldn't believe that a process which I thought was perfectly natural could cause so much pain! A little more knowledge of the subject of childbirth, as well as mental handicap and Down's Syndrome, would have been invaluable to me at that time. I was unaware that many Down's babies are very sleepy and can sleep themselves to death. One would have thought that the hospital staff knew about this problem. If they did know, why didn't they tell me? If they didn't know, why didn't they know?

I remember, very vividly, the first time I took James to see the chap who was then our GP. I cannot honestly remember my reason for going — it may be that the hospital had recommended that I visit my doctor. Anyway, the doctor asked how the baby was and, without a word, I just thrust the little bundle towards him so that he could see for himself. The doctor gazed at James for a few seconds then looked at me and said, 'Mongol?' I nodded and I suppose he must have made a few soothing remarks but cannot have said anything of great moment or I am sure that I would remember it. I really must have been in a very 'scrambled' state in those early days. Also, of course, it is twenty-seven years ago!

My advice to any young (or not so young) mother of any uncomplicated handicapped baby is to treat him or her as you would any other baby. They all need tender loving care and not much else in the first few months. By the time you have got through that period you have made a great many mental adjustments and life does indeed settle down to the usual small baby chaos! The trend is to start teaching handicapped babies from as early an age as possible, but I really think that most mothers need several weeks to come to terms with their baby's handicap. However, there are also those mums for whom activity is therapy (I have never been one of those!) and the sooner they can start their handicapped baby on an advised course of stimulation, the sooner those particular mothers will settle their own minds. One aspect of having a Down's Syndrome baby when I had James (and which is very different today) was that we were urged by Dr Morris to have another child as soon as possible (I never asked why). Today the mother of a Down's Syndrome baby would almost certainly be offered genetic counselling. This would involve attending a centre specially for the purpose — there is, for instance, the Newcomen Centre at Guy's Hospital, London — and some handicaps have their own specialized centres. Sydenham Children's Hospital in south-east London specializes in children with spina bifida (I feel I should say 'specializes for' those children) and I, if I were having Christopher today, would have been advised to check whether it would be possible or likely for me to have more than one Down's baby. It is very important that if you are not offered any of the services mentioned anywhere in this book, you should ask for them. And don't take 'No' for an answer — these things are important.

With certain types of handicap it may be possible for brothers and sisters to be carriers, so genetic counselling for the whole family is no bad thing. The consultant should be able to give guidance on whether this is necessary. I was present at a conference a couple of years ago and wanted to ask a question. As the place was full of professionals I, needless to say, didn't feel like standing up and making an ass of myself; during the lunch interval I waylaid Dr Morris, who was chairing part of the proceedings, and told him about it. 'What question did you want to ask?' he queried and I told him that I had wanted to ask whether my boys ought to have genetic counselling. 'You should have asked that — it's a very good question,' he said, and led me over to meet a doctor who was, at that time (and still may be, for all I know) doing research into Down's Syndrome at Great Ormond Street Hospital, London. I told this particular doctor what I wanted to know and he said that he thought it probably wasn't necessary but, if they would be reassured, then have it. I, there and then, offered myself and my entire family for his research programme; he expressed great delight and gratitude (apparently people don't rush to take part in these projects), wrote down my name and address in his diary and to this day I haven't heard a word!

We persevered in caring for James (and in trying to have this other baby for Dr Morris — never let it be said that we were lacking in our duty to our paediatrician!) and life was really rather tranquil, I remember. We had a lovely new house, a lovely new baby and everything in the garden was, if not exactly orderly, at least 'coming on'. The worst part of those first few weeks was breaking the news about James to our friends and neighbours. I knew that if someone told me that they had given birth to a handicapped child I wouldn't know what to say, so I, not unreasonably, assumed that people wouldn't know what to say to me when I told them about James. My friend Mary provided a welcome distraction by having to be revived with a glass of water (she tended to faint on stressful occasions) so the immediate need for words was postponed! It is a frightful position to have to put people in, but there really is no alternative — it would be too cruel to leave your friends knowing that you have a handicapped child but not knowing whether you are aware of it.

One of the best things about having James first was that I had no other child with which to compare him. Everything he did was accepted as natural progress, whether it was late for his age or not. Half the time I didn't know what his milestones were, anyway. When I took him to the clinic, which I did every week, everybody just cooed over him and took him as he came. There was none of this sense of urgency which seems to have invaded the rearing of children these days, including those who are handicapped. The doctor at my clinic, Dr Chase, was very good to me and never let me consider for a moment that James was anything but a Down's Syndrome baby. They hadn't given me a flat diagnosis at the British Hospital for Mothers and Babies and Dr Morris had merely said, 'We will watch his progress together,' so Dr Chase's support was extremely valuable. She must have got sick of the sight of me bowling in with James for our weekly chat — which would now be called counselling, I suppose. To get to the clinic I had to pass my local church and, as our church was open at all times in those days, I used to haul James out of his pram, march up the aisle with him, plonk the woolly bundle down on the altar rails and pray like billy-oh for peace of mind. Acceptance doesn't necessarily bring that asset with it but, as the months went by, I gradually felt that my prayers were being answered and I did, indeed, feel quieter in my mind. As a matter of interest, I have only ever once been prescribed tranquillizers and that was many years later when the boys were in their teens and the doctor felt that I was a bit jittery and needed calming down. He put me on a month's supply of Librium and when I went back the following month he insisted that I should have a further course. I argued with him and said that I felt that I really didn't need them but he insisted, and wrote the prescription accordingly. And I accordingly went home and crossed the Librium off before getting the rest of the prescription filled. Just because the doctor writes it on the form doesn't mean you have to have it. I think, if you feel strongly about something like that (and tranquillizers are the most controversial, it would seem), it is better to cross the item through on the prescription than to get the pills and leave them lying around the house, or consigned to the dustbin. Why pay for something you have no intention of either starting or finishing?

None of my relatives, friends or neighbours ever asked me what James was expected to do. He really was a very nice, jolly baby and I suppose everyone, including Neville and I, was content just to wait and see. How different things would be today. Actually, for about the first year

Neville and I didn't discuss James's handicap, as Neville had quite a lot of difficulty in coming to terms with it. I understand this perfectly. Fathers have a different approach from mothers, I think. They tend to look ahead to the football-playing times, the school days and ultimately what sort of a 'man' they have fathered. Will he be interested in the sort of career his father has? As a mother, or at least the sort of mother I was, I would have been extremely disturbed if James (or any son) had been interested in the sort of career I had (wife and mother!) so to me he was just a baby to hug and squeeze — not that Neville didn't do his fair share of hugging and squeezing, but basic attitudes were different. I think we probably both felt very isolated in those days — Neville more than I, though, as I was at least able to talk about James to my friends, if I wanted to.

When James was eleven months old, Dr Morris got tired of asking where this other baby was (I told him we were doing everything possible — I mean, there is a limit!), so he sent me up to the Royal Free Hospital Fertility Clinic. I can tell you, here and now, that those people there really know their stuff. They blew my tubes (it gave me such a pain in the top of my chest that I nearly fainted) and, bingo, after one more period I was pregnant. I think they used dynamite. When I was about two months pregnant I took James once more to see Dr Morris — we were going to see him about every three or four months. I told him about the pregnancy, he was highly delighted and wrote it all up in our file. When I went to see him again with James, about three months later, I took my mother with me. Mistake number one. As we bowled in (Mother as well), Dr Morris took one look at my nice little bulge and said, 'Hallo, what's all this then?' I pointed out to him that he knew already and had written it all down at our last visit. He gazed at the file, and at me and said, 'Oh yes, I got you pregnant, didn't I?' I didn't dare look at my mother, and just replied, rather weakly, 'Well, in a manner of speaking,' and started talking about James in rather a hurry!

Practical support, in those early days, was not exactly forthcoming. I suppose, really, you had to go out and look for it and not everyone can do that. My health visitors were very good at the clinic, but if I hadn't actually attended the clinic each week I don't know if anyone would have come in to see if I was all right. I suspect not.

With most of the people I have spoken to, there seems to be a great lack of counselling in those early days. Some parents also feel that where there have been complications the consultants have not always given the whole story. Paul was a few months old before Chris was told that he had two holes in his heart and that surgery was not possible. Up to this time the only inkling that Chris had was when a welfare-clinic doctor asked her if she knew that Paul had a murmur. Paul used to turn very blue, but no treatment was given to him for his heart condition. Chris can't believe that no one knew about this shortly after he was born and feels very strongly that she should have been told. She could at least have been able to make sure that Paul didn't exert himself more than was good for him. On the reverse (and better) side of the coin, Chris's health visitor put her in touch with another mum, Pat, who had a Down's Syndrome daughter, Sandra, who was just six months older than Paul. Chris and Pat became good friends and it was obviously a happy meeting.

I hope it was happy for Doff when she met the parent she had been put in touch with, because it was me! We met when Gavin was about a year old. Prior to our meeting Doff had been taking Gavin up to Guy's Hospital for genetic counselling: first at six-weekly intervals, then quarterly, then six-monthly until Gavin was three. After that they just went at Gavin's fifth and eighth birthdays. Until we met, Doff and John had felt no great desire to become involved with any organizations and were coping well on their own.

Doreen and Don, after receiving Kathrine's diagnosis from the locum, were quite fatalistic. In Don's opinion their very supportive marriage was their main prop at this time (in the absence of a religious one or a great deal of help from the family) and Don was able to chat at work to one of his colleagues, Lawrie, who, though not the parent of a handicapped child, was one of the leading lights of the local MENCAP society. Doreen and Don both wanted more children but no advice on this subject was given to them. Doreen remembers being quite sure that the next baby would be perfect.

Elsie had a particularly difficult time in the early days. She had been running a playgroup for four years when she became pregnant with a baby she didn't want, and while she says she would never have had an abortion because the baby was inconvenient, she now wishes she had had the amniocentesis. The playgroup was held in a hall just opposite Elsie's house and when Mark was about ten days old, the new term started. Lots of the mums knocked on Elsie's door to see how she and the baby were and Elsie found it very nerve-wracking. Her closest friend was so upset by the news of Mark's handicap that it was six weeks before she could visit Elsie — something which Elsie can understand now but found very hard at the time. She also found that when she had broken the ice and visited the playgroup once, it then became very important to her and says it 'saved' her. The mums and staff were very supportive and Elsie went back to work there when Mark was three months old.

Not only was Pauline left to get on with it by the professionals but she was also left by her husband. Keith was a month old when Edward left Pauline for the first time and Pauline had to cope with Jaqui, Bruce, Clare and Keith on her own. Edward came back when Keith was four months old but life didn't improve much as other circumstances (personal to Pauline) hadn't changed. Pauline told me that when she first knew, very soon after he was born, that Keith was a Down's baby her first thought had been, 'How will Edward take it?' Pauline's health visitor had mentioned the Greenwich MENCAP Society to Pauline, but she wasn't interested at that stage. With four young children and an unreliable husband, it is hardly surprising. I don't know how she was ever able to put her nose outside the door. She was able, however, with the health visitor's encouragement, to get to the clinic regularly and didn't mind mixing with the other mums.

Sue had absolutely no doubt whatsoever as to whether she was going to be able to cope with a handicapped baby or not. She knew she could not. She had had no special visit from the paediatrician (and Sue had known about the handicap from the day of the baby's birth) but he did turn up two days later. He told Sue that there was no doubt about the diagnosis; no suggestion had been made that Sue's husband, Mike, should be present when the paediatrician came to see Sue. One thing he did was to offer

Sue a contact — it was a lady who had a Down's Syndrome daughter of nineteen! Christopher had to stay in hospital to get his tummy upsets sorted out (he also, if you remember, had a mild cleft palate) and Sue didn't stay in with him. She was still undecided over the baby's future and in the end decided to go to the hospital and tell them that she wanted to put him up for fostering. She told Mike what she was going to do and Mike said all right, they would go to the hospital — and bring him home! It seems that Sue thought that Mike wouldn't be able to cope and she knew that she couldn't without his support, so while she loved the baby 'desperately', she was prepared to give him up for what she thought was the good of the family. Mike suspected how her mind was working and Sue said they 'laughed hysterically' all the way to the hospital at the trouble they could have saved themselves if they'd each spoken their thoughts. The staff at the hospital, needless to say, were absolutely delighted at their decision and Sue said there was quite a party atmosphere. So Sue and Mike took Christopher home with them and he settled into his rightful place in the family, being taken regularly to the clinic and having the loving care lavished upon him which he so nearly missed.

There are babies whose mothers are reluctant to take them to the clinic for a number of reasons. The handicap may be obvious and the mother embarrassed by it or she may just never have come to terms with it at all. Whatever the reason, if a health visitor has a mother on her 'patch' who won't take her baby to the clinic she should, if she's worth her salt, make regular home visits to the family, weighing the baby and generally keeping an eye on things. If, for some reason, a health visitor has a personality clash with a mother, then the case should be handed to somebody else — they should not just be left 'in limbo'. A health visitor, by the way, has no statutory right of entry into a house.

Early counselling is particularly relevant in the case of parents who have had a Down's Syndrome baby, because this is one of the most common observable handicaps at birth. There are others, such as spina bifida, of course, but in those cases the degree of mental handicap is very varied and may not be present at all, while in Down's it can be taken for granted.

On the ever-fascinating question of how and when the news should be broken, I was talking last year to a group of medical students who were doing their psychiatry course at a well-known medical school. We got on to this subject and my instinct was to say to them, 'Toss your textbooks out of the window and try to imagine what you would want to be told yourself,' a concept they took up with some enthusiasm. We were all shot down in flames by their tutor, however, who told us that in doing that we were using 'empathy' which is getting inside the mind of someone else, and we all agreed that that was not really possible. Also, so much depends on how much the parents themselves know about their child's condition. Alas, there is no easy way to break the news. One question which does arise is whether, in fact, the paediatrician is the best person to do the job. It would require an unusual degree of honesty from the paediatrician; he or she would have to have a long hard look at him or herself (and who enjoys doing that in a critical light?) and wonder if there may be somebody on his or her team who would be better at it. Being good at making children's illnesses better does not necessarily mean that you are a fantastic counsellor. A paediatrician should have the courage to say to him or herself, 'This is not the thing I'm best at and Sister Whoever or Nurse So-and-so have a greater gift of communication than I have,' which, after all, is what it all boils down to. Once the news has been given to the parents the paediatrician will need to be on hand to answer such medical questions as they may ask and there should also be someone — possibly the hospital social worker — to tell them what their next steps should be. It cannot be emphasized often enough that parents need to be counselled and advised a number of times; if anyone had told me anything of vital importance at the time we were told about James (apart from the fact of his handicap) I would have been quite unable to take it in the first time. Counselling should continue until the mother and father (either or both) have got this situation under control. It takes time, and they are entitled to as much as they need. I do have quite a bit of sympathy for the doctor who finds himself in such an unenviable position. Any minute now a perfectly nice pair of adults (generally) is going to start hating him; I suppose, being flippant for a minute, it's a good thing we are not living in the age when the bringers of bad news had frightful things done to them — I have a feeling the doctors would delegate the task a lot more often than they do now.

One of the main supports to parents who have recently had a handicapped baby must surely be a close and loving family. I felt terribly bereft when I came home with James, knowing that my mother and father were in Australia. Looking back dispassionately now, I don't think they would have been much 'verbal' help — after all, nobody knew anything about mental handicap, but support doesn't necessarily entail knowledge. They would just have been there, listening sympathetically to what I had to say and doubtless offering practical help such as looking after James while I had a morning wandering round the shops on my own. (I have never minded being on my own in the normal way.) James really presented no problems in those early weeks; certainly no more than any other baby. He was much admired by the neighbours — and quite rightly so, he was delicious — but there was always that great big question mark hanging over him and which every parent of a handicapped child sees. Will he sit up, will he grow teeth, will he walk, will he talk, will he go to school, will he be strong, will he be any sort of person with whom we can communicate at any level? All questions which nobody in the world, in the early days, can answer and all vital. Uncertainty is difficult and unsettling to live with and the parents of handicapped children have much more than their fair share of it.

An experienced parent can be a boon at times like this, but not every new parent (or parents) wants to get involved too soon with other handicapped people. It takes a while to come to terms with what you have got yourself, without having to make polite noises to someone else with something similar. When the time does come that you feel you can face another parent, their experience can be very valuable. You discover that the things which your child has are shared by others in a lesser or greater degree. Heart problems, chest infections, chronic catarrh — these are all things to which handicapped children are prone and somebody else's remedy could save your sanity. In my case

I discovered that garlic capsules were not a good idea for James's catarrh as he tended to have what we will politely term 'digestive problems', but sugar-coated garlic tablets work much better. They don't hang on the breath. I would also heartily recommend that where there are self-help groups of mothers meeting together, the health visitors should try to sit in. They could glean a large amount of helpful information which could be passed on to new mums, making life that bit easier in the first depressing weeks.

When talking to Pat, my health-visitor friend, she told me that where a family is having difficulty in coming to terms with a handicap, it is often very helpful to recommend services which do not necessarily connect with mental handicap. She has found on a number of occasions that a family is able to accept help from a physiotherapist or speech therapist, where the emphasis tends to be on the physical side, thus giving them time to adjust to the possibility of mental handicap. Several of the mothers I have spoken to have had a sympathetic and helpful health visitor; for instance, when Ann brought Julie home from the hospital she remembers that her health visitor came 'all the time' and Ann obviously appreciated her doing so. I was interested, when talking to Ann, to realize that she didn't know that 'spastic' and 'cerebral palsy' were the same thing. I wonder if I am the only person who thinks that the proper name for these handicaps is the preferable one? It occurs to me that some of the professionals could be a bit more forthcoming about educating parents in their own child's handicap. After all, you would hardly make a study of a subject which was never going to touch your life and nobody ever expects to have a handicapped child. Once a health visitor or social worker has a mother with a handicapped child as part of their case-load they should make sure that they are able to answer all the questions the parents may ask, or perhaps not even wait for them to be asked. A great many parents do not have any idea what questions they should be asking and probably some of those they do ask will be unanswerable — those of the 'What will he do?' variety. I wonder how many parents of children with cerebral palsy have asked, 'Will he walk?' Another problem with some parents seems to be the age of the so-called experts who are supposed to be helping them. I heard one mother say, recently, that she felt her young social worker had no insight whatsoever into her problems as she had so little experience of life herself, let alone the sort of problems this particular mother had. Perhaps the social services should be looking a little more carefully at the suitability of the people they are sending out to do this difficult and delicate job.

In the early days it is very easy for parents who have just heard the news to be what I can only describe as 'punch drunk'. In *Right From the Start* (Spain and Wigney, published 1975) the authors suggest that 'at least two or three sessions are usually required before the parents can comprehend the diagnosis'. I would bear this out. Pain blots out thought for most of us and I, as I said previously, can remember very little that was said to me by Dr Morris at our first interview. This, of course, is where it would be a great help to have a health visitor or social worker sitting in. They could always write down any salient points which the parents may overlook, especially where a baby has a physical handicap needing special care — such as the teats you need to have on the bottles of babies with a cleft palate — or any sort of medication. I get very impatient with the view which some professionals seem to hold that if you tell a mother what sort of illnesses her child may suffer from she will spend all her time looking for them. Actually, this attitude is not particular to the professionals, is it? I know quite a number of people who won't read medical books (of the encyclopaedia type) because they know they'll end up thinking they've got every disease they've read about. I'm the reverse, actually, in that I assume that all the symptoms of cancer, heart disease, diabetes, thyroid imbalance, etc. etc., which I suffer from are all mere menopausal imaginings! They will probably write 'She died of the menopause' on my tombstone! The thing is, with the complaints that handicapped children get (chest infections, bronchitis, etc.), the symptoms can be very frightening indeed. When James had bronchitis in his first eighteen months, I couldn't believe the noise he was making and if I had known that he was likely to fall foul of this sort of thing I would have made sure I had something in the house which would have eased the condition and maybe not have necessitated bringing the doctor out in the middle of the night. He wasn't in danger of his life, as it happens, but I certainly thought he was going to breathe his last any second. A little more information from those who know would alleviate a lot of anxiety for those who don't.

That counselling is a largely undiscovered art is made obvious, it seems to me, by the amount of publicity given in the press to the various cases concerning Down's children which have appeared in our courts over the past few years. It would appear that 'they' still haven't got it right and it has to be admitted, of course, that what is the right way for one family will not be for another. I suppose it is all back to education. I look forward to the day when handicapped and 'normal' children are sharing playgroups, visiting each other's primary and secondary schools and learning from a very young age that we are not all the same in this world and that those who are mentally or physically 'infirm' have a right to our care and attention. There, but for the Grace of God . . . .

4

THE EARLY YEARS

The first few years of a handicapped child's life can be quite busy in comparison with those of a normal child. (I apologize for the continued use of the word 'normal', but it serves a purpose.) All sorts of things can start happening to a handicapped baby almost as soon as it arrives home from hospital, especially if the baby has an observable handicap. First of all the health visitor will make her statutory 'home visit' and, if the baby has been diagnosed early, the health visitor should be in a position to be of positive help to the family. She should offer her information on the local societies connected with the child's handicap, or if the mother is not particularly organization inclined at that time, the health visitor may offer to put her in touch with another mother with the same problem. Sometimes, so Patricia tells me, a mother (and/or father) can't or won't acknowledge that the child has a mental handicap and on these occasions Patricia emphasizes to the parents that it would be a good idea to do something about the child's physical development and recommends the speech therapist or the domiciliary physiotherapist, both of whom Patricia considers parents find what she calls 'non-threatening'. As I indicated in the previous chapter, it is, very often, the 'mental' aspect which forms the barrier for these parents. These agencies are also very helpful when the handicap or degree of handicap is genuinely unknown. There is no point in sitting around, waiting to see what happens and neglecting to do all you can for the child's physical development.

A baby who is worrying the hospital staff when he is born will be put on the medical follow-up register.

Sometimes the fears will turn out to be unfounded, but the reasons a baby may be on the register could be, for instance, anything abnormal at birth, i.e. premature or difficult delivery, poor uterine growth, any low APGAR result (a system of testing the heart rate, respiratory effort, muscle tone and reflex irritability in a new-born baby) and resuscitation for any reason. Once the baby has been 'noticed', the health visitor, at her first home visit, will encourage the mother to bring the baby to the clinic where he or she can be monitored in the usual way. If a mother doesn't take her baby to the clinic it gets very difficult to watch the baby's progress, especially if there is no follow-up at the hospital. It is to be hoped that the GP will keep an eye on the baby — I well remember taking my third son, Michael, to the doctor's to have an injection when he was about ten months old. There was, would you believe, a locum in attendance and he, without referring to any notes the doctor may have made, looked at the little strawberry mark on Mike's scalp and said, with great intensity, 'Is he keeping up to his milestones?' Not very subtle! If I had been a panicky mother I would immediately have started to have a very bad time indeed.

Let me just sum up why — if everybody is doing what they should — no handicapped baby should escape notice for too long. Of course, there will always be exceptions. So, if a handicap is noticed at birth, the parents should have been told of it and, if they have accepted it, they should have regular visits to the paediatrician or whoever the expert is in the field of their child's particular handicap. If the handicap is only suspected and nothing has been said to the parents, the GP will be informed by the consultant (hopefully) and the baby will be put on the medical follow-up register. The health visitor and the Medical Officer of Health will also get copies of the hospital reports and, if everyone links up correctly, the baby will be known. The next step is whether or not the mother takes the baby to clinic. If she does, then the baby's progress can be satisfactorily monitored there and the clinic doctor will write to the GP if she (or he) feels that further action needs to be taken. If the mother does not take the baby to clinic, then everything depends on either the health visitor being on good terms with the mother and making home visits, or the mother taking the baby to the GP who will (or should) know that the baby needs watching. It is essential, incidentally, that the health visitor puts in a report to the Nursing Officer if she is not allowed into the house.

In high-mobility areas there are special difficulties as people may move around quite a lot and a handicapped baby could escape being seen by anybody. This may then become the problem of the Department of Education and Science when the child is presented for school at five years of age.

So, once a family has accepted that their child does indeed have something to be concerned about in its development, there are a number of agencies which can be called upon to help. The health visitor is one of the best contacts for a mum to have. My friend Patricia should, without doubt, be cloned and sent to every clinic in the British Isles! She is quite one of the most caring and practical health visitors I have ever come across (and I have met a few). This is not to say that there has been anything actually lacking in the ladies who have helped me in the early years, but Pat definitely has something special. She believes that, wherever possible, the health visitor should accompany the mother of a handicapped child on visits to consultants (especially in the early days) and also to assessments. She thinks that mothers very often don't understand what the consultants are talking about (do they do it on purpose, these consultants?) and she quotes one memorable occasion when she went with a mother to visit the consultant who explained the baby's condition to all his students while Pat sat close to the mother and translated for her in a quiet voice as he went along! This is a ridiculous situation and someone really should take consultants to task for their attitudes towards parents. In my opinion they can be rude and offensive and it makes me very angry. It is very important, for obvious reasons, for the health visitor to establish good relations with the family. The local clinic is, or should be, a place where a mother can get advice from experienced nurses (health visitors are, after all, nurses), doctors and sometimes from other mothers. It is highly desirable that the mother of a newly-diagnosed handicapped baby shouldn't cut herself off from her contemporaries at the clinic. They can be very kind and supportive to a new mum and, dare I say it, it is very good for the mothers of 'normal' babies to see that they themselves could be considered lucky. It is also, of course, the first step in the long journey of integration into society. How are people going to become accustomed to handicap if they are never allowed to see it? This was exactly my own problem as a child. The handicapped person was kept indoors and never had a chance to become familiar to those around him.

MENCAP is very concerned indeed about counselling and support right from the start — and we have seen what can happen if either or both of these is lacking. Stamina Paper No. 5 sets it out as follows:

Family support services
MENCAP believes that every Health District should provide a comprehensive service for children with mental handicap.

A *District Handicap Team*
In the first instance parents will be referred to the District Handicap Team for advice and assessment. It will be the responsibility of the District Handicap Team to refer to the Community Mental Handicap Team as soon as mental handicap is diagnosed or suspected.

B *The role of the Community Mental Handicap Team*
The role of the Team is to provide specialized advice and help with problems related to mental handicap. It should do so on request by families and by professional workers coming into contact with the child or his family, making use of specialist mental handicap and other services provided by the NHS, local authorities and MENCAP.

Functions of the Community Mental Handicap Team
(i) To act as the point of contact for parents and to provide advice and help.
(ii) To co-ordinate access to services — far too often provision is fragmented.
(iii) To establish close working relationships with MENCAP and other relevant voluntary organizations.

A comprehensive service will take into account the varying degrees of dependency and the age of the child and, consequently, the different kinds of support required.

In putting these recommendations before you, I feel I should point out again that they are what MENCAP considers should be the *minimum* services available to families with a handicapped child and not what actually *is* available. The Stamina Papers were written for local societies in order that they could see what was lacking in their own areas. I am passing the information on to you so that, if these services are lacking in your area, you may add your voice to that of your local society — or any other help agency working in this field — if you have not done so already. Stamina Paper No. 5 proceeds thus:

C *Family Support*
MENCAP believes that in every Health District there should be a jointly funded and managed FAMILY SUPPORT SERVICE which will ensure the provision of:
(i) base for the Community Mental Handicap Team;
(ii) diagnostic and assessment services;
(iii) residential phased care and short-term care;
(iv) child care, development and management support.

Check
8 That there is a co-ordinated policy for the provision of a comprehensive service for children with mental handicap.
9 That the 'comprehensive service' includes a full domiciliary service.
10 That the service provides appropriate professional expertise and aids to enable parents to stimulate their child's development, e.g. Portage, speech therapy, physiotherapy, etc.
11 That a Community Mental Handicap Team has been established and is working.
12 That the Community Mental Handicap Team select a named person to whom the family can refer (see Warnock Report).
13 That the LEA [Local Education Authority] is informed when developmental delay of a significant kind is observed with a baby.

14 That there is a FAMILY SUPPORT SERVICE.
15 That these services are easily accessible for parents.
16 That these services include facilities for diagnostic and subsequent monitoring and regular reassessment of each child's progress.
17 That these services should enable, if necessary, daily attendance of the children in a nursery equipped and staffed for remedial therapy as well as for social training and education.
18 That nursery education opportunity groups, playgroups, toy libraries, etc. are provided as essential components of day provision.
19 That other members of the family have the opportunity to discuss their feelings with members of the Community Mental Handicap Team.
20 That every effort is made to help parents, grandparents and other close relatives to understand the nature of the handicap.
21 That special consideration is given to the emotional and practical needs of other children in the family.
22 That priority for home help, aids and family relief schemes is given to families with a mentally-handicapped child.

The last section of the above paper (which I won't quote here) is an exhortation to local societies to establish their own welfare and advisory services. MENCAP at Golden Lane, London EC1, run excellent courses on welfare — a delicate subject — but once having mastered it I believe that parents of the mentally handicapped are very well equipped to offer support (of the verbal variety) to other parents. There is no way that the society's welfare visitors should do the work of the social services — they are not trained (whatever that implies) social workers, but they are well able to provide a sympathetic ear and to point the family in the right direction should they be in need of help from the professionals. Being a welfare visitor (and I would emphasize the word 'visitor') is not everyone's cup of tea, of course, and while many parents have their own experiences to call upon in offering assistance to other parents, not everyone is either suited to the task, or even inclined to take it on.

The Community Mental Handicap Team would, I

imagine, come between the local society welfare visitor and the social services — I mean in pecking order, not in a divisive way! I had a long chat with Dominic, the social worker attached to the Community Mental Handicap Team in Greenwich (the first of three) and he sees the role of the team very much as working alongside the social services but as specialists and certainly not doing their job for them. He felt that the CMHT should have more time to spend with clients, hopefully not having the huge workload which generic social workers have, and he sees counselling as being an important part of the service. He summed up his job as that of someone who should be able to give information, advice and guidance on all matters which relate to any age group of mental handicap.

The nurse of the team agreed that she saw herself as being to the over-fives what the health visitor is to the under-fives. She said that it was necessary to have a nurse on the team to go, for instance, with mothers to out-patients' clinics and to help to back up a diagnosis. In a case where epilepsy has been diagnosed the nurse can spell out what this means and also help explain the medication (as consultants seem to be notoriously bad at explaining anything at all). She will also come in and give support to the family where the mentally-handicapped member has to be admitted to hospital.

Referrals to the team do not necessarily have to come through official or professional channels. Parents were perfectly free to telephone whenever they needed help and Colette (the nurse) told me that all local society members should have access to the telephone number of the Community Mental Handicap Team.

One of the fastest growing areas of help must surely be that of the toy libraries. We didn't have one in Greenwich when James was a toddler and I'm sure it would have been most welcome (by Christopher, Michael and David if not by James!). I went down to the Greenwich Toy Library and talked to Pat Gardner, the librarian, who herself has a handicapped child. I honestly do not know where these indefatigable people get their energy. She told me that the library is funded partly by Urban Aid and partly by the local authority. This pays for the full-time assistant and other help (non-financial) comes from the Voluntary Workers'

Bureau. Community Service Volunteers are sometimes sent along to the toy library and Pat said that this has worked very well. The library does not charge a subscription.

The Greenwich branch caters for 350 families which Pat said was really much larger than usual but this tends to be the case in London. It started, in fact, as a pre-school playgroup, but expanded later to cover the gap between the very young and the older ones who need support but not toys and there is now a youth club, a spin-off from the original venture, which provides a social evening for youngsters in the 7–19 age group.

Another interesting offshoot of the toy library in Greenwich is the Sit-In Service. Over a long period of time volunteers and families meet together and eventually a volunteer is allotted to a family with whom he or she is compatible. The volunteer can then be called upon to sit in at, for instance, tea time — which might be a very difficult time of day for the mother (or father) — and also by taking charge of the handicapped child, perhaps for outings, which will enable the rest of the family to come together. This is in addition to the normal baby-sitting requirements which are usually to allow the parents an evening out together. The expenses of the volunteer are paid (and this may involve taking a cab home if this is deemed the wise thing to do) and expenses are also paid if the volunteer takes the child for an outing. I should explain that these expenses are paid by the association, but if the family require a service from a volunteer on a regular and frequent basis they are, not unreasonably, expected to pay the expenses themselves.

On the day I visited the toy library there was a very relaxed atmosphere and I particularly noticed the large number of young people, obviously brothers and sisters of the handicapped children, milling around. It seems that the toy library performs a very specific function in allowing parents to meet together in a play situation with no pressures attached. Mrs Gardner seemed to be well-informed on the family background of most of the people there and I got the impression that there was a lot of quiet 'welfare' going on. Mrs Gardner did inform me that if, on their home visits, they were appraised of any difficulties, they considered it part of their service to put families in touch with the people whose business it would be to help them. There was no obligation whatever to attend the toy library at its base and many families relied solely on home visits.

In order to maximize the amount of help a parent can give to a mentally-handicapped child, it really is very necessary to have regular assessments. It is a word which tends to frighten parents (well, me anyway!), as it does seem to have a slight 'pass or fail' feel about it. This is a pity as it is so much in everybody's interest, especially the child's, to know as early as possible what is the correct treatment and education for him or her. The process normally starts at the clinic and, I suppose, in the early days mothers looked upon assessments as 'check-ups' — that was what I always called it. The word 'assessment' only came into our vocabulary when our children approached the age of five and something had to be done with them. The screening tests at the clinic — which all babies should have whether handicapped or not — are carried out at six weeks, six to eight months, eighteen months, two and a half years and pre-school. It cannot be stressed too strongly the importance of taking a child regularly to the clinic. If the staff are doing their job properly all sorts of conditions (both mild and serious) can be picked up and dealt with before they become alarming. If a child is shown to be behind in his milestones, remedial help will be provided and this could be with the speech therapist or the physiotherapist. Any dietary problems will be dealt with and, in the case of Down's babies, where there is very often a feeding problem, the clinic is a much easier proposition than forever carting the baby back to the hospital or spending hours sitting in the doctor's waiting room. Have you ever sat in the doctor's waiting room with a grizzling baby? It's always at those times that the waiting room is full of frowning pensioners! At least at the clinic you can be fairly sure that your particular grizzler will be part of a duet or even a trio! If a mother is reluctant to go to the clinic — and in some cases it would be cruel to apply pressure — the screening tests can and should be done at home. It is in cases like these, of course, that the health visitor has to work very hard at achieving and keeping a good relationship with the mother. A personality clash could be very detrimental to the baby. The tests done on the occasions mentioned are for vision, hearing, social skills and locomotion. If the baby is severely retarded in its development then a longer assessment will be arranged which could take several hours. I would point out here that there are several methods of assessment — find out which one is going to be used for your child and try and get a book from the library on the subject. Forewarned is forearmed and you will know what they are doing — and why.

The assessments may have improved from when James and his friends were expected to make bridges from little bricks (and not much else) but in some cases the doctors' attitudes haven't. When Pauline took Keith for his assessment just before his second birthday, the health visitor went with her. The doctor didn't ask Pauline any questions about Keith; she made no explanations as to what the various tests were for but merely said to the health visitor, 'Does she know what this is all about?' and the health visitor said, 'Yes.' What a pity she didn't turn to Pauline and repeat the question. As far as Keith's tests were concerned, Pauline said he 'fell down' (Pauline's words) on pointing out his own eyes, nose, etc. He 'passed' on the knives, forks and tea set — he was used to playing tea parties with his sister. The doctor asked the health visitor (it really is incredible!) if Pauline had any preference as to which school Keith went to and Pauline (who is able to hear and speak!) said, 'Maze Hill' (Maze Hill School for Mentally-Handicapped Children, Greenwich). The doctor thought that Keith would benefit from going to school at two and didn't offer Pauline any alternative. As Pauline's marriage was going through a very difficult phase (her early fears about her husband accepting Keith's handicap were being realized) she felt that she needed the break which Keith being at school would give her. She did tell me that she had felt very much that she was an observer at her own child's assessment. I think it is shameful she should have been made to feel like that.

In Margaret's case, by the time Lisa was a year old she (Margaret) was beginning to get very worried about Lisa's progress (she told me that Lisa 'looked and behaved like a six-month-old child'). The GP told Margaret that she was neurotic and offered her Valium. (I can hear thousands of you saying, 'Hmm, typical!') Margaret's only ally at this time was her health visitor who wrote, herself, to the GP and Margaret subsequently obtained a letter from him to Great Ormond Street Hospital, London, where Lisa was assessed as being mentally handicapped, but no explanation was offered of the possible cause.

After initially not wanting the baby, Linda's husband, Robin, adopted a very responsible attitude towards Stephanie and when the health visitor was arranging to make a home visit, Robin asked that she should come on a day when he was also at home. I think many of us make a mistake in not bringing dads more into the centre of things. In this day and age when a girl has to give up a possibly lucrative job in order to have a family, it seems logical that the sharing — which is so much the trend these days with wives working outside the home — should also extend to taking an active part in bringing up the children.

From when Mark was three months old until he was just over two years, he underwent assessments with the same doctor James had. When Mark was six months old, his mother, Elsie, enquired of this doctor what school she thought Mark might attend and was told not to worry about it but to train him socially. Elsie was very cross! When he was two Mark had to go to the same doctor for a further assessment and on this occasion the doctor required Mark to pile up a few building bricks. Instead of piling the bricks up Mark made a train with them — the doctor said it was wrong and once again Elsie was very cross. She can laugh about it now, but obviously at the time she had very good reason to be angry with the doctor's extraordinary attitude. As Elsie refused to take Mark to any more assessments they were forced to come to her home and fortunately it was a different doctor.

Once a handicap has been diagnosed the parent (or parents) should have been offered the services of a Home-School Liaison Teacher. In order to find out about this service which, of course, was not in existence when James was little, I invited Ronnie Seabrooke round to tell me all about it. She is the Home-School Liaison Teacher attached to Maze Hill School. It had disturbed me for some time that parents were being pressured to get their babies into the education system at the earliest possible moment and I was glad to know that Ronnie had a very relaxed approach to the subject.

When she first makes contact with a family, either through the health visitor, the doctor, paediatrician, educational psychologist, social worker, speech therapist or physiotherapist (a family could, I suppose, be involved with all of these people at the same time — terrifying thought) she tells them straightaway that she is a teacher from Maze Hill School for Mentally-Handicapped Children and also which agency has referred her to the family. She is very aware of the need to tread carefully at the first visit as parents are very vulnerable and words like 'backward', 'slow in reaching milestones', 'handicap' and 'special school' are very painful to them. She is quite emphatic in pointing out that she is there to work in a team with the parents, gaining strength and ideas from each other. Another point she tries to get across is that, although she herself is based at a school for mentally-handicapped children, that is not to say that the child she is working with will go to that school and, in fact, many are physically handicapped and will go to Charlton Park School in south-east London, where it is possible for children to take O- and A-Level examinations. She does not, obviously, commit herself on the subject of school as that is the job of the people who are assessing the child regularly.

So, what can she do for a baby of six weeks — which is the age she likes to 'get them'? She tries to get the baby to focus on her face then she moves from side to side and up and down so that he can follow her with his eyes. She will call his name from these different positions and perhaps blow gently on his face. She will move a toy that rattles or chimes or rings in the same way; put the toy in his hand, helping him to hold it, wave it and shake it, etc. Later he will reach out to grasp it, if only to drop it again immediately. As time goes on he will learn to follow toys rolled on the floor near him — he won't understand that what he can't see still exists. At first, if he drops a rattle he won't look for it but gradually he will come to look for it. All children learn this concept when playing 'peek-a-boo' with the family. The face hidden behind hands or under the scarf is still there saying 'boo' when uncovered. The toy is still there when covered by the scarf or box and when the baby starts to look for it his memory is developing. Much later on he will look for half a chocolate button under a pot or a raisin on the bottom pot under a pile of pots. And so he progresses.

All the time Ronnie and the parents together are training the baby to listen to their voices — talking to him, bouncing him gently to the songs so that he gets the rhythm of the speech; tapping his hand on theirs and perhaps lying on the floor with the baby on their chest so that he can watch their lips closely and feel the vibration of their voices through to him.

The last thing any Home–School Liaison Teacher wants to do is breeze into a home and tell the parents what they have got to do and the emphasis is always (or jolly well should be) on helping each other to help the child. After all, teachers know that they are only with the child for a very short time (Ronnie can only get to each one of her children once a fortnight) so if all her work is not to be a complete waste of time it is essential to have good and friendly relations with the parents who are going to implement what she is doing.

She places much importance on little ones listening to as great a variety of sounds as possible and each sound the baby makes should be repeated to him many times. She uses the Portage system of structured learning only as a guide as she feels (and I agree with her) that if she left checklists (which is the Portage system) with the parents the playtime could become tense, anxious and fraught instead of the happy, natural and loving time it should be. I must say that some of these programmes of early learning are quite terrifying and require degrees of dedication from the family which I personally think are over and above the call of duty. Parents of mentally-handicapped children are often carrying a sufficient burden of guilt over their child's handicap without being made to feel that you are a failed parent if you don't spend twenty-five hours out of twenty-four playing with and teaching your child. I can't imagine anything less conducive to relaxed family life and let us not forget that there may be other people in the family who also need love and attention. I have never forgotten the clinic doctor who said to me, many years ago, 'Don't sacrifice the rest of the family for one child.' I have always considered them wise words. It often pays just to stand back a bit and look at what you are doing.

Ronnie sees talking to the parents as a very important part of her job and considers that having brought up two sons herself (neither of them handicapped) gives her a little insight into the problems which families may wish to discuss with her concerning other members of the family. She can get very involved with families and has been invited to christenings, weddings, parties and funerals — which I think says volumes about how supportive a person can be in doing that particular job.

She expressed her concern about those children who are eventually taken into the nursery class of a school for children with special needs. This can happen at the age of two and Ronnie feels (as I and a great many others do) that a whole day away from mum is much too long. No normal playschool or nursery school (excepting those run by local authorities for working mothers) expects to keep a child for more than two-and-a-half to three hours and why should it be any different for a handicapped child? Ronnie thinks it is as wrong for the parents as it is for the child. It is asking parents, who are probably only just recovering a little from their dreadful shock and grief, to break the bonding that may just be beginning to strengthen. The reason given for not having the little ones for half a day is transport (the old bugbear). It seems that no coach can be provided for the children to go home at midday. One does wonder why some of these school buses which one sees in the streets all day cannot be used. If a mother shows a preference for a place in a local playgroup or day nursery Ronnie encourages this; it means that the child need only be at his class for two to two-and-a-half hours, and will also be with his mother. This is not only good for the handicapped child but hopefully will instil good relations with normal children at a very early age. This is where integration should start.

I must point out that at Maze Hill School there is absolutely no objection to a child going for a couple of half-days a week if the parents can organize their own transport. The fact that a child has been assessed as suitable for school at two does not mean that he or she has to go — Dr Morris told me, when James was a toddler, that all babies need their mothers up to the age of three and I can't think that anything has changed, except the fact that there are now places in school for two-year-olds.

The current favourite among learning programmes seems to be Portage (until something else takes its place) and Sue Stevens has used this American system for Christopher. While she finds it successful and rewarding she said that you do have to be rather ultra dedicated! The great thing about Portage (called after a town in Wisconsin, by the way) is that you don't have to be a trained teacher to assist a mother in teaching her baby because the basic lists of tasks are in the form of progress charts with an explanatory book; and the system can be learned by health visitors — which is what has happened in Sue's case. In Greenwich the Home-Liaison Teachers are also versed in the Portage system and it is all run a little differently from Bexley, in Kent, where Sue lives. In that borough the scheme is run by educational psychologists. It costs £120 (at the time of writing) to buy the Portage system, which is too steep for many parents, but it can be borrowed or, I would have thought, a local branch of MENCAP or the Down's Children's Association might offer financial help if it was thought necessary. The system has a lot to recommend it provided the family (and why should it just be Mum?) can look upon it as a useful method of helping a child along and not feel that if they don't do it to the letter all is lost. Family life is important too.

The life of a handicapped baby or toddler can be very busy indeed. Sue's Christopher has speech therapy once a fortnight; Portage every day; and occasional physiotherapy at the playgroup which he attends. There are also appointments at the Brook Hospital with the paediatrician every six months, appointments at the Queen Elizabeth Military Hospital in Woolwich in south-east London, to check on the palate, also every six months, and regular visits to the Newcomen Centre at Guy's Hospital, London, for assessments. It was on a visit to the assessment centre that a slight hearing loss was picked up and in order that he will be able to swim, Guy's will put in grommets and tubes at the appropriate time — so Christopher won't miss out on an activity which so many children enjoy. When Sue mentioned genetic counselling to the paediatrician he said she could have it if she liked, but so far she has not pursued it. She feels, however, that she will probably do something about it at some time in the future.

While I personally am in considerable disagreement with that part of the Warnock Report which recommends integration (in the classroom) in normal schools, I think it can be done very successfully at nursery-school age. If we parents want to help the general public to understand and accept our children we have got to work on the rising generation — and where better to start than at nursery-school age. Of course, it is not always possible; the only nursery school nearby may have neither the facilities nor the staff to cope with a handicapped toddler but, having said that, they may allow the mother to be in the group with the child and they have immediately got the extra staff they need. It is good for a handicapped child to mix with its unhandicapped peers and it is very good for unhandicapped children to learn from an early age that there are other little children who need extra care and attention from the rest of us. Opportunity Playgroups present just such an opportunity for the handicapped and non-handicapped to mix and this is, I am glad to say, very much a growing area.

James, of course, missed all this (and as I am writing it is the day of his twenty-seventh birthday!). Looking back, I don't know if I would ever have actually got him to a nursery, even if there had been one. I certainly wouldn't have wanted him to go before he was three and by that time I had got Christopher (who would have been ten months old when James was three) and was expecting Michael. Life was hectic and tiring. I suspect that I am not being strictly honest with myself. I have a feeling that if a school bus had called at the door I would have let James go to school; it is with hindsight that I say I would have wanted to keep him at home until he was three. I felt at the time that my own survival was rather important. As there wasn't anywhere for James to go, the conflict never arose.

There are always going to be babies who slip through the 'care net'. One of these has obviously been Rhoda's little boy, Edward. While travelling about (and Rhoda's sister, Priscalla, left her to cope on her own when the child was two), Edward had constant colds and chest infections. Life in a caravan is pretty spartan by my standards but not by Rhoda's. When we talked together I asked her what was the best thing about living in a flat and do you know the only thing she could think of was not having to fetch and heat all her water! I had expected a great long list! When Edward became ill enough to need medical treatment, Rhoda simply took him to the nearest hospital. I suspect that what he missed in companionship at nursery school he made up for within the family. There seemed to be a lot of children milling about for him to play with. Incidentally, at the time of writing, Greenwich is in the process of appointing a social worker whose specific task it will be to look after the gipsy families in the borough. It would be nice to think that there could be some liaison between the areas so that there could be monitoring of any handicapped children even when they are travelling around. The travellers do, after all, seem to be fairly consistent in their habits.

Some associations run coffee mornings just so that young (and not so young) mums can get together, and these are very low-key. The Down's Children's Association runs a pop-in parlour in Bexleyheath, in Kent, and the toy library in Greenwich look upon their coffee mornings and regular lunchtime sessions as an important part of the function of the association. Celia, when Paul was very young, used to go to the coffee mornings at the clinic to get the things she wanted — in other words, she 'lobbied' them. Somewhat relevant to Celia's case was a conference at which I was asked to speak in September 1984. The theme of the conference, which was organized by the Inner London Education Authority (ILEA) (for teachers in special schools and parents of handicapped children) was 'Working with Parents' and my particular brief was 'Parents as Partners'. If only this concept could start from the birth of the baby. After all, no one is likely to know more about a child who lives at home than his mother and there are still too many instances of the professionals treating parents as though they were deaf mutes as well as stupid. I myself experienced a fairly typical example of the treatment which can be dished out to parents. Towards the end of James's first year of life he kept bringing up little bits of his food — not sick exactly, but he continually regurgitated small quantities of the meal right up until the next one. There seemed to be no respite. He was perfectly fit and really this was just a blessed nuisance. On one of our three-monthly visits to Dr Morris I mentioned this 'nuisance'. He leaned back in his chair, turned to one of the 'entourage' and said, 'It's funny how some of these children have a slack cardiac sphincter,' then he turned back to me, the child's mother, and said, 'Give him lots of sticky food — Irish Stew and that sort of thing.' He made no explanation to me at all of the reason for the condition. I took James home and gave him lots of sticky food, as instructed; I also looked up cardiac sphincter — not at all as instructed! The next time we went to see Dr Morris he asked how James was. 'Fine,' I said casually, 'still having problems with the slack cardiac sphincter, though.' Dr Morris pounced — 'How did you know about that?' he said, so I told him. I think he was totally unaware of having given any offence; he presumably assumed, wrongly, that I would be unable to understand any explanation he might have offered. So much for parents as partners. How nice it would be if this idea was taken up by the medical profession and the social services, as well as the schools.

Before James had his fifth birthday David, our fourth son, was born. David's birthday was at the end of January 1963 and James was five on the 2nd April following. Life became a sort of conveyor belt of nappies. The house smelt constantly of *Persil* (usually boiling over somewhere!), to say nothing of other odours. It really was a baby-orientated establishment. When anyone asks me what alterations I would make if I had my time over again, I usually say that I wouldn't make any. No, I'm not in need of urgent psychiatric treatment! It's just that having all the boys so close together was very good for James. Of course, if I had my time over again and James wasn't handicapped, that would be a very different can of beans, but it really did him the world of good being slung out of the nest so early. When schoolchildren want to know if James got more than his fair share of attention, I point out to them that James was lucky if he got any attention at all! It amuses me, looking back, to realize that none of them ever really noticed the next one coming along. I suppose my easy attitude was subconsciously taken up by them as well. None of them ever said, 'Mum, why have you got such a big tum?' I look back on those days with nostalgia now, if you can believe it!

So, let us just sum up the people who, in the early years, should be supporting you, the parent of a mentally-handicapped child. In the first instance it should be the health visitor and the social worker. The health visitor will have made a home visit during your pregnancy and should visit you again within ten days of arriving home from hospital with your new-born baby. If she doesn't materialize (and I imagine that there could be difficulties in rural areas — I haven't extended my research beyond London), your GP can put you in touch with her. If you are taking your baby to the welfare clinic regularly you will know who she is and if, for personal reasons, you don't take your baby to the clinic she should be making regular home visits to weigh and check the baby. She will be able to give you help and advice with such things as nappies (they can be obtained free after two years) and special bedding; washing and bathing your child if you can't do it yourself, and problems requiring nursing skills, such as enemas and dressing sores and wounds. General health matters like diet, exercise and sexual problems can all be referred to her. I should say straightaway that some of the difficulties mentioned above will be passed on to the Community (District) Nurse, who will be notified of your needs by the health visitor. Different areas have different structures and it may be that your GP will be attached to a Health Centre where all these people can be seen under one roof. I should mention that health visitors these days seem to have enormous caseloads and while she shouldn't forget you she is but human and you may just have to keep on at her a bit. If you do find that you have to press for the services you require, please don't be embarrassed about it. Tell yourself you are helping them to do their jobs properly!

The social worker comes under the jurisdiction of the social services (as opposed to the health visitor who comes under the district health authority) and you should be able to call on him or her for help with personal problems and worries which you may have — and the early days can be very fraught from sheer ignorance of your child's handicap. We all feel it — it's a perfectly natural reaction, fear of the unknown. Do remember, though, that you are looking after a baby first and foremost — it is so easy to allow the handicap to dominate your life and it needn't. If you can be relaxed about it, so will your baby. And we all know that a relaxed baby is better than a tense one!

The social worker can give you advice on benefits, and that is a tangled web if ever there was one. Actually, until your child is sixteen the process is fairly straightforward. After that it can get somewhat complicated but that will be dealt with later. There are facilities for helping your day-to-day living; adaptations can be made to your home if they are needed. For instance, hoists can be put over the bath to make it easier to lift the child, and ramps put in for wheelchairs, and that sort of thing. Your social worker should also be on hand to provide respite or relief care. On the subject of respite care I do beg of you not to wait until you are on the very brink of insanity before taking advantage of this very helpful service. It may not have occurred to you, but even other members of your family can be going quietly mad while you are occupied and busy with the handicapped child. Not all handicapped children disrupt the home but others in the family do deserve a bit of your undivided attention now and again. Also — and it is a very important also — it keeps your child's existence in the consciousness of the social services and, believe me, that is no bad thing. If and when the time comes for permanent care they will know exactly what sort of person they will have to accommodate.

I went on a course recently and met a marvellous girl called Lesley. She and her husband offer respite care to mentally-handicapped children and young people in their flat close to the sea in Bournemouth. They are assisted financially by MENCAP and the social services. This, to me as a parent, seems infinitely preferable to a hospital or hostel because, of course, it has an essence of 'mothering' and 'fathering' about it and sounds the sort of care we want for our young children. However, don't pass up respite care because you can't get this sort — it isn't very common, yet. Incidentally, if the social services are hanging back on respite care, get in touch with your local Association for the Disabled (known in Greenwich as 'GAD' — they have a transport service called GADabout!). They may know of other ways of obtaining what you need. Failing that, there's always the local press or television!

5

ASSESSMENT: EDUCATION AND TRAINING

As James approached his fifth birthday and with his one and only assessment now behind us, the time came for school to be considered. For 'school' read 'junior training centre'. My baby of four and three-quarters was going to a training centre. Schools for the mentally handicapped were not, at that time, in being. The children were still being educated by the Ministry of Health. My husband was informed by the local authority that there was a waiting list of children for the training centre, and they would let us know in due course when a place became available. Neville promptly wrote to them, asking to be furnished with the list of names and the list somehow miraculously evaporated, and James was offered a place. Doesn't it pay to be just a bit articulate? A fact of life which never ceases to enrage me. It shouldn't be necessary. There are far more parents who are unable to speak up for themselves than those who can. At the time that James started at the Cecil Rooms Junior Training Centre, he was toilet-trained during the day (not at night) and he really was not yet speaking in even short sentences. I was never able to find out what he did at 'school', but as time went by I used the hear the names 'Auntie Potter', 'Auntie Bryce' and Miss Dell. He loved his teachers and I am sure that they loved him. He was a most loving, good-natured and bright little boy.

It was during this period that I had my first brush with a social worker. In order to get James to the training centre each day I had to leave David (then two months old) alone in his cot (the sort of thing you read about in the papers!) while I got James, Christopher and Michael dressed and I then had to wheel the three of them up to the Sidcup Road (the A20; a main arterial road) in order to wait for the coach. After some time of this the social worker came to see me one day and I asked her if the bus could make a diversion (not involving any great difference of route and certainly not putting anyone out) so that I could put James on the bus at a spot which was not quite so far to walk, thus leaving the baby for a shorter time. And it would also be less dangerous — I was always expecting Christopher or Michael to make a sudden dash into the road. I shall never, ever, forget her reply. 'I'm not going to help you,' she said, 'because if I change your stop, all the other mothers will want their stops changed.' You don't forget something like that, do you? She was a 'Miss' (the old-fashioned sort) and she had about as much compassion as our cat. Less. So we continued, until the buses started calling for the kids at home, and that was absolute heaven. Didn't matter how late they were then, at least we were warm and dry. The coach drivers were really nice chaps. I well remember on one occasion I was waiting in what turned out to be the wrong spot (due, if I remember rightly, to an unexpected re-routing of the bus) and the coach driver brought James across the road himself — which is, of course, more practical than taking the escort away from all the others!

It was shortly after starting school that James started banging his head on the end of his bed. We had had no problems of this nature with him before, and I really wondered where we were going from there. We tried all sorts of things — going into his room, turning him over and waking him up. He would settle down straightaway, then minutes later — thump, thump, thump would start again. The doctor prescribed a course of mild phenobarbitone (the things I've done to that child in my ignorance — it's a wonder he has survived!) but I wasn't at all happy about it and in the end the problem was resolved accidentally. When David had to be moved out of our room (he was a few months old) one of the other boys went in with James, who had up until then been sleeping on his own. From the first night that he had company in his room James stopped banging his head. We found it very interesting and incidentally were also very relieved. He was beginning to get a lump on his head and I was very concerned about it.

When Colin was rising five, Doreen went to see the

headmistress of the school her daughter Christine had attended and explained about Colin's speech and hearing defects. She also mentioned that she thought he seemed behind in his mental development. The headmistress agreed to take Colin, and Doreen felt that it was the logical thing to do even though she didn't feel it was the right school for Colin. He didn't like it, in fact, because he had always been very averse to any change. Fortunately he had a sympathetic teacher (who, Doreen discovered years and years later, was a great friend of Doff and John's) and in time he settled down. He didn't make any progress to speak of (and this is a pretty high-powered primary school) and he found the playground very nerve-racking. Poor old Colin spent the whole of his lunchtime holding the hand of one of the dinner ladies (who also in later years turned up in the local MENCAP society!). At the end of his first year Doreen visited the school to see what they were going to suggest regarding Colin and was rather disturbed to find that they intended putting him up a class, despite the lack of progress. When he went into the next class (and it was his correct age group, if nothing else) he had a very strict teacher who couldn't give him anything like the amount of time he needed but, and let it not be said that she didn't have a kind heart, gave him a budgie to help him with his speech! Colin was totally bored by the budgie, but Christine thought it was great and it became her pet. At the end of the second year Doreen asked what suggestions they had for Colin and she was told that nothing was to be decided until September. Doreen and Jack were extremely concerned about leaving it as late as that and decided not to send him back to the school. This was the best thing they could have done as, in Doreen's words 'it brought all the forces of the law down on them'. Apparently it didn't matter if Colin didn't make any progress at school as long as he was there! After a lot of to-ing and fro-ing (the details are lost in the mists of time) Colin saw the educational psychologist and an assessment was arranged. During all this, it was made quite plain to Doreen and Jack that they were being an awful nuisance. After the tests and medical examination (some of which took place at home) it was decided that he was retarded. To quote Doreen — 'Mr and Mrs Sanders, you are right.' It took the educational authorities seven-plus years to discover that a child with a mild hearing problem, no speech and a very low concentration level was mentally retarded. Bully for them. It is interesting to speculate what would have happened if Doreen and Jack had continued to send Colin to the same school. They instigated all the proceedings to get Colin correctly assessed and received neither sympathy nor apology for the terrible delay in getting him the correct tuition.

As Joan had never been able to persuade anyone that Penny was retarded she decided to send her to a nursery school — this was well before Penny's fifth birthday. Every doctor Joan saw said that Penny would 'probably grow out of it' and none of them would consider retardation. The head of the nursery school was sympathetic and Penny stayed there until it was time for her to go to 'big' school. She was assessed at this point and the doctor told Joan that there couldn't be much wrong with Penny because she was able to close the door when told to do so! Penny ended up at the same school that Colin went to, and after only one-and-a-half terms Jim had a fresh assignment and the family took off for Australia. Out there things were a little easier for Joan and Jim as there was no special procedure for sending a child to a special school and Penny was able to get the correct tuition without a lot of bureaucratic palaver. Joan still couldn't get anybody interested as to why Penny was handicapped. While she was in Australia she saw a programme on television about phenylketonuria and went from Canberra to Sydney to see a doctor who specialized in the field of handicap. Professor Lorimer Dods was the only person who ever showed any interest in Joan (and Penny's) problem, but all the tests he did were inconclusive and he was unable to offer Joan and Jim any reason for the girls' handicap — Cathy had been born by this time and with the same condition. When the family returned to England in 1964 (Cathy was six by now), Joan rang the authorities to inform them that she required places for Penny and Cathy. The assessment tests were, to use Joan's word, 'desultory' and the girls were placed in the Cecil Rooms Junior Training Centre, with James and his contemporaries.

Chris's Paul was a very active child and when he was about three, one of the clinic doctors became very concerned for Chris's state of health and arranged for Paul to be assessed (this would be about 1969), the outcome of which was that Paul was recommended to the nursery which was then being run by Greenwich MENCAP with funding from the London County Council (as it was then). This nursery was one of the best things which the Greenwich Society ever undertook. It started in Woolwich, south-east London, in 1965 with four pre-school handicapped children and, when the 1971 Act made it possible for children to go to school at three (or even two) the nursery became redundant. My friend Pat (the health visitor) had been running it for several years up until it closed and it was this experience which gave her such a deep and lasting concern for mentally-handicapped children and their families. Paul stayed at the nursery until he was five and then he went to Maze Hill School.

I must tell you about Maze Hill School — which is a shining beacon among special schools (well — we in Greenwich think so, anyway!). The mentally-handicapped children of Woolwich and Greenwich were being looked after in the Cecil Rooms (one of those grim 'upper and lower' hall buildings of, I suppose, Victorian or Edwardian origin and much beloved by holders of jumble sales). It was really tatty and the Society had to pay for lino for the floor as the children were coming home with splinters in their knees. This state of affairs existed for some years before Maze Hill School was built and this really was an innovation. It was actually called 'a school'. It opened in January 1966 and up to 1984 (when she was seconded to the Inspectorate of ILEA for two terms) was run by Betty Godfrey who is another shining beacon among teachers in special schools (which is why, I guess, she was grabbed by the Inspectorate!). To my mind she is the perfect teacher — she combines a totally professional approach with compassion and (lacking in far too many teachers) a keen sense of humour. I well remember her amusement at Yvette (one of her more difficult pupils) who, on being told that 'Miss Godfrey will not be in school today', was heard to say (rather loudly), 'F...ing good job, too' — and this in front of the whole school and staff at Assembly! Once Betty was ensconced in the school she got started on the structured learning programmes which are now (hopefully) a normal feature of special schooling for the severely subnormal child, and this was well before the 1971 Education Act. At the beginning there was no nursery provision, of course, as this also came under the 1971 Act. The nursery in Westmount Road, Eltham (the one Pat ran) was therefore still very much in demand. This also, though, brought its traumas to some parents. Transport, as usual, was a major problem, but as the nursery had expanded so much since it was first opened, and it was no longer possible to ferry the children around in private cars, it became essential to have a minibus and the Variety Club of Great Britain, as is their wont, came to the rescue. Doreen and Don well remember the first time the nursery bus came to collect Kathrine — it had 'Mentally-Handicapped Children' written all along the side and made Doreen's tummy turn over. It is so easy to put it out of your mind when you are just occupied with the day-to-day care of your child. Kathrine stayed at the nursery until she was five, when an assessment was done and it was decided that she was a suitable candidate for the nearest ESN (Mild) school. The assessment was done at the nursery — Patricia always tried to get the children assessed there if she could as they functioned so well in those surroundings.

After his pointless two years at his first school, Doreen and Jack were told that Colin could have a place at Rose Cottage in Plumstead, south-east London, which is also an ESN (Educationally Subnormal) Mild school. Fortunately transport was provided as the school was virtually inaccessible from where Doreen and Jack lived. Colin was eighteen months in the first class and it got to the point where he really couldn't stay in that class any longer. They tried him in the next class (he was nine by now) and as no progress was being made by him, it was arranged that further tests should be made by the educational psychologist at Great Ormond Street Hospital in London. This came about because once again it was suggested that Colin's lack of progress may have been due to his faulty hearing. When Doreen and Jack took Colin to see the educational psychologist he was very sympathetic and, after the tests had been analysed, told Doreen and Jack that Colin was retarded! He contacted Rose Cottage and the outcome was that Doreen and Jack received the 'your child has been deemed ineducable' letter which it pleased the authorities to send out in those days. So much for 'no child is ineducable'. Things have improved somewhat. Doreen and Jack were a bit alarmed when they saw how much more retarded the children at Maze Hill School were than Colin but, looking back, Doreen can see that this was greatly to Colin's advantage as it was a terrific boost to his confidence to be one of the best. He took less time to settle at Maze Hill than at any previous establishment and his hearing seemed perfectly adequate. Incidentally, during all this educational and emotional upheaval, Doreen and Jack never saw a social worker. Judging from my own experience, that might have been no great loss!

Sandra, mother of albino baby Elizabeth, is an example of how easy it is to close one's eyes to a child's handicap, and how lack of communication between the professionals and the family can confuse the issue. Sandra had been taking Elizabeth back to King's College Hospital, London, once a month; she had also been taking her to the local clinic regularly and no mention was made by anyone at either of these places that Elizabeth was very slow in her progress. It appeared, subsequently, that something had been said at King's to Sandra's husband, and it has to be assumed that the hospital thought he had passed the information (whatever it was — Sandra never found out as she is now divorced) on to Sandra. This, of course, was not so, but nobody every queried whether Sandra was in possession of the truth about her baby. It is interesting that Sandra (who is not unintelligent by any means) was able to accept the baby's lack of progress right up until the educational psychologist came to the house to assess Elizabeth at the age of three. The psychologist recommended Maze Hill School and Sandra 'blew her top'. It was the first hint she had been given of mental handicap and she had convinced herself that Elizabeth would be going to a school for the partially sighted (the common disability of albino children and adults). Sandra was persuaded to go and see Maze Hill and her first impression was that 'it was really lovely'. Sandra's mother is very supportive and I suspect she was instrumental in helping Sandra to face the truth about Elizabeth's handicap. Sandra is quite certain that it is only the dedication of the school which has got Elizabeth where she is today. It was quite amusing, actually, that when I asked Sandra what Elizabeth could do when she started school, Sandra said, 'Nothing.' I queried this. 'Absolutely nothing?' 'That's right,' said Sandra, 'Absolutely nothing,' and then went on to tell me that if Elizabeth wanted anything from the other side of the room she had to shuffle across on her bottom! In other words, the 'absolutely nothing' was, in fact, sitting up and shuffling across on her bottom! In terms of handicap that can hardly be described as 'nothing'. Sandra has had some rather unusual difficulties with Elizabeth as a result of her poor sight — she is extremely frightened when sitting in the pushchair. Sandra thinks that this is because Elizabeth just sees large shapes (often holding bags) coming at her and is unable to identify what they are. This is one of the problems of forward-facing pushchairs. What a very simple adjustment this would be, but of course many children (handicapped or not) would be more stimulated in a forward-facing pushchair as it is much easier for Mum to point things out before you get to them than to mention them after they've gone past.

School, I think, has a much more important role to play if a handicapped child has no one else at home with whom to play. James would have benefited from a Home-Liaison Teacher, rather than going to school before he was five, because he had the other boys for company and I suspect that they too would have benefited from the teacher coming to the house. If I had my time over again (and I did say that I wouldn't change anything), it could be like running my own nursery school. Actually, it was a bit like that anyway. The boys were really very sweet when they were all small together (not that they still aren't, of course, it's just that the term seems inappropriate for children the size mine are now!) and the main game they played, and which I now look back on with such amusement, was 'Hospitals'. I have no idea why they played 'Hospitals' — it might have been after Michael had his tonsils out when he was three — but it was all a very serious matter. The teddies all had their respective roles to play, as did the boys, and guess who was the doctor? Yes, that's right. It was James! My nursing students and I get a lot of laughs out of that. (I show James's film to nursing students — but more of that later.) There were very few disagreements in those far off days and when I look back through the mists of time (and the horror of adolescence!) they really were comparatively tranquil times. Of course, nobody wanted to know us — there were too many of us. Mary, who by this time was raising her own family not ten minutes' walk from where we lived, was the only person upon whom I called with any degree of regularity and even her husband was once heard to remark, 'I see the demolition squad has been round again!' They did tend to — er — explore, and on this particular occasion had had a good nose round the shed, which had involved having to remove quite a lot of the contents which, it seemed, they had quite forgotten to put back. They have improved over the years, I would hasten to say. A bit.

My older sister, Pamela, I look back on as being someone rather akin to Mother Theresa. She used to house all six of us for Christmas almost every year until 1972, when Peter was born. How about that! The year I had Christopher (he was born in June 1960) I arrived at Pam's house in a very ill state and went straight to bed. I really did have awful pregnancies (except with Peter). Pam coped marvellously with us all and I shall be ever grateful to her. Let me state it publicly! She had one son of her own, Paul, and the year I arrived and went to bed she herself was pregnant. It turned out that Monica, my younger sister, Pamela and myself each had a baby in 1960. Pam's Paul was born on 17 May, Monica's Matthew was born on 15 June and Christopher was born on 17 June. Is it any wonder that Mother came tearing back from Australia. When we three girls got together that year, it was like Tweedledee, Tweedledum and Friend! One of the reasons that Mother and Father had returned was, of course, James. I hadn't said anything about his handicap in my letters but we had sent out some photographs and there was one in particular which gave the game away and, while my brother in Australia had a large family of daughters (subsequently six!) his wife's family were all on hand, so Mum and Dad's support wasn't needed to the extent that it was here. It was a nervous moment when Neville and I went to meet them at Southampton and I cried all over Mum! We had never, Mum and I, been what you would call very close but I sure had missed her during that traumatic couple of years — James was coming up to two when they arrived home. Their return marked a change for the better as far as I was concerned because they were always ready to be called upon, and frequently made the awful journey by public transport (my family had never once owned a car) from Ilford to Mottingham in order to give me a little time on my own — or just to be around. They were fantastic with the kids and never spoiled them, which is the only criticism I would dare to make. I think grandparents ought to be allowed to spoil their grandchildren a little. It's much better than the parents doing it because the grandparents aren't around nearly so much, so spoiling becomes a treat instead of (as it seems to be now) a right. One of the things I remember that upset Mum was the way James sucked his flannel in the bath. It was at the time when we were having problems with his tummy and were restricting his liquids a bit. Mum always thought he must be dying of thirst but I suspect that a lot of toddlers suck their flannels in the bath! Bathtime, when the four boys were small, was really quite fun and Mum used to love doing their hair. Christopher's hair tended to be curly and Mother used to roll it into a great big curl on top of his head — he looked so big-eyed and innocent! Mary said of Christopher, when he was a small boy, that, 'He looks as though butter wouldn't melt in his mouth but we all know it would fry.' It was a pretty accurate summing up! Once James started school the pressure was reduced somewhat, and even more so when the school bus called at the house.

When I was about five months pregnant with David (James would have been about four and a half) my elder sister Pam took charge of Christopher and Michael, I left James at home in the care of my mother and father, and Neville and I went off to the continent for ten days with Neville's sister, Janet. On this occasion it was James's bottom which became a problem! He was still in nappies (and I suspect that we hadn't started toilet-training him with any great degree of enthusiasm before this holiday as we we didn't want Mum to have the hassle of running round after him all the time). You wouldn't think that nappy rash could do what it did to that child's bottom before we went away. We used everything that had ever been invented to try and clear it up, and Mum and Dad absolutely refused to

allow us to consider cancelling the holiday — it really was
that bad. So, we went (and had a super time) and when we
came back we learned that Mum had called in the doctor
and he had told them that if it didn't show some
improvement in the next thirty-six hours, he would have to
take James into hospital. Fortunately, under Mum's
marvellous ministrations and, I have no doubt, her prayers,
it never came to his having to go into hospital, but I think
my lovely parents went through some very bad moments.
In fact, I wasn't at all worried at leaving James with Mother
as, when her doctor saw how she nursed my bedridden
grandmother for several years without a single sign of a
bedsore, the doctor told Mother that she could find her a
job doing similar work any time she asked. Mum was really
clever at making you comfortable when you were ill and I
think that's what I missed most after I got married!

A few years later I heard David (he would have been
about four) telling the others that he knew all about
Switzerland because he had peeped out of Mum's tummy-
button! How's that for one-upmanship! This summer we —
Neville, James, Peter and I — will be going back to the
places we visited on that holiday for the first time since
then and I am sure that it will bring back lots of memories.

These days, mothers and fathers are kept much more
closely in touch with their children's educational progress.
At Maze Hill School (and these improvements have been
built up over the years since James was there) each child
has a Home/School Book. The work which the child does
at school is recorded and, hopefully, so are family events.
The object of this is to give the child and his teacher topics
of conversation as well as to enlighten the parents as to
what is going on. If there are any problems (i.e. with
feeding or some other developmental task) the parents are
invited to the school either singly or (if the problem is
shared among several children) as a group of parents.
Parents are also welcome to visit the school at any time
(preferably making an appointment first as the teachers may
not be able to free themselves at a given moment) and in
Maze Hill it is not necessary to contact the Head first in
order to see one of the class teachers. Betty Godfrey did
say, though, that she would expect the class teacher to
inform her if a parent wanted an interview.

Yearly reports are sent out for each child during June and July and these are followed by interviews, on a definite appointment basis, with the class teachers. On these occasions, the Head, Deputy Head, Speech Therapist, Physiotherapist and School Social Worker are all available if the parents have anything they wish to discuss with any of these people. There are occasional workshops for parents, the purpose of which might be to enlighten parents on specific areas of the curriculum. This could be on how number or letter recognition is taught or perhaps the Maketon sign language — which is really essential for parents to know if they have a non-speaking (aphasic) child. Maze Hill School runs these workshops in the evenings or occasionally on Saturdays and, in order that both parents (where applicable) may attend, they provide supervision for the children. One wonders what there is left to do.

Maze Hill also has a thriving parent/staff association (of which I was secretary until well after James had left the school!) and even there great strides have been made since James went on to the adult training centre. They now put out a newsletter with contributions from parents as well as teachers and this goes out at least three times a year. It is not very surprising that parents wonder what has happened to them when their child leaves a school like Maze Hill to go to the adult training centre.

The school can be a tremendous support to parents, in addition to providing the child with the education best suited to his ability. It was the school physiotherapist who told Sandra that she didn't have to keep buying expensive (and breakable) pushchairs for Elizabeth but that she was entitled to one provided by the social services. The school can also implement some of the care that all children need; for instance, regular visits to the school by the mobile dental unit and regular medicals. The dental unit can show up any problems which may occur in-between visits to the child's own dentist. This may be particularly useful with children like James who don't complain until crisis point has been reached. You wouldn't believe the number of times James has said, 'I've got a sore spot,' and has lifted his shirt or rolled up a sleeve to expose what is, in fact, practically a boil. Nobody wants a moaner but there must be a happy medium!

Maze Hill School was very good indeed at backing us up when there was a problem to be tackled. James, when he was about twelve, went through a phase of using the most frightful language and as I am the sort of mother who doesn't ignore bad language (on the principle that if you don't tell them that you don't like it and don't want to hear it, how are they to know?), I decided to rope in the school to help. So, Betty Godfrey and I agreed that if James continued to swear (bearing in mind that he had young and impressionable brothers at home) he should not be allowed to go swimming with his class. In order to make sure that James realized what was going on, Miss Godfrey took him into her room, explained how distressing to everyone his swearing was and that it was up to him. She asked him which he would rather do, swim or swear. Now my handicapped son can be as bloody-minded as the rest of them and, of course, he said, 'Swear.' 'Right-ho,' said Miss Godfrey, and left it there for the time being. However, one day it became necessary for me to phone Miss Godfrey and tell her that James had not got his swimming things because the time had come to carry out the threat. James, of course, didn't think about such boring things as swimming trunks and when the time came, he went and lined up with his class. He was spotted by Miss Godfrey. 'Where do you think you're going, James Thompson?' she asked him. 'Swimming,' replied James. 'Oh, but you said you would rather swear than go swimming, James,' came her answer, 'so you may go into my room and swear,' and he was duly bundled in so to do! This is now called behaviour modification! I don't actually know how long James spent in Miss Godfrey's room swearing aloud (and being urged to continue when he stopped) but it sure did the trick and the swearing, after that time, tended to be very *sotto voce*.

At about this time it was observed that James seemed to be in need of a sight test. I took him along to the local clinic in Greenwich (local to the school) and a most kindly doctor sorted him out and prescribed spectacles. One has to have terrific confidence in the people who test our children's sight as, at this point, James was unable to point to letters and I was never sure whether he knew what the pictures were supposed to be! As the years have gone by he has decided for himself when he feels he needs to wear the spectacles and we leave him to it. He has also graduated from National Health frames to smart 'private' frames, which do look much nicer on him. Also, we often see people on the television with identical specs to James's and that's always good for morale! I do think that Down's people need all the help they can get, appearance wise, stopping short (as far as we are concerned, anyway) of cosmetic surgery. The only problem James has with his glasses now is that he tends to put them down and forgets where they are. Something he has in common with his parents!

When the handicapped child reaches school age, many parents feel they ought to start on the business of allowing him or her to go for short visits to local hostels. This has a two-fold purpose. In the first place it allows the family a break from the continuous 'vigilance' which is necessarily entailed in caring for a handicapped child or adult and secondly it helps the child to become gradually accustomed to living away from his or her own family. This second point is, for me, very important indeed, though as far as the 'vigilance' is concerned, you don't realize how much of it there is until you are relieved of it. We try to get James into the hostel for at least a week each year (he didn't go at all last year, I'm afraid) so that if there was a crisis and he had to go into care quickly (and who knows what's around the corner?) it wouldn't be too traumatic for him. It is necessary for us to give the social services a considerable amount of notice as there are only six short-stay places in Greenwich at the time of writing. I do think it is cruel to keep handicapped sons and daughters (or sisters and brothers — the carers are not always the parents) at home, with no experience of living away, until the bitter end. The end may be very bitter indeed. Parents and carers are sometimes required to be really unselfish in arranging short-term care for their children. They know that they care for them most and best and really do not want to part with them for any reason. Patricia has always said that parents of handicapped children are among the most caring she has met as a health visitor and never ceases to be amazed at the personal hardship they will endure to do the best for their child. I think that Rhoda, my 'traveller' lady, is a good example of what Pat meant. Rhoda sold her caravan and took to life in a flat (which doesn't on the face of it seem a very great hardship) because it was better for Edward, her Down's son. I would consider separating myself from my family, as she did, to be considerable hardship, actually.

There are several establishments in Greenwich which cater for short-term care: Eastcombe Avenue and Ashburnham Grove cater for the younger ones and Hervey Road and Westcombe Park Road take the adults. Ashburnham Grove Hostel has been adapted into a number of small flatlets where the youngsters come together in very small groups and a considerable amount of training is incorporated into the duration of their stay. It is hoped that there will be more establishments of this nature in the borough and that they will be of benefit to older people, like James, who have missed out on so many of the innovative philosophies and practices.

Doing the best for your handicapped child can sometimes end up being a real pain. James has been made very comfortable at home, and God knows, he's no trouble, but I suppose we have made it difficult for him to adapt to hostel life, even for a short time. We have provided him with his own room where he has his music centre, his dartboard (with proper rubber mat — a recent birthday present!), his colour TV, and downstairs he has his quarter-size snooker table. Follow that, social services! Should I be advising parents not to do these things for their children? No, I have to give James the benefit of the doubt and accept that he is more adaptable than I give him credit for. This probably applies to the majority of handicapped children — or even the non-handicapped. It is a fact, though, that when James comes back from sharing a room with three other people, he tends to take to his own bedroom for quite long periods — and I don't disturb him.

Being a single parent, Pauline finds it very helpful for Keith to go to the hostel at Eastcombe Avenue. It gives her a chance to spend a little more time with the rest of the family (and the importance of this should not be underestimated) and also it just helps to relieve the tension. Elsie and Jim have also started Mark going for short stays at the hostel in Ashburnham Grove and he absolutely loves it. Elsie told me that as soon as he gets home he wants to know when his next visit is! We parents regard this reaction with somewhat mixed feelings! I shall never forget (and this really is digressing for a moment) when James went into a local hospital for a couple of days when he was about ten to have a sinus wash-out (the usual old catarrh problem). He settled into the ward beautifully, they all spoiled him rotten and when I went to bring him home, he cried because he wanted to stay! How about that! This stout party was very collapsed indeed. Needless to say, I did think that it was better for him to be like that, really, rather than mopey and whiney.

Our friends, Doff and John, go about their short-stay problem in a different way. They are opera enthusiasts and when they go on one of their 'operatic' holidays they arrange an adventure holiday for Gavin at the same time. It serves a similar purpose in adjusting him to being away from the family, but I feel that being in the hostel while attending the usual school or training centre does extend the experience to a valuable degree.

Goldie Leigh Hospital, in the borough of Greenwich, is quite a nice little subnormality hospital but of course, its days are numbered as the children in there (supposedly up to sixteen years, but there are a few older) are to be accommodated in new buildings of a more acceptable nature. It is still serving a valuable purpose, of course, as there is, in addition to the residential part, a day centre which caters for children up to the age of five; the main purpose of them being there is, on the whole, to relieve pressure at home. These children tend to be profoundly handicapped; the sort whose parents never get a good night's sleep and places like the Goldie Leigh Day Centre can be a life-saver — literally. Patricia has found, on a number of occasions, that even mothers of terribly demanding handicapped children are reluctant to let them go to any sort of nursery or centre but a visit to the day centre 'just to look' can often change their minds.

The day centre can also be a marriage saver. It doesn't require much imagination to see the amount of tension a marriage is put under if the parents are never getting a good night's sleep and a job of work has to be done the next day. In fact the work is almost incidental — not getting enough sleep is conducive to intolerable wear and tear on the nerves and few marriages can stand up to this sort of assault for any extended length of time. There are other aggravations; a baby who rarely stops crying can have the same nerve-jangling effect as sleeplessness and the day-care centre brings a most welcome relief to parents in either or perhaps both of these situations. Another consideration always to be borne in mind is the welfare of the other children in the family; I avoid saying 'brothers and sisters' as the others could well be being fostered. Without the relief of the day-care centre they may only see their mothers (and/or fathers) as tense and sometimes distraught people who spend too much time with the handicapped member. It's not their fault the child is handicapped, they may reason; why should they pay for it by losing out (it seems to them) on the love and attention they feel they deserve? This jealousy is perfectly understandable and may, equally understandably, lead to bad behaviour at home, at school or outside, with the usual result of worsening relations all round. It makes a great deal of sense to let your profoundly handicapped child go to a day-care centre at least for part of the school holidays so that your other children can recoup a little of the 'mothering' and 'fathering' which they may have missed out on.

Ron, somebody I haven't mentioned until now, has a daughter in Goldie Leigh. Jenny is a profoundly handicapped girl of twenty-three and Ron earned my unbounded admiration when he told me that he had had Jenny home for a fortnight at Christmas. Ron is divorced and only had his younger daughter, Michelle, to help him. Gary, his younger son, was there in a, shall we say, supervisory or advisory capacity (Gary is eighteen) and a certain amount of help, which was much valued, came from Ian who is Ron's Down's Syndrome son. Ron was very emphatic about the amount of affection and companionship he gets from Ian, who is twenty-two years old, and I am afraid Ron and I exchanged a lot of experiences on the difficulties of raising 'normal' children!

Chris and Bill's little boy, Paul, wasn't at Maze Hill School for very long and never went into short-term care at all. I can't imagine that Chris would ever have let him go, even if he had survived his heart attack — unless it was very much for Paul's own benefit. No big deal was ever made of Paul's heart murmur by any of the doctors that Chris took him to and even Guy's Hospital never suggested any treatment. When Paul was eight he had a heart attack at home, which Chris had to cope with (and her GP told her he thought she had saved Paul's life), but in the hospital, after a few days, he had another from which he didn't recover. While Paul was in a state of collapse (and Chris stayed with him all the time he was in the hospital) the team was unsuccessful in getting a new oxygen cylinder going and it was only after Chris had phoned Bill to come to the hospital, and he had collected one of their other sons on the way, that the cylinder was assembled. As Bill walked into the ward, the last nut on the cylinder was screwed into place. Chris feels very bitter about the way Paul died and also cheated. She resents the fact that it was assumed that no heart surgery would be performed and she resents the apparent incompetence which may have hastened his death. It has taken since 1974 for Chris to come to terms with what has happened to her and this has been even more difficult since Bill died in 1982. Paul and Bill both died in December and Chris finds Christmas a very trying time indeed. She gave me the impression, very strongly, that she hadn't been allowed to finish a job she considered well worth doing. I remember Paul very well — he went to the nursery in Westmount Road, Eltham, which Patricia used to run. He really was a dear and I know Chris isn't exaggerating when she says that everybody loved him. She obviously took Paul's rearing very seriously and related, with justifiable pride, the occasions when, on holiday, she met people who had worked with Down's children and who complimented her on Paul's progress. One lady she met told Chris that she had a boy of ten but he 'wasn't like Paul', even though he was a Down's. Chris asked the mother where the child was and was told that he was in a home. 'Well,' said Chris, 'that's your answer, isn't it?' She takes the view that you only get out of these children what you are prepared to put in and she was obviously prepared to put in a hell of a lot. What a pity she couldn't finish the job.

It is not uncommon for people who haven't got a handicapped child to assume that their death at an early age must be 'a blessing' for the family. This is not so. The death of a child, whether handicapped or not, is terrible and the sense of loss is, if anything, increased where the child has been so very dependent upon the parents for every single one of its physical and emotional needs. The gap in the life of the family cannot be described. Having said that, I have talked to parents who feel that if, when they themselves were too old to look after their adult handicapped offspring, those offspring were to predecease them, they would be spared the worry of wondering what would happen to them when they were no longer around to care for them. What an indictment upon the society in which we live.

This point of view is more common among 'believers' who often (and should always) feel that death is a beginning rather than an end. I'm one of those 'believers' and it is a great comfort. Don and Doreen — who don't have a particular faith — have a very down-to-earth approach. Don said that whatever Kathrine's future may hold he knows that he will have made her life as happy as he knows how for as long as he is able. 'Spoiling' is a word you don't hear very often in connection with bringing up mentally-handicapped children, at least not with the people I have met. I wonder if this is because these children (the younger ones at least) tend to be much less demanding of material things than normal children?

When my boys were all very young, the non-handicapped ones thought that being mentally handicapped must be the greatest thing that could happen to you — life consisted of nothing but parties, presents and outings, or so it seemed to them. I'm sure they felt James was some important and privileged person! The local MENCAP society certainly did lay on a lot of things in those days, some of which have, of course, been superseded by other activities. There is now a Regional Sports Day at Sunbury-on-Thames in Surrey, at the lovely Salvation Army training establishment and the local society hires a coach (or two) each year for those members who want to go (not everyone's cup of tea, of course), and instead of the usual Christmas parties, our particular local branch holds Easter parties on the grounds that there are many other parties and events going on around the Christmas period.

When James was about seven he started going to Fanny McRobert's house in Blackheath, south-east London, where a class had been started for a handful of young children. The numbers had to be restricted, of course, by the size of Fanny's room and the transport factor (as ever), but those who went each week had a marvellous time. The class started through the interest of one of the tutors at Goldsmith's College in London. Her name was Marian North and she was the tutor in charge of the Laban Art of Movement. She supplied two of her students each week and these young men and girls gave up their Saturday mornings (they were paid expenses only) to come and instruct this small group of children in music, painting and movement. This went on for some years without interruption until Miss North left Goldsmith's and the supply of students then became the responsibility (gladly taken on, I would hasten to say) of Mary Newlands at the Sydney Webb College. The students at Sydney Webb became so interested in this Saturday morning group that it became a form of teaching practice and most of those who passed through the hands of Mary Newlands turned up at Blackheath at some time or other. It was an extremely valuable experience for those students who were going to make a career in education of children with special needs. The group eventually moved to Kidbrooke House in Greenwich and the society provided transport. This was good and bad — it meant that children who may not otherwise have been able to get there could attend the group; on the other hand it put an end to the delightful meetings we mums used to have round Fanny's kitchen table in the basement of her house. Fanny made lovely coffee and that hour or so was a real oasis in the week. The group finally disbanded, owing partly to the closing of the Sydney Webb College and partly to Fanny having to have a hip operation and being no longer able to supervise the running of the group.

In those days our family car was a Renault 4L estate and in order to pack in as many as we could for the Saturday morning group Neville had bought four little wooden stools (made in Yugoslavia, I seem to remember!) which the boys sat on in the boot of the car when the main body of it was full of mums and handicapped children. Shows how safety conscious we are now — the very thought of it makes me blush! Once the need for ferrying large numbers had gone I became as critical as anyone else of that sort of thing, of course. Our cars now have seat belts front and rear!

6

HOLIDAYS

Holidays play an important part in family life and in 1964
we took all the children on holiday together for the first
time. David, then the youngest, was about eighteen months
old and I remember it as the most back-breaking holiday
we ever had — including all the camping we have done
since (with the possible exception of once having to push
the caravan up Okehampton Hill in Devon because the car
engine was too small — but that's another story!). David
absolutely loved paddling but in order to save his life it was
necessary to bend over and grasp his harness in the middle
of his back (for some reason it didn't seem to work with the
long strap) while he staggered and splashed about in the
shallow water. We stayed for our summer holidays, from
1964 to 1968 inclusive, in a little cottage at St Agnes in
Cornwall and we look back, Neville and I, with very mixed
feelings to those days. The advantages were that we were
free to do as we liked and there was no danger of the
children disturbing anyone. Self-catering was the only type
of holiday which was practical from the financial as well as
the physical aspect, but dragging that huge pushchair across
the beach with all the towels and paraphernalia which four
small children require was an experience which Neville will
never ever forget. The other thing I remember was that we
only ever seemed to go to the beach. I mean, if it was
sunny we went to the beach and if it looked like rain we
hoped for the best — and went to the beach. If it did rain
(which it usually did) I sat with an umbrella up (the misery!)
while the children took no notice of the weather
whatsoever. As I think I was a hot-house plant in earlier life
this sort of behaviour did not suit me one little bit! The

cottage was owned by some friends of ours, Ursula and Bert DeVos, and I am sure that if it hadn't been for them renting it out to us at such a low sum (I can't remember what it was but it must have been low or we wouldn't have been able to afford it!) we probably wouldn't have got away at all. The journeys were a nightmare and it used to take us, on average, twelve hours to get from South London to St Agnes with just a couple of short stops — no eating in restaurants in those days — and keeping the children happy was such fun!

Sometimes, during the five years we went, my mother and father would come along with us (or join us down there) and it really can't have been a very relaxing holiday for them but it was marvellous to have them there. Oddly enough, Neville and I never took advantage of their presence to go off and 'do our own thing'. It was more likely that the family would have to split up according to who needed a nap at that moment — and not always the children, I might add! Dad was untiring at amusing the boys and I still laugh when I remember him playing cricket on the beach with them. He had a very good eye for a ball and was also pretty nippy on his feet, which was just as well because when it was James's turn to bowl, Dad used to have to run all over the beach in order to hit it! There was never any question of James not taking his turn to bowl because he couldn't throw straight. The ball was hit by Dad whichever direction it happened to be bowled.

The cottage we rented for these holidays was one of a group of about five which in fact were originally farm cottages. The farmer and his wife were very good about the amount of 'trespassing' the boys used to do. One morning James got up very early, let himself out of the house and the farm dog out of his shed and they both went for a walk. The farmer's wife did actually mention it to us and none of us thought it was a particularly good idea (although I think the dog approved), so we discouraged him from doing it again. On another occasion James told us that he had had a chat with Timmy, the bull, and that Timmy had licked his face — and wasn't he a nice friendly bull! We agreed, with slightly ashen faces, and impressed upon James that all conversations with the bull must take place with him, James, outside the field and Timmy, the bull, inside. These holidays gave the boys a chance to be close to animals which they wouldn't normally have seen — and we all enjoyed the delicious clotted cream which Mrs Benney used to make in her kitchen with milk from cows which the boys had watched being milked.

We had a few nerve-racking moments on these holidays (in addition to the ones previously mentioned!), caused mostly by our losing James. He never lost us — he always knew where we were, but we didn't know where he was and we didn't know that he knew where we were, if you see what I mean. One afternoon, on the beach, we searched for him for what seemed like hours and finally discovered him sitting up in the rocks — you know what most Cornish beaches are like. What had made it more difficult to see him was the fact that he was wearing a rock-coloured T-shirt. It was a greeny-brown striped shirt and it blended in perfectly with the rocks around him. So, if you don't want to lose your handicapped child on holiday, don't camouflage him! Another occasion for alarm was when we went into Newquay on a Saturday afternoon and James disappeared in the High Street. If you can imagine what Newquay High Street is like on Saturday afternoon in August you will probably understand the reason for our immediate (but controlled!) panic. Once again, he had just wandered a few doors along from the newsagent's where we were shopping and it didn't take long to find him but again it seemed like weeks. He was never distressed on these occasions. He presumably had some purpose in mind and when we found him he hadn't yet realized that we weren't around.

Holidays for mentally-handicapped children don't necessarily entail tagging along with the rest of the family. MENCAP organizes holidays for unaccompanied children all over the country every year and of course many schools take parties of children on holiday in the same way that ordinary schools do. It was on one of these school holidays that James and a couple of his friends invaded the coal cellar of the house where they were all staying. Doreen, Colin's mum, had gone with them to help and she said that the bathing and scrubbing which followed probably quite ruined the fun that they had had making themselves black in the first place! Mischief of that sort obviously is not confined to the non-handicapped!

It was before a school holiday to East Anglia that James developed the most enormous blister I've ever seen on one of his heels. There was a new lady doctor at our surgery and she looked at this blister, listened to my tale of woe about the school holiday and asked if he was going to be sea bathing. I said that I supposed he probably was and she told me to let him go on the holiday, if I could find suitable footwear, as the sea water would very likely clear it up more quickly than anything she could prescribe. My opinion of doctors went up a bit after that!

In order to arrange a holiday for a handicapped child through MENCAP it is necessary to write to the MENCAP Office at Rochdale, Lancashire. There is a wide range of unaccompanied holidays which are specially geared to suit a wide range of handicaps and ages. They tend to fall into three groups as follows:

1 *Special care holidays*
These cater for the profoundly handicapped (severely subnormal) including those who also suffer severe physical disabilities and children with behaviour problems. Some holidays are for children aged six to sixteen years, some for adults over sixteen years and some for both children and adults. Additional handicaps, such as epilepsy, diabetes and special diets, can be accommodated. These holidays usually take place in residential special schools.

2 *Adventure holidays*
This type of holiday is designed to suit less handicapped children and adults who can usually at least help to wash and dress themselves. They must be ambulant, continent and with no severe behaviour problems. Adventure holidays provide mostly outdoor activities which the guests otherwise would not often have the opportunity to enjoy or participate in.

3 *Guest-house holidays for adults*
These take place in guest houses in seaside resorts for adults over sixteen years who would enjoy the 'traditional' type of seaside holiday including local outings, shopping expeditions, going to shows and, of course, visits to beaches, etc. Guests must be ambulant, continent and preferably able to wash and dress

themselves, although help is always available. Severe behaviour problems cannot be catered for on these holidays.

I think family holidays are very important, but don't be tempted to think that, if the family can't afford a holiday together, there is little point of allowing the handicapped member to go away. There is every point. It allows the rest of the family a break from the eternal vigilance (not to say sheer hard work) of caring for a mentally and/or physically handicapped child all the year round and it gives the child a welcome break from its own possibly boring routine.

John Oliver, who is 'in charge' at the MENCAP Office at Rochdale, puts it as follows:

> It [the holiday] provides parents with an opportunity to break out of the vicious spiral of tension that can be created through caring for a mentally-handicapped person for twenty-four hours a day, seven days a week, for fifty-two weeks of each year. Parents have an opportunity to pick up their lives together again. Mothers, in particular, have a break away from the normal, daily household chores associated with caring for a handicapped person. It provides the other children in the family with some recompense for the limitations often necessarily placed upon family life. It gives everyone an opportunity to recharge their batteries, to enable family life to continue, without parents seeking what may often be inappropriate residential care, if not for their sakes, then for their other children.

And you can't argue with that. One section of the population John hasn't actually mentioned by name and about whom I am very conscious (by virtue of knowing Pauline) is single parents. Of course, this doesn't just include young single parents but those middle-aged and elderly parents who have lost husbands and wives. There is a very large number of widows and, I am sure, widowers who are still struggling to keep their handicapped child at home with them (very often for company) and I think the term 'single parent' too often tends to mean the unmarried and divorced. Doreen has had to cope with Colin on her own since Jack died unexpectedly a few years ago, and while she has found Colin's companionship very welcome, he has always been averse to change and, of course, the death of his father was traumatic. Doreen feels that having to concentrate on keeping his life on as even a keel as possible took its toll and that she should have been able to allow herself more time to grieve. She admitted to me, in a burst of honesty, that she often found Colin irritating (he is very repetitious) and the respite of holidays for people in her situation is essential. Actually, Colin is a dear and all my boys think he is great. I was doing the Club run (that phrase will be very familiar to huge numbers of you!) and Colin bowled out of his house. 'Cold, isn't it?,' he said, 'Cold enough for snow.' He repeated it a couple of times. When I could get a word in I said to him, 'Cold enough for snow? I never heard such rot!' (we all tend to shout) and Colin roared with laughter. He seems to enjoy being mildly abused verbally! I have always found him very good-natured but I have to confess that I don't envy Doreen having to live with him.

However, back to holiday provision. In addition to the three types of holiday mentioned and which are for unaccompanied handicapped people, MENCAP Holiday Services will also provide details of self-catering establishments, boarding houses and hotels where there are facilities for wheelchairs, laundry and special diets, and so on.

On the subject of finance, a small number of avenues are open to families who cannot afford to finance a holiday themselves, particularly if the degree of handicap of the child or adult to be catered for demands specialized or unaccompanied provision. The degree of care and attention required to provide for a handicapped member can place great pressure upon family budgets. Also the income potential of families can be greatly reduced if the demands of caring for a severely handicapped person preclude the mother (or whoever the carer may be) from returning to full or part-time employment. Fathers may have to forego overtime, shift work or occupations that may take them away from home, in order to be on hand to share some of the household chores and strains. In practice this often means that many families simply can't afford to take a holiday or may have to accept many limitations and restrictions in the choice of holiday, unless additional financial help is made available to them. We all know (or should know) that it is incumbent upon local authorities within their policy of community care to provide for the needs of their handicapped or disabled citizens and their families. However, assistance with holidays is not often seen as a service of high priority and spending in this area is more vulnerable to reduction in budget estimates than other social service functions. Local authorities are empowered to provide assistance with holidays for handicapped or disabled people under a number of Acts of Parliament, the most commonly used of which are:

The National Assistance Act 1948
The Mental Health Act 1959
The Children and Young Persons Act 1963 (or its
    equivalent, The Social Work (Scotland) Act 1968)
The Chronically Sick and Disabled Persons Act 1970

There are wide variations in the range of help available and in the criteria adopted by local authorities so far as financial assistance is concerned. Some local authorities allocate their budget on the 'first come, first served' basis; others consider each application according to its merit. Few give any indication of planning to match known demand to the resources available.

Perhaps the widest variation between local authorities occurs in the extent to which parents are expected to contribute to their holiday or that of the child. The vast majority of social services departments make some assessment of a family's circumstances and are prepared to help according to their own criteria. Some may make a flat charge or an automatic grant. Others will assess the contribution required from the family against guidelines, such as the cost of holidays provided by the authority itself; the equivalent of the minimum charge made in Part III accommodation; supplementary benefit rates; or the equivalent of the charge payable if their child was in care. Some will only give assistance every other year, whilst others do not expect any contribution towards the cost of the holiday from parents, particularly where the holiday is provided as a result of a social worker's report for urgent need in this respect. Authorities are also empowered to provide transport or contribute towards the cost of an essential escort for the holiday. Again there are wide variations, not only in the provision of help with transport but also whether that help is provided free of charge or a contribution is required. Although Section 2 of the Chronically Sick and Disabled Persons Act 1970 imposed a duty on all local authorities to provide a specified range of supporting services to any disabled person in need of them, one of which was by facilitating the taking of holidays '... whether at holiday homes or otherwise and whether provided under arrangements made by the authority or otherwise', great differences in the provision made by local authorities for assistance with holidays still continue.

If you need help for a holiday you should apply to your local social services department (and it seems logical for this to be done through a social worker. Don't let them put you off — be polite but *firm*!). Once a local authority has admitted that the need for a service under the Acts exists, they have a duty to meet it. The problem at the moment is that even when they do admit a need exists, many local authorities plead that they do not have enough money to provide that service. If you are refused help because the local authority says that, although they recognize the need, they do not have the resources available to help you, or if you are refused help and no reason is given, you should ask for one and ask them to state whether they consider the need exists or not, and then take the following course of action. You should send a complaint to the Minister for the Disabled at the DHSS, Alexander Fleming House, Elephant and Castle, London SE1 6BY, giving full details of your needs and circumstances and, if possible, evidence of the local authority's acknowledgement that you need the service requested. The Minister can declare the local authority to be failing in its duty and issue instructions as to how it should carry out its duty.

Local MENCAP societies will often assist parents and their families who cannot afford quite enough money for a holiday and who may have been unable to gain financial help elsewhere. Another possible source of financial assistance is the Family Fund. This is a government fund administered by the Joseph Rowntree Memorial Trust, established to complement and not replace existing statutory services. It exists to provide help in the form of goods, services or a grant of money to families with severely disabled children under sixteen. The fund has wide discretion to provide any help which would relieve stress arising out of care of the child, which includes assistance towards family holidays or outings. There is a lengthier description of its services at the end of the book.

The Family Fund's policy of not giving a grant for a family unless the local authority contributes towards the child's share of the cost does, however, place it in a difficult position. This could, for instance, discriminate against families who live in areas of poor local authority provision and who, in some ways, are most in need of a positive discrimination. Interestingly enough, however, social services departments who state that they have only limited resources have, when approached by the Family Fund social workers, sometimes agreed to pay the child's cost of the holiday. The Family Fund also operates outside the limit of local authority statutory responsibility; by taking, as its premise, the relief of *family* stress rather than, as in the Chronically Sick and Disabled Persons Act, the meeting of individual need, it enables parents and others caring for a handicapped child to take a holiday on their own, i.e. by grant aid. You can apply for help from the Fund by writing to The Secretary, The Family Fund, PO Box No. 50, York YO3 6RB, giving your name and address, the name and date of birth of your child, the way he is disabled and the help you need. You will then be visited by a representative of the fund, which has a team of about 180 visiting social workers throughout the United Kingdom.

As is the case with the rest of life, the kind of response you evoke is often determined by the way in which you put your case. If you are seeking financial assistance from a local authority for an unaccompanied holiday for your child, despite all that has previously been said about the need for holidays for handicapped people and their families, you may receive more sympathetic consideration if you ask for help with 'a period of short-term care' rather than 'a holiday'.

While on the subject of holidays for mentally- and/or physically-handicapped people, I should just mention the splendid army of volunteers who make it all possible. The success of the holidays depends upon them; on 'special care' holidays the staff ratio is one helper for each child and other holidays may need one helper for every two children, so that altogether almost as many helpers are needed as there are guests. (Have you spotted the commercial?!) The volunteer helpers are responsible for all the personal care each child needs: washing, dressing, helping them in the toilets, changing napkins and other essential tasks. Some of these jobs may appear unpleasant at first but all volunteers share them and they soon became routine. At times help is needed with cooking and cleaning, making beds, laundry duty and so on and these duties are shared on a rota basis, which is nice if you have a chronic aversion to any one of the tasks mentioned! At least, if you are on a rota, you shouldn't get stuck with the one thing you can't abide! Volunteers are always needed and anyone reading this who thinks they may be interested should write for further details to MENCAP Holiday Services, 119 Drake Street, Rochdale, OL16 1PZ. The minimum age is eighteen and there is no upper age limit, but you need to be fit and persevering, with a mature and responsible attitude to demanding work of this sort. There must be a lot of laughs, because I've known youngsters who have helped on these holidays time and time again. The volunteers consist of people from all walks of life — students, teachers, school-leavers, nurses, social workers, and so on. They will be helped with travel expenses to and from the holiday up to a maximum fixed for the year and, of course, full board and lodging is provided. I was interested to note on the blurb from MENCAP from which I am gleaning this information for all you prospective volunteers, that you are able, up to a point, to choose on which holiday you would like to help. Some fill up more quickly than others, of course.

Some of the clubs manage to take members away for holidays and James's club, Focus, in Eltham, south-east London, has had some really smashing holidays. They have been to Switzerland a couple of times, to Scotland, to the Lake District, to the New Forest — oh, all over the place. James really loves these holidays and it would be more than my life was worth to allow anything so unimportant as a family holiday to interfere with a club holiday. In 1984, when we came back from France, I had one day's turn around before I took off for the New Forest and our caravan. Neville was due back at work the day after we got home from the Gironde and I was taking James and Peter down to Brockenhurst for the remainder of the summer break — except that James was interrupting his time at Brockenhurst with Peter and me to go to a very nice holiday centre nearby called Avon Tyrrell near Burley, Hampshire. As I said, I had one day (and one night) at home before taking off again and I arrived home to a broken washing machine. I had to leave the cleaning of the house (the other boys had gone off to France as we were coming back — we passed each other on the road somewhere, I suspect) and nothing had been done by the boys, of course. I knew the washing machine was broken before I left home and had left instructions with David to get an estimate for repair but not to have it done if it was over £100. I also (with my heart in my mouth) left him a blank cheque. Upon discovering the washing machine was unrepaired, I set out to try and find the blank cheque — there was no note left as to its whereabouts, of course. I don't know where my heart was by this time. It had stopped. Eventually I found an estimate for repair — cost £11, which was where the cheque had gone — but the repair itself, alas, would have cost £150 which was why the machine was still broken. I spent all morning rushing backwards and forwards to the launderette which God in His wisdom had put at the end of my road (it's a very short road) and apart from not being able to sort out the rather high degree of dirt and untidiness in the house, everything proceeded fairly well. Until lunchtime. At lunchtime (we were due to start off for Hampshire at about 4 p.m. in order to get to the campsite while there was still plenty of light) dear old James broke a tooth. There was good reason for my wanting to burst into tears at that moment. We had returned from France the previous day and left our caravan on a site where it was not supposed to be unattended overnight. Neville, man-like, was convinced that a couple of nights wouldn't hurt but I am a very law-abiding person (or perhaps I don't like being found out!) and there was no way I was going to leave it for more than one night, which was why it was essential that we got back on this particular evening. So, I had to down tools (the poor house was absolutely fated never to be cleaned!) and get on the phone to James's dentist. Fortunately they told me to bring him along to the surgery and they would fit him in between appointments, which is exactly what we did. I got into the car with the boys and started off for Hampshire at about 5.15 p.m. (which wasn't bad), but I must say that I felt like a piece of chewed rag! The situation wasn't helped by having to have all James's clothes ready for the Avon Tyrrell holiday; camping in the New Forest isn't conducive to easy washing and ironing — not the way we camp, anyway! However, it all came together OK and James went off from our campsite to join his friends on the appropriate Saturday and we collected him a week later, a good time having been had by all. It was a very hot week while James was away and Peter and I were going to do all sorts of trips out, as there were only the two of us, but in the end we were too hot to do very much except 'lay about'! James takes very well to camping and his muscle comes in very useful when it comes to getting water or lifting the loo into the boot of the car to be taken to the emptying place (well — it's better than digging a hole!). James is very muscular and is the envy of his brothers for the number of press-ups he can do. They try to do as many as he can and I just sit and admire! He has occasionally gone off on his own for walks in the forest, giving us a few worrying moments, but it is on these occasions that you have to have faith. He has only got lost once (if I remember rightly a police car delivered him back to the site!), and he generally wanders back when he's had enough and sometimes in a rather muddy condition! I often wonder what the other campers think when they see this Down's Syndrome young man wandering along the river bank or walking through the woods. Well, perhaps familiarity will breed not contempt but friendliness and I wouldn't for the world stop James from exercising his independence in one of the comparatively few ways open to him.

Camping is, in fact, a very good holiday for a mildly handicapped child, especially for those who only know city life. Of course you have to use a bit of common sense as to what sort of site you are going to camp on and this varies with the degree of disability of the child or adult concerned. I would think that the physical difficulties would preclude a profoundly handicapped child from taking this sort of holiday — incontinence is bad enough with a baby, where you expect it, let alone an adult, but if you have a child who is not incontinent and who you know won't wander off (or if you have sufficient 'staff' to keep an eye on him), being out in the country and thus having a complete change of environment can be very stimulating to a child who has never put his feet in a stream. Our local MENCAP society has a static caravan on a site in Sheppey, Kent, and I know from advertisements in *Parents' Voice* (the MENCAP national magazine) that there are other caravans available for hire. Some campsites are very well equipped with washing and drying facilities so if *you* can cope, perhaps even an incontinent child could enjoy a camping holiday on a formal site. I personally never enjoyed combining camping and nappies, however good the facilities, but that could just be me being a bit 'wet'!

7

WIDENING HORIZONS

'He may be mentally handicapped but he's not daft.'

I'd like a shilling (sorry, 5p) for every time we've said that about James. One day, when he was about ten, I took him shopping with me. It was in the days before the big new precinct had been built in Lewisham, south-east London, and the road from the car park to the supermarket was a very rough unmade track. We went round and got all the shopping necessary to feed four small people and two large ones for one week and at the end you can imagine I had a fair old trolley load. I thought of the walk to the car park with some dismay and voiced my feeling about it to James. He said to me, 'Why don't you go and get the car while I wait here with the trolley?' It was the obvious solution and I had never even given it a thought! He has always been the most willing to do anything indoors — or even out of doors. If you ask James to run up the road and post a letter you will never hear him say 'Hang about' — a phrase which has been known, on occasions, to provoke me to near-violence!

While he has missed out on a lot of things during his life, for example the nursery at Westmount Road and being able to do a college course after he left school, he was able to benefit from some of the progressive thought which allowed the mentally handicapped to express themselves positively and not through others. The Christmas plays at Maze Hill School have gone from strength to strength and it has been fascinating to see, each year, the further demands which the staff have made upon the children in getting them to do quite difficult speaking parts and how magnificently the children responded. They started, in

James's day, by taking part in tableaux while the narrator told us what was going on, and have progressed to a point where the narrator is no longer necessary — the children tell us the story themselves. At the end we have a jolly good sing, if it's Christmas — which everyone enjoys. I am constantly amazed at how little the teachers have to intervene during the performance and this applies equally to the musicians. They love their percussion instruments and, of course, the talents of the mentally handicapped don't stop at percussion. I was present at a Gateway Festival recently at the Royal Festival Hall in London where the clarinet and recorder were most beautifully played by a blind and mentally-handicapped young man. I am always fascinated to find myself envying a mentally-handicapped person, and it has happened a number of times. They can be very gifted.

Fresh changes in the education of mentally-handicapped children are in view. The 1981 Education Act followed the paper produced by the Committee of Enquiry into the Education of Handicapped Children and Young People, chaired by Lady Mary Warnock (as she is now). This Act, for the first time, sets out to lessen the gap between the concepts of education for handicapped and non-handicapped children. It is a further move in the direction of the Education (Handicapped Children) Act 1970 (the corresponding 1974 Act in Scotland was not implemented until 1975) which stated that all handicapped children, however severe their disability, were included in the framework of special education. Henceforth, no child, however great his disability, was regarded as ineducable. If I may quote from Mary Warnock's booklet *Meeting Special Education Needs* (HMSO 1978), she sets out, far more succinctly than I could, the recommendations of her Committee. First the wider concept of special education:

The concept of special education employed by the Committee was therefore appreciably widened, as was the notion of the children who might need it. The Committee rejected the idea of two distinct groups of children, the handicapped and the non-handicapped, of whom the former had special education, while the latter just had education. On the contrary, just as needs were seen to form a continuum, so special education itself was seen as a continuum of provision, ranging from temporary help to permanent and long-term adaptation of the ordinary curriculum. The Committee therefore recommended that the distinction between special and remedial education should be dropped and that the assumption should be that perhaps as many as one child in five might need special educational help at some stage during his school career. In this sense, then, special education becomes a far broader and more flexible concept.

The far-reaching implications of this widening of the concept cannot be too strongly emphasized. If up to one in five children may need special educational provision in the course of a school career, this does not imply that up to one in five are to be thought of as handicapped in the traditional sense of the term. With proper help, the educational problems of the majority will be temporary; without it they will be compounded by a continuing experience of failure. The Committee referred to any child who needed such help as 'a child with a special educational need' and it is with such needs, however long or short their duration, however severe or minor, that the report is concerned.

I think it is important to define the aims of education and the Warnock Committee holds that these are, whatever the advantages or disadvantages of the boy or girl concerned, first of all to increase a child's knowledge of the world he lives in and his imaginative understanding, both of the possibilities of that world and of his own responsibilities in it; and, secondly, to give him as much independence and self-sufficiency as he is capable of, by teaching him those things he must know in order to find work and to manage and control his own life. Children have manifestly different obstacles to overcome in their path towards this double goal and for some the obstacles are so enormous that the distance they travel will not be very great. But for these children any progress at all is significant. For the most severely handicapped, education seeks to help them overcome their difficulties one by one.

Writing as the parent of a child (sorry, James — 'young man') who was, at a very early age, deemed 'ineducable' the preceding words of the Committee are music to my ears. It really ought to be very difficult indeed for any consultant, when faced by grieving and resentful parents, to say, 'Put him away — he'll never do anything. Forget you ever had him,' and all the extraordinary things which

parents have, in the past, been forced to listen to from the
person who should be first in the queue to help them make
the most of their handicapped child. As Chris said about
Paul, 'the more you put in the more you get out'. I wonder
if there is any liaison between the Department of Education
and Science and the medical schools to educate those who
are in at the beginning?

I guess there are a lot of parents of profoundly
handicapped children who might be saying to themselves,
'None of that is for my child.' You would be making a
mistake if you thought that. Your child might be lying on a
bean-bag all day but he is, hopefully, being cared for by
people who are being inspired by those who feel that life
must have more to offer all handicapped people, and are
being helped to take a fresh analytical look at how your
child's life could be improved.

When the time came for James to go to school, we asked
Dr Morris whether we ought perhaps to consider Rose
Cottage, which was then designated ESN (Mild). He advised
us to send James to the Junior Training Centre. He had, up
to that time, never known a Down's child really to succeed
in a school of the Rose Cottage type and was of the opinion
that it would be much better for James to be a big fish in a
small pool than a small fish in a big pool. He also told us
that he sometimes felt that it was necessary to advise
parents against his own inclinations for their benefit — in
other words some parents really couldn't face their child
being in a severely subnormal school. I was always glad that
he didn't think it necessary to give us that advice. We
realized, of course, that he was quite right. It is nearly
always better for a child's morale to be the big fish and I am
sure that more children would succeed in comprehensive
education were not the schools so vast. I am personally in
favour of comprehensive education (but not all-ability
classes) and see no reason why the handicapped child
should not have its school as part of the same 'campus'. Let
us have a look and see what the 1981 Education Act is
going to do for (or should I say *to*?) our handicapped
children.

In the first instance, children are to be assessed as having
special educational needs. Which children? The Act defines
them as being children who have: (i) significantly greater

difficulty in learning than most of the children of their age; or (ii) they have a disability which either prevents or hinders them from using the educational facilities generally provided in schools, within the area of the local authority concerned, for children of a comparable age. It also covers children under the age of five who could fall into either of the previous categories if special provision were not made.

Previously local education authorities had to fill the needs of pupils 'who suffer from any disability of mind or body' either in special schools or otherwise. This duty has now been replaced by the more general one of having regard to the need to make sure that special educational provision is made for children who have special needs, and, provided certain conditions are satisfied, that children for whom 'statements' are made are educated in ordinary schools. When I look at the resources there are in 'ordinary' schools today and consider the resources which would be needed even adequately to fulfil the terms of the 1981 Education Act, I am deeply thankful that James has completed his school life.

The conditions previously mentioned are that account has been taken of the views of the parent (and parent can mean guardian or whoever has custody of the child) and that education in an ordinary school is compatible with: (a) the child receiving the special educational provision that he or she requires; (b) the provision of efficient education for the children with whom he or she will be educated; and (c) the efficient use of resources.

It is also incumbent upon the Governors of county and voluntary schools to ensure that the special provision required by a child is made; that teachers should be aware of the importance of identifying and providing for children with special educational needs; and that where the 'responsible person' has been told by the LEA (local education authority) that a student has special educational needs, those needs are made known to all who are likely to teach him or her.

The 'responsible person' may be the Head, Chairman of Governors, or another Governor appointed by the governing body. In the case of maintained nursery schools, which do not have governing bodies, these duties are given to the LEAs and the responsible person is the headteacher.

Children with special needs have to take part in 'the activities of the school together with children who do not have special educational needs', provided conditions (a), (b) and (c) above are satisfied and it is 'reasonably practicable'. Local authorities also have a duty to keep their arrangements for special educational provision under review.

If a local education authority considers that special educational provision, or any part of it, cannot be provided in a school they may, after consultation with the parents, arrange for all or part of it to be provided, 'otherwise than in a school'.

It is not very difficult to see from all this that it is extremely important to have good liaison between the local health authority which (in the guise of the hospital staff and health visitor, etc.) is the first agency likely to spot a candidate for special educational needs, and the education authority. Under Section 10 of the Act it is stated that if an area or district health authority considers that a child under five has or probably will have special educational needs, it must inform the parent and, after providing an opportunity for discussion with a health authority officer, must bring it to the attention of the relevant local education authority. If it believes that a particular voluntary organization is likely to be able to help the parent, it must inform the parent accordingly.

Assessment over the last twenty years has ceased to be the dreaded experience it was when James was young. Then, it was either 'educable' or 'ineducable' and we didn't want to hear the second. Now, constant assessment is the very best way of making sure that your child is receiving the provision best suited to his or her needs. Section 6 of the Act allows local authorities to assess a child under the age of two only with the consent of the parents; in addition to that, if the parents make a request to have a child under two assessed, the LEA has to do it.

In the case of a child over two, once the education authority has decided that it has to make a 'statement' for a child (in other words, the child is going to have special educational needs and these must be 'stated' before they can be provided — obviously), Section 5 on assessment comes into force. Before making the assessment, the LEA must inform the parents: (a) that it is proposing to make an assessment; (b) of the procedure to be followed in making it; (c) of the name of the officer of the authority from whom further information can be obtained; and (d) of the parent's right to make representations and submit written evidence. within a specified period which must be not less than 29 days from the day on which the notice of the assessment is served. Having taken into account any representations made to them the local authority may proceed with the assessment or decide not to make an assessment.

If it does decide to assess the child, the local education authority has to inform the parents in writing of its decision and the reasons for making it. If it decides at any time it is not going to proceed with the assessment, again it must inform the parents in writing.

If, having made an assessment, the authority decides that it is not required to determine the special educational provision that should be made (i.e. make a statement), it has to inform the parents of its decision and of the right of appeal in writing to the Secretary of State. The Secretary of State may direct the local authority to reconsider its decision.

Once a statement has been drafted, the LEA must indicate therein what sort of provision will be made to meet the child's needs. Parents must be given a copy of the intended statement and must be told that they have a right to contribute to the statement, to ask for interviews with an officer of the LEA and afterwards, if they wish, with any person who gave advice on their child's assessment or another suitable person the authority may nominate.

The LEA must take into consideration any contribution the parents wish to make to the statement. The authority may then make the statement in its original form, or with alterations, or it may choose not to make the statement at all.

Once the statement has been made, parents must be given a copy of it and be informed about their right of appeal. They must also be given the name of a person to whom they may apply for information and advice about their child's special educational needs.

In the event of parents being dissatisfied with the LEA's plans for the special educational provision set out in the statement, they have the right to appeal to the local appeal committee (established under the 1980 Education Act). An appeal committee can't overrule an LEA if it disagrees with the plans, but it can make comments on the plans and ask the LEA to look at them again. The LEA must then reconsider the case, taking the appeal committee's views into account. If the parents are still not satisfied with the authority's decision after the proposals have been reconsidered, or if the appeal committee supports the LEA's original plan, they have the right to appeal to the Secretary of State for Education. The Secretary of State has the power to confirm the statement, make changes to it or tell the LEA to abandon it.

If a local education authority decides not to assess a child but the parents feel an assessment should be made, they can appeal to the Secretary of State.

I know a lot of people will be very anxious to know what will happen to our excellent special schools. The Act states that before a local education authority can close a special school, it must inform parents and other interested people what it plans to do — they must then be given time to raise objections to the closure. The Secretary of State must also be informed and must be sent details of any objections made. The Secretary of State can then approve or reject the LEA's proposal. Let's hope that no special schools are closed through apathy on the part of the parents — this could be another area in which combining with a local organization could be of great use as a pressure group.

As usual, where a vital part of a handicapped child's upbringing is concerned, MENCAP have produced a Stamina Paper. A great deal of what I have already written is listed in Stamina Paper No. 1, which also makes the following important points:

Admissions and placement
IT IS ESSENTIAL TO ENSURE:

1 That all children who require special education are receiving it.

2 That continuing special education is available for all mentally-handicapped children and young people up to at least the age of nineteen.

3 That the education available is 'full time'.

4 That children in hospital receive full-time education.

5 That in the event of the suspension of a mentally-handicapped child becoming unavoidable, because of behaviour problems, LEAs should immediately seek alternative educational provision.

Transport

6 That children are on the bus for the shortest practicable time.

7 That bus escorts are provided.

8 That bus escorts have some training.

9 That there are arrangements for parents to discuss transport difficulties.

School programmes and assessment

10 That there is a minimum staff ratio in each class of 1:6 children (including helpers).

11 That there is a varied diagnostic social/educational/emotional assessment and regular reassessment.

12 That parents, teaching staff, therapists, residential care staff and welfare staff are closely involved in assessment.

13 That written programmes for individual children are devised from these assessments.

14 That individual programmes are monitored and re-corded in writing, continually revised and made available to parents and, where appropriate, and subject to parents' consent, to residential care staff.

15 That there are regular case conferences of parents, teachers, care staff and therapists.

16 That parents and care staff are involved in the child's educational programme.

Note: The purpose of assessment is for programme planning. If results and programmes are in writing, teachers and parents know where they stand and can monitor progress; all those involved can see the overall goals for the child.

Curriculum

17 That education in basic numeracy and literacy is available to all.

18 That social education is available to all.

19 That language development is available to all and

should include, where appropriate, Makaton, Bliss, etc.
20 That speech therapy is available to all who need it.
21 That there is a progressive programme of motor development.
22 That physiotherapy is available for all who need it.
23 That the curriculum includes music.
24 That the curriculum includes drama.
25 That the curriculum includes domestic science.
26 That the curriculum includes physical education.
27 That the curriculum includes self-care and personal hygiene.
28 That the curriculum includes personal relationships, citizenship and sex education as and when appropriate.
29 That there is adequate equipment.

Note: If no speech or physiotherapy is provided, approach the headteacher. Physiotherapy is usually provided by the DHSS — approach District Health Authority — or the Community Health Council could be asked to apply pressure. Speech therapy can be provided by the education authority. Seek the help of the school governors.

Individual programmes should contain an appropriate variety of subjects as part of the overall teaching plan.

Communication
30 That there is a parent–teacher association.

Note: PTAs should be the most important method of communicating with the school, not merely a fund-raising organization. Ensure there is one; don't be put off with 'parents can come in at any time'. Ensure, also, that there is a parent on the school governing body.

Holidays and leisure
31 That there is a local programme for children during school holidays.
32 That there is an educational holiday programme away from home.
33 That there is a planned leisure programme.

Note: Social Services have power to provide support for joint planning with the Education and Social Service Departments. In many cases local MENCAP societies and other voluntary organizations co-operate with holiday arrangements.

Education of the profoundly retarded and multiply-handicapped child

34 That there is a ratio of special care staff to pupils of 1:3.

35 That stimulation in special care is intensively programmed by appropriate trained staff.

36 That the child's progress in the programme is recorded.

37 That specialists are consulted when difficult problems arise.

38 That the school has a specialist social worker.

39 That medical and nursing assistance are available.

40 That physiotherapy is available.

41 That all school medical screening and treatment programmes are operated.

Note: All these points are of particular importance for profoundly retarded and multiply-handicapped children. These children need a changing environment, specific goal planning and highly trained teachers.

Education and social integration

42 That educational integration with normal schools is encouraged, where appropriate.

43 That social integration with normal schools is encouraged.

44 That there is transfer from special school to normal school or ESN(M) when appropriate.

45 That there is a programme to inform pupils in normal schools about mental handicap.

46 That teaching staff have access to a programme of personal knowledge and staff development.

47 That there are appropriate contacts between school staff and those providing adult services, to enable proper forward planning and follow-up to take place.

48 That parents, teachers and social workers should be involved in planning adequate transitional arrangements for children in their final stages at school — including the provision of a detailed leaving report outlining progress made while at school, together with immediate needs for educational and personal development.

Note: Encourage understanding of mental handicap in other schools.

There is nothing I can say to improve on what has gone before except that I do feel a little sadness that no thought appears to have been given to the children's spiritual life, but perhaps schools prefer to deal with that on an individual basis, given that most schools now are multi-racial. For myself, I still think that as we are (or supposed to be) a Christian country, then that is what should be taught in our schools. Personal view.

I think it is a good idea to try and spread your own load a bit. Try to get other members of the family and your friends interested in what you are trying to do. I always think that it is the last straw for a family, who may be really struggling for survival with a difficult handicapped child, then to have to turn their attention to fighting for that child's rights. It's good for other people to help — good for their souls! Too many people wander through life in their own cosy little cocoon, looking neither to the right nor to the left. See if you can grab a few of them and awaken their social consciences. It sometimes surprises you — the people who unexpectedly show an interest in your cause. I have been going to a local hairdressing salon recently and the young girl who does my hair has been very interested in the book and, of course, in James. I had been telling her about the house in Greenwich for which our local society is raising funds; it is to house eight mentally-handicapped adults whose parents can no longer look after them. Lee (my stylist), it transpires, lives directly across the road from 'Project 28' as it is called, and when she suggested doing her sponsored parachute jump for the mentally handicapped I asked her if she would like to do it specifically for No. 28, 'the neighbours'. She was delighted with the idea as it gave her an added interest to what was going on opposite. Incidentally I did ask her if she was at all bothered at the use to which the house was being put and she looked at me in great surprise. 'Good heavens, no!' she said, and made me feel that I had committed a social solecism for even having suggested it!

In spreading the message about mental handicap, brothers and sisters have a very important part to play, but unfortunately psychological (and practical) problems can seriously get in the way of them doing so. Michael, Kathrine's brother, told me that he had never mentioned to his friends that she was handicapped as he had not considered that it was necessary. Leaving aside any psychological reasons for this (I am not and don't want to be a psychologist), I think it is a shame that brothers and sisters feel this reluctance to mention the existence of a handicapped member of the family. The more matter of fact the family is about it, the less it will be seen by others as an undesirable phenomenon. I am sure that Michael would say that he was being 'matter of fact' about it in not mentioning it — perhaps boys never do talk about other members of their family, but it would be interesting to know what he would have written if he had been asked to do an essay on 'My family'. Perhaps teachers should do this more often — they might get a greater insight into possible problems. Somehow or other we have to put it across that nature's 'hiccups' can be lived with, tolerated and loved. If only we could help those brothers and sisters to be amused at bizarre behaviour instead of embarrassed. Parents have to give the lead in this and, for the sake of the other kids, it is worth working at. I have to say, from my own experience, that it is something which needs a positive effort. A schoolgirl asked me recently if I was ever embarrassed by James and I was forced to say, 'Yes, sometimes,' but I hope I tempered it by telling her that I felt that I shouldn't be embarrassed by him. I wished I'd had time to talk to her longer but it was the end of our session and they were all anxious to get off home. I felt that in answer to my question, 'Does anyone here have a mentally-handicapped member of family?' she might have been one of the children who should have put her hand up but didn't.

It is helpful, of course, to give the brothers and sisters of a handicapped member of family a positive role in the life of the child, without turning them into slaves! How much better to draw an awkward-feeling child into the circle than to keep apologizing to it for your handicapped child's weird behaviour. It seems to me that parents take a mentally-handicapped child terribly for granted and frequently forget that the older (or younger) brothers and sisters haven't had the advantage of talking to consultants, health visitors, social workers or any of the myriad people who mill around (if you're lucky) where there is a handicapped child. Take time — as much as is needed — to sit with your normal children and, in the absence of the handicapped child, explain to them as fully as you can (and in terms they can understand) why their brother or sister is not the same as they are. Make allies of them. If they go to a school where they have a 'prayerful' assembly you could ask for prayers for the handicapped child if he or she falls ill — a cold will do. You will find it a very useful way of letting people know that there may be other problems than just the sort the school is used to. Headteachers should always be aware of a family with a mentally-handicapped member as it could cause behaviour difficulties with the other brothers and sisters. There are many handicapped children who are terribly demanding and there will always be others in the family who, despite the efforts of the parents to give them as much time as they can, will have difficulty in coping with their lives. I think, also, it is important not to let the guilt factor get a hold of brothers and sisters of handicapped children, and there is no logical reason why it should. It is nice if, after seeing that there are needs to be met, they go out and help in clubs or become teachers in special schools, but I have met normal youngsters who have been so churned up by their handicapped brother or sister that they have thrown themselves head first into organizations and clubs to the detriment of their own mental health. If you have had a bad time with a mentally-handicapped brother or sister, rushing and working with other people with the same disability probably isn't the answer. I am a parent of a mentally-handicapped person and there is no way that I would choose to work with them. I have four other normal children and there is no way that I would be a teacher. So what? To each his own and if it is those who don't live with the problem who come forward to relieve the lives of those who do, let we parents (and you brothers and sisters) thank God for them and *don't feel guilty*!

MENCAP is very aware of the special problems and needs of the brothers and sisters of mentally-handicapped people, and is encouraging these young people to get together in groups to talk — talking can be very therapeutic. There is a MENCAP information sheet giving some guidelines on setting up groups for brothers and sisters of mentally-handicapped people and this is available from the MENCAP National Centre. It covers every age group. Some brothers and sisters end up as carers; they may have their own needs and they may also have some very useful experiences to impart to their younger partners in possible adversity.

I have wandered away from school somewhat, but before I leave the subject altogether I would like just to comment on a part of the curriculum which is becoming more important. Part of the new philosophy of improving life for people with all types of handicap is the realization that sexual awareness and the relations which ultimately stem from this are as important to this section of the community as to those with no handicap. Thus, it has been necessary to re-think the curriculum in schools for children with special needs, and look at how they can be helped towards leading, where it is appropriate, a more full life.

Sex education, to be as comprehensive as possible, has to start from a very early age — primary-school children are given a programme of carefully selected information, and the needs are similar in schools for children with special educational needs. Miss Godfrey was kind enough to furnish me with details of what is going on at Maze Hill School and I quote below from, firstly, the suggested outline for a sex education curriculum and, secondly, the curriculum itself:

There is a growing climate of opinion that sex education for the mentally handicapped is necessary, as part of their training in socially acceptable behaviour as well as a part of their general education. The two ideas, that the mentally handicapped are potential satyrs or nymphomaniacs, or conversely are lamblike in their sexual feelings, are fortunately less prevalent than they were. Undoubtedly, although much ignorance still exists concerning the sexual feelings of the mentally handicapped, it is becoming increasingly recognized that their sexual feelings can be the same as others, not necessarily greater or necessarily less. What is certain, however, is that with their limited intellectual capacity, the mentally handicapped are poorly equipped to deal with the emotional and hormonal changes that occur at puberty and the physical reactions they will experience during their lives. The Plowden Report states:

1 We have no doubt that children's questions about sex ought to be answered plainly and truthfully whenever they are asked.
2 The answers must provide an acceptable and usable vocabulary for the child.
3 Every school must make the arrangements that seem best to it and should have a definite policy which, in consultation with parents, covers all children.
4 It is not good enough to leave matters vague and open, hoping for the best.

Although this was written specifically with primary schools in mind there is no reason why these four recommendations should not apply to ESN(S) schools. Natalie Perry writes that 'teachers and parents should co-operate in providing each child at his level of understanding with facts about sexual growth and behaviour.'

As teachers then, it behoves us to prepare our pupils for their sexual development as much as we try to in other areas of the curriculum.

The 1959 Mental Health Act aims, among other things, at the normalization and integration of the mentally handicapped into the community, and indeed much of the work done in school is done with this principle in mind. A Danish point of view is that the normalization principle means that 'all talk of protection, not to say over-protection, should be stopped'. Most of us would agree that this position is far too extreme for our children. Our children will always need protection and care but the degree of protection and care will be greater in some cases than others. If, then, the mentally handicapped are coming into the community, and whether we like it or not this would appear to be the trend, it is necessary for us to prepare them, so that their sexual behaviour is socially acceptable.

Sex education in normal schools is quite common, but because of our pupils' handicaps it is not desirable to include everything which might be on such a curriculum, neither can we take over the whole approach, but we can select and adapt.

In many respects our approach to sex education needs to be very careful; there are many qualities in our children such as their ingenuous displays of affection, which it would be unfortunate to make them self-conscious of. At the same time they should be aware that not every stranger can react to these displays in the same way that relatives and teachers can, neither is their lack of self-consciousness about their bodies always acceptable to the public. It is sometimes felt that this carnal innocence is a 'good thing' and should be encouraged rather than discouraged. However, although we may feel that education should change society, our first duty is to our pupils and their acceptability by society. Our aim should, therefore, be to inculcate socially acceptable behaviour while, at the same time, not destroying those ingenuous qualities which are often suppressed in normal childhood.

One of the aims of sex education in normal schools is to dispel the sexual ignorance which people encounter when entering into sexual relationships. Whether we feel our children should be prepared for sexual relationships is a matter for personal conjecture; what is certain, however, is that they are unlikely ever to be able to show the degree of responsibility necessary to raise a family. From this point of view, it is arguable that we would be irresponsible in suggesting or encouraging the notion that our children should lead a full sex life. It would be inappropriate, therefore, to teach coition except as part of conception.

Perhaps then the content of any sex education devised for our pupils should concentrate on the following areas:

1 Socially acceptable behaviour.
2 Knowledge which will enable our children to come to terms with their own sexuality.
3 Hygiene.
4 Knowledge of reproduction.

I would suggest therefore the following outline curriculum:

A three-stage scheme:

Stage 1: Pre-puberty
Knowledge Parts of body, male and female, recognition of male and female. Growth of young inside body. Knowledge of families.
Skills Related skills of health hygiene.
Attitudes Naturalness of childbirth, pregnancy, affection, consideration for others, nudity not indecent but convention demands modesty in certain places.

Stage 2: Outset of puberty
Knowledge Male, female contribution to conception, egg and sperm, reinforcement of proper names of sexual organs, development of secondary sexual characteristics, preparation for menstruation, nocturnal emission, normality of masturbation.
Skills Further development of hygiene skills, including menstrual hygiene.

Attitudes   The normality of menstruation, nocturnal emission and masturbation.

Stage 3: Adolescence

Knowledge   Conception, birth, sexual urges, irresponsible behaviour, homosexuality in adolescence.

Attitudes   Considerate lifestyle, affection, care for self and others.

Some of our children will derive little or no benefit but others will find it helpful in coming to terms with their own sexuality and adjusting to the standards of socially acceptable sexual behaviour. It would be inappropriate therefore for all our children to receive instruction on the lines suggested; rather, it is up to the teacher, in accordance with the parents' wishes, to assess the child's degree of need for sex education and to act accordingly. Instruction should be ongoing with certain children, much of it incidental with specific instruction when a teacher feels it is appropriate. The overall aim should be to give knowledge of sexuality in accordance with the needs of individuals in order for them to participate acceptably in society.

I am extremely grateful to Betty Godfrey for allowing me to use Maze Hill School as an example of the sort of sex education parents might expect to find in special schools. It should be pointed out that Maze Hill comes under the Inner London Education Authority (ILEA) and other LEAs may have a different approach. It is up to you, if this is a subject about which you are particularly concerned, to confer with the teachers at your child's school. People may challenge the statement that it is inappropriate to teach coition as the mentally handicapped are unlikely to show a sufficient degree of responsibility necessary to raise a family. I think it is fair to say that while, in general, mentally-handicapped children mature that much later than ordinary children and thus teaching coition may not come within the brief of the sex-education programme of the special schools, any parent (particularly of those children who are able to stay on at school until they are nineteen) who is concerned about this aspect of their education should contact the headteacher of their special school. Alan Course, the acting Head of Maze Hill at the time of writing, admitted that when the original programme was devised in 1976 the whole subject of sex education in special schools was in its infancy and that the school was now very prepared to expand the scope of the subject where they considered it appropriate, always bearing in mind that parents, as well as children, have needs and that not everyone has a broad-minded approach to the subject. He also expressed his concern that as soon as sex education is mentioned, it is in terms of being a 'problem'. He feels very strongly that we should move towards seeing it as a necessary part of education in the same way as learning to go to school by public transport and where the individual is able to cope with it.

I am inclined to think that it is not quite so neat as that. It seems abundantly clear to me that a great many ordinary people are quite unable to cope with their own sexual urges and appetites. Perhaps it is a question of education — for everybody. The fact that so-called normal people are unable to manage their own problems (I use the word advisedly in this context) only serves to emphasize the need to take even greater care with the sexual education of our mentally-handicapped children.

When James was just over fourteen Peter was born. I had been having contractions off and on ever since my delivery date two weeks previously and one night, knowing I had an antenatal appointment the next day, I told Neville that I had decided to go in as I guessed that they wouldn't send me home again. Neville went and told Christopher (who was asleep in a tent in the garden) where we were going and off we went to the British Hospital. Well, of course, all the pains went away once I was settled in and the next day it was decided that an induction was the best thing for me — and presumably the baby. As I was thoroughly fed up by this time (I was enormous!) I didn't really care what they did. I just knew if they didn't do something I'd go on carrying the baby for the rest of my life! The drip was put in at 11.00 a.m. and Peter was born, with a great deal of huffing and puffing on the part of his rather elderly Mum, at 1.10 p.m. The mental vision I had of forceps did somewhat spur me on to greater efforts and, in spite of him weighing 9lb. 6oz. I didn't have a single stitch. The nurses were, in fact, humming and ha-ing over whether I ought to be stitched but I pleaded with them not to spoil my record of never having had any and, bless their kind hearts, they indulged me. I am by nature a quick healer (too quick actually, I tend to get adhesions) and I feel confident that they used their discretion. I know they wouldn't have listened to my pleas if it had been unwise not to stitch. It was horrid, being induced, and I am certain that, on the whole, nature does it better.

Just after Peter was born (I had the foresight to arrange it on a clinic day) Dr Morris came in and gave him the once-over. He was very good about checking my babies as soon as he saw me in the ward and it was much appreciated by me. Peter was the youngest baby he'd looked at (of mine, that is) and I was fascinated to see how Dr Morris was able to walk him up the bed at just about 20 minutes old. Thank God they stop again for a while! During the time I was in hospital Neville was very busy with the others (it was during the school holidays — Peter was born on the 10th August) and getting James ready to fly to Switzerland with the Club. He was also putting everything together to take Chris, Mike and David camping in Wales for a week or so. Talk about a glutton for punishment. What made life very difficult and worrying for both of us was that James had succumbed to one of his occasional bouts of diarrhoea. He really was quite bad and Neville didn't know whether he was going to be fit to go or not. As it happened he got enough Kaolin and Morph. into James to render him sufficiently recovered to go away but I remember that he came back with tonsillitis and I guess that was what he was cooking up beforehand. So, having got James off OK Neville took the other three to Snowdonia (having first made sure that I was recovering satisfactorily from my sterilization operation) leaving Peter and me to our own devices. And very nice it was too! I had an amenity bed in the hospital (because I felt so old and I knew I'd feel terrible after the operation) and the nurses often used to pop in for a chat. So different from the first time I had a baby in that particular building.

Pam's husband, Gerald, and Mum came to get Peter and me from the hospital and I have to confess (with some shame) that it was really rather nice to go home to a quiet house! I knew the kids were all having a great time in Wales (they had been introduced to their new brother) and I appreciated the few days I was to have with Mother, getting the new baby into some sort of routine. Pam had prepared food for us and laid in a few things I might need for the first couple of days and after she and Gerald had returned home, Mum and I settled down to a very companionable interlude. I wanted to breast feed Peter but it hadn't taken off very well and I started giving him a bottle shortly after arriving home. Realizing what life was going to be like once all the family was back together again I decided to abandon what seemed to be a failure anyway and put Peter completely on the bottle. After they arrived home and made fresh acquaintance with the baby all the boys took turns in giving him his bottle, even James. It was really great in the mornings. There would be a queue of small pyjama-clad figures in the bedroom arguing over whose turn it was to feed Peter! They weren't in the least in awe of him, quickly learned how to support his head and really took an interest in his development. One of my proudest moments was when Christopher was content to wheel Peter in his pram past the church where a number of his friends were coming out of the late Mass. He was totally unembarrassed! Considering how much time a new baby needs, their attitude made my life a great deal easier.

During these years, following Peter's birth, James was progressing very well at school and it is difficult to look back and pick him out from the rest of the family. He wasn't presenting us with any particular problems and it was a tranquil period. The other boys hadn't yet fully entered into the dreaded adolescent phase of their lives and I am glad that I didn't know what was ahead of us. Not with James, of course, but with the others.

When Peter was a year old we all went camping to the south-west of France where we were meeting up with our good friends from Bath, the Parrys. In order to make life a bit easier we had borrowed a 'lobster pot' playpen from Mary and Paddy Joyce (from my Church) and we laid it over the top of the trailer tent, well tied down with elastics. I can tell you that that playpen was the most valuable piece of equipment we took with us. We used to have to stop by the side of the road for lunch (it took us a couple of days to arrive at our ultimate destination in the Gironde) and can you imagine what life would have been like if that year-old baby had not been able to get out of his car seat for an hour? I can heartily recommend a playpen as part of your holiday equipment. It also made life much easier when we were in camp. We put the playpen well out in front of the tent, put Peter in it and then got on with what we had to do, leaving the boys (and usually quite a number of other people from the site) to entertain the baby!

It is in these middle years that a handicapped child's social life can really take off in Greenwich. The Federation of Gateway Clubs is designed to provide leisure interests for mentally-handicapped people from the age of twelve upwards and in our area there are Clubs almost every night of the week — though not all under the aegis of Gateway.

Focus Club, which was the first, has been running now for about fifteen years and for the last twelve had been under the guidance of Don Simms (whom you met in the first chapter). He is now retired from the police force but I strongly suspect that Doreen hasn't yet noticed that he has retired! Doing nothing is not Don's idea of an occupation! The Club provides a number of different activities including table tennis, snooker, darts and, of course, the inevitable dancing! James absolutely loves disco dancing and I think he's very good at it. Peter, James, Neville and I went to Spain for a week during the October half term (a couple of years ago). We stayed at a little place in Almeria called Mojacar and, during the course of the week, one of the advertised attractions at the Hotel was the usual Flamenco night. I was determined not to miss this as I am a Flamenco addict (I once went all by myself to the Fairfield Hall at Croydon to see Paco Peña!) and we made sure that we arrived early in the Bar just outside the Hotel where the show was to be held. In fact we arrived an hour early and somewhat to our dismay (having very sensitive ears) they were playing records until the dancers were due to begin. There were a few people there already and more were arriving all the time and James kept everyone entertained as he danced, alone, to the records for three quarters of an hour. He got a round of applause as he left the floor!

Another marvellous activity James enjoys with the Club is, of course, the holidays. He has, as mentioned before, been to Switzerland twice with them; once when Maria Goddard was Club Leader (that was thirteen years ago) and again about three years ago with Don. On one of the Club holidays to Scotland they all went out for a walk 'up the Glen'. It was a wooded and winding path and, according to Don (and he remembers the event with awful clarity!) James Thompson led the way. He was leading the way from rather far ahead in fact. Don saw him disappear round a corner and decided that he was getting too far in front and that he should call him back. Don (who, while being reasonably fit is not, shall we say, in the first flush of youth!) ran up the path, looked round the corner to find that there was no sign of James. He ran on up the path (and apparently it really was 'up') calling James and getting very fearful of having lost him. They were staying at Loch Awe and it seems there was nothing between James and John O'Groats except wild country. As Don puffed round the millionth bend James came into view and Don just had enough breath left to call him to heel! I have always been thankful, knowing how I would have reacted, that Don did not have enough energy left to belabour James physically! It says a terrific lot for his dedication that he continues to take the kids away in spite of these sort of incidents — and I guess James isn't the only one who has given cause for alarm in the past.

A lot of Clubs spend a certain amount of time on producing an entertainment which will eventually be seen at their Regional Gateway Rally. In London, the Metropolitan Region Rally is held at Sadlers Wells Theatre and about twenty or so Clubs take part, producing some very good entertainment indeed. It is a few years since Focus Club took part but not all Club leaders want to spend the amount of time needed on this sort of activity and I feel that the Clubs should stick to what they do best — which, I am sure, is what Don thinks. There are over sixty members in Focus Club and producing an entertainment which would include all of them is difficult and time consuming. Other activities are just as important. Having said that, I must mention that whenever a Rally takes place, be it in Sadlers Wells or at the National Rally at the Festival Hall (no less), the Club helpers from Focus are there in force helping the whole production to run smoothly. Getting all those Club members on and off the stage with a minimum of fuss takes a great deal of organization and they all get better at it every year. If you ever get a chance to attend a Gateway Rally, do go. You will get a surprise.

Don had a training day recently for Club helpers and asked me to go along with our film, 'James Is Our Brother' (of which more later) as part of it had been filmed at the Club and he thought it would be of interest to the newer helpers. He also asked me if I would have a chat with James about any improvements or alterations he would like to see at the Club. I sat with James one evening when everyone else was out and we had a little chat about the Club. He started off by giving me a list of the things he thought needed renewing (table tennis balls, etc.) and with just a little prompting from me said that he would like drama and yoga added to the Club activities. He also said that he very much enjoyed going on visits to other Clubs and playing in table-tennis or darts tournaments with them and he wished they could do more of that.

Having connections with a Gateway Club does a lot to restore your faith in human nature. I was at a rehearsal of the Eltham Choral Society (to which I belong) when a new member approached me and introduced himself. 'I'm Michael Parfitt' he said, 'I know James — I help at the Focus Club'. These lovely young people pop up everywhere! He knew who I was because James leaves his literacy class on Thursdays at 9.00 p.m. and walks to the school where I am rehearsing. I finish at 9.30 p.m. so he waits in the foyer doing his reading and writing (he and the school keepers are great buddies!) and we come home together, very occasionally by way of the White Hart pub!

On many occasions, when I have shown the film to school children, one or two of them have come up afterwards and expressed an interest in the Club and a desire to help. It does make a change from everlastingly hearing about the antisocial behaviour of young people. I do try to get across to the young people how grateful we parents are for their help and interest and point out that a great many activities for the mentally handicapped simply could not take place if it were not for the unselfishness of young people like themselves.

Gateway and such like Clubs help to bring some social enjoyment into the life of mentally-handicapped young people but they cannot and should not always be shielded from the harsher aspects which are, none the less, part of everyone's experience. In the past it has been thought that the death of parents or other close members of family had little or no effect upon the mentally handicapped. This, of course, is not so. Even a profoundly handicapped child, while not comprehending the finality of the death of someone near, will surely be disturbed and upset by the grief of those around him and have a sense of loss.

In 1970, when James was 12, my father was taken into the London Hospital for blood tests. He had been complaining (and that was something he *never* did) of pain following a fall (he would run for buses) and we all thought he was being tested for arthritis. While he was in the hospital it was discovered (and teaching hospitals are good at this sort of thing) that he needed a prostate operation. He had the operation and was making such a poor recovery that one day, as I was leaving after visiting him, I waylaid the Sister (I ought to have known better) and said 'What the hell's going on here?' (I was extremely fond of my father). She then asked me, did I not know that my father had leukaemia? Even I, with the little medical knowledge I had, wondered how a person my father's age was expected to make any sort of recovery from an operation when he had that sort of blood problem. He died on 3 October, 1970, and (to date) it is the worst thing that has happened to me. I think my sisters probably feel the same.

When I came back from mother's on the evening of the day that Dad died, I gathered up the boys from Mary's house — she had collected them from school and picked up James as well. A friend in need indeed. I told them that their Grandpa had died and kept as cheerful as I could as I didn't want to upset them too much. Later that night (Neville was out at a dinner of some sort) Michael suddenly burst into tears and said 'I feel so sad about Grandpa' and while I was comforting him my attention was taken by James who was lying on his tummy on the settee watching Mike. As I looked at him James squeezed his eyes tight shut and when he opened them again two large tears rolled down his face! I have never really known whether he was genuinely moved or whether he just felt obliged to produce tears either for Grandpa or to keep Mike company! In the time that followed he didn't seem to be feeling any sense of bereavement. When Neville's father died James was much younger but he still remembers things about him which he has stored away in his memory all these years.

James only attended my mother's funeral, which was fairly recent, and I greatly regret not taking him to the funerals of my father and uncle and aunt, whom he well remembers. It has come to be recognized that the funeral is the finality which a mentally-handicapped person may be able to accept, rather than just be bewildered at someone's continuing absence. Death (and bereavement) is the one sure thing that will happen to everybody in this life and we are doing our children no favours at all in shielding them from this inevitability. In my own case, having a faith makes explanations much easier and it always seems to soften the blow to be able to tell the children that we will all meet up again in the world to come. If you don't believe in the world to come I suppose you just try and explain to your handicapped child that each one of us has a life span which lasts for a certain time and when that time comes to an end, we are no more. I should think, in the case of people who have no belief in an after life, it is even more important to demonstrate the finality of death by taking the handicapped bereaved person to the funeral. It could also be pointed out, of course, that in many cases death is a release from suffering.

During what we thought was going to be James's last year at Maze Hill School I was occupying myself one morning at home with the usual rivetingly-interesting domestic chores when the phone rang. It was Neville. 'How do you fancy being on television?,' he asked, somewhat to my surprise. You'd be amazed to know how rarely people phone up to ask me to appear on television. 'No thanks,' I said, 'Was there anything else?'. He was a bit taken aback that I didn't seem to want to know more and went on to explain, regardless, that the BBC wanted to make a film about a handicapped child of school age who had brothers and/or sisters, also at school. They contacted MENCAP, knowing them to be the main organization for the mentally handicapped and MENCAP had, in turn, contacted Neville knowing that his family fitted the description. And how! I really didn't want to do it. It seemed like a lot of hassle and the whole idea didn't appeal to me at all. Then Neville uttered the magic words, 'It's for schools'. Well, that did it. I had been so very frightened of mentally-handicapped people when I was a child that I was prepared to do almost anything which might allay the fears of children nowadays and perhaps bring a little of the enlightenment which I, as a child, never had. In fact, when Roger Tonge (producer of the 'Scene' series of Schools films for the BBC) came to see us it was not finally decided that we should be the chosen family. Roger also had to see another family in North London. I think that it was James who swayed the balance. Roger and James got on like a house of fire and I think it was James being able to speak up for himself (to an extent) which tipped the scales in our favour. Apparently the child belonging to the other family was very profoundly handicapped and I imagine that even in those early planning days Roger was hoping that he would be able to interview James.

Roger came over to spend a day with us a few weeks before he wanted to start filming, just to get to know us and tell us what he wanted to do. I asked him, in all innocence, if there would just be him and a cameraman. He looked at me pityingly, 'There will be me, my assistant, the cameraman, the cameraman's assistant, the lighting man and the sound man'. 'Oh,' I said, a little faintly, 'And will I have to feed all these people?' 'Oh no,' said Roger, 'They'll all push off to the pub to eat.' Which is exactly what happened — but I do remember rather large quantities of home-made cake being consumed!

On the whole making the film was a very pleasurable experience. The only exception was when they decided to film the family at Sunday lunch. Instead of all sitting at the kitchen table, as usual, we had to set it up in the dining room so that the crew could fit in — that was the start of the awfulness. No — the start was when I was dishing up the roast lamb, roast potatoes and vegetables on the kitchen table prior to the dreaded lunch in the formal surroundings. I had cooked baked parsnips (which looked and smelled delicious, even if I say it myself) and I felt absolutely dreadful when Dave, the young assistant cameraman, leaned over the baking dish wherein they lay and said 'They're my favourite vegetables'. I hadn't prepared lunch for the crew, of course, and after that I didn't enjoy mine at all! Anyway, we sat around the dining table, with bright lights and camera watching every mouthful, making the most stilted conversation you ever heard in your life! Needless to say, that episode went in the editor's bin! They were a really super crew and made what could have been a very difficult experience most enjoyable; they were Dave (the parsnip man), Les, the sound man (who greatly admired Tabitha, my pretty tortoiseshell cat); Joe, the lighting man (who hit it off really well with the boys — he was a golf addict like Chris); John Hooper, the Chief Cameraman (and a name of considerable note amongst cameramen); Diana, Roger's assistant and, of course, Roger himself who has become a valued friend, sending James beautifully printed postcards from the depths of Thailand and Sri Lanka — or wherever he happens to be on holiday. They are much appreciated both by James and us.

A lot of amusing things happened during the making of the film, not the least on the day that Roger came down to see us before it all began. I must just tell you that before he went into television Roger had taught physics in a school in the east end of London. On this particular day he was sitting on the settee with James looking through James's holiday scrap-book. James had been to Switzerland with his Club and the first picture that came up was a postcard of a village with snow-covered mountains in the background. 'Ah,' said Roger, 'What's this?' 'We went walking up there,' said James. 'Right up those mountains?' asked Roger, 'Yes,' said James. Roger looked at the picture again. 'In all that snow?' (this in tones of frank disbelief). James looked at the picture also. 'Yes,' he said, staunchly. The mountains were very high and *very* snowy. 'What sort of boots were you wearing?' asked Roger, challengingly. 'Bovver boots' replied James unhesitatingly and Roger very wisely turned to the next picture in the book!

The next picture was of a very pretty cow (similar to a Jersey) with a bell round its neck. 'Now, James,' said Roger, suddenly turning into a schoolteacher. 'Do you know why the cows in Switzerland have bells round their necks?' He obviously expected James either to say, 'Yes, so the farmers can hear them in the mountain mists,' or 'No, I don't know why cows have bells round their necks,' in which case Roger would have welcomed the opportunity to instruct him in the matter. In fact James said, 'They wear bells round their necks because their horns doesn't work' (grammar was never his strong point!). Roger just roared with laughter and said, 'We must get that in' and in it went. It has caused a great many laughs among the schoolchildren who have seen the film and it just goes to show how very instructive those jokes in Christmas crackers can be! Very little of the film was in any way rehearsed. When they filmed the drama lesson at Maze Hill School, Roger just took James on one side and made a few suggestions as to things he might do (in the way of most drama teachers, I imagine) and left the rest to James. It has amused me ever since that in the restaurant scene James says, 'Sorry — chips are off'. I mean; for heaven's sake, who ever runs out of *chips*? The only thing on the menu you fancy maybe, but not chips!

I think one of the most difficult aspects of making the film was getting the three middle boys to let Roger interview them. They were aged 12, 13 and 14 respectively and were all very self-conscious. Roger was trying to persuade them to respond to his questions by the use of sweet reason. When I couldn't stand to see him suffer any more I took him on one side. 'Look,' I said, 'there's no way you're going to persuade them with argument. For heaven's sake stop using reason and start using brute force!' Poor Roger. That wasn't at all his idea of how to get the best out of young people; however time was getting on so he thought he'd give it a try. 'OK, you lot,' I heard him say, 'Shall we stop wasting the time of those people here and get on with it, NOW?' It worked, of course. They didn't like it but they recognized that the moment had come to co-operate. It takes experience to know when the time has come to stop asking and start telling!

Making the film has had a very broadening effect on James. He is enormously pleased if he meets anyone who tells him that they have seen it and he considers himself to be something of a television star — actually, so do we! I show it to fifth year pupils at a comprehensive school in Eltham and one day one of the teachers was explaining to the form what sort of film they were going to see. It was a kind of preparation and she made such a good job of describing the film and its 'local' location that one of the children recognized James from her description. 'Oh,' he said, 'I know that boy. He travels on my bus in the mornings. He doesn't half know a lot about football'. Such is fame. It is very heartwarming to hear this sort of thing and know that James is going about his job of ambassador to the mentally handicapped so competently. I'm sure it is only a matter of time (and integration from nursery-school age) before handicapped people (whatever their handicap may be) can take their rightful place in the community.

8

AWAY FROM HOME

While I am writing this book for parents and carers who have decided to keep their handicapped child at home — whether they are their own children, fostered or adopted, nonetheless there will be times when these children will have to spend some time in care and it is right and fitting, I think, that they should do so. As I have said before, it can only be to a handicapped child's benefit to spend time away from its own family as this will, inevitably, be his or her ultimate destiny. As indeed it is for nearly everybody. Before actually going on to the Stamina Paper about residential care, I would like to pay tribute to some parents I met during the course of my research. They are Sue and Mick, Ann and Tom, Joyce and Alan. Each of these couples either had or were in the process of adopting a mentally-handicapped child.

Sue and Mick were very experienced 'fosterers' and on the occasion that they got a call from the hospital to foster Rosemary they had no idea that she was to change their lives. The baby's mother had given birth upstairs in the bedroom in her mother's house (the baby's mother was aged fifteen) and the baby, who had a Nigerian father, was put up for adoption. Sue fell in love with Rosemary (who was of normal intelligence at birth) from the minute she saw her and asked the local authority if there was any chance of them being allowed to keep her. The local authority was rather doubtful as to whether this would be allowed. Sue did have some qualms about adopting Rosemary as she and Mick had already adopted Thomas, a child they had previously fostered, and Sue felt quite guilty about 'hogging all these lovely babies' as she put it! A few weeks before Sue and Mick were due to go on holiday with all the children the social services telephoned to say that they had a family who was interested in Rosemary; they already had two mixed-race children, apparently. They visited Sue and Mick twice with a view to getting to know Rosemary a little before actually attempting to 'live' with her and each time the baby cried almost non-stop. Eventually the day before the holiday arrived and the prospective adopters came and collected Rosemary. Sue and Mick went off with their children and Sue admits to feeling very glum. She had made up her mind that she wouldn't telephone to see how Rosemary was getting on for a week, and when she actually did phone, she was told that the baby was in the Hospital for Sick Children at Great Ormond Street and that it was 'touch and go'. Sue immediately telephoned Great Ormond Street and was told that Rosemary was in an oxygen tent and that all they could say about her condition was that it seemed to be some mystery virus. Sue wanted to go straight up to London to see Rosemary, of course, but realized that she really had no claims over the baby, so had to be patient until the two weeks were up. When she eventually went to see Rosemary, the day after she got home from her holiday, she found that the baby was out of danger but had no sight and apparently no responses. However, when Sue sang her their 'special song' the baby smiled and Sue was thrilled that Rosemary had responded to her. As the adoptive parents had been somewhat thrown by all this, Sue agreed to look after Rosemary while they made up their minds what they really wanted to do. This situation continued until Rosemary was seven months old — she still had no sight but had been transferred to a local hospital out-patients department. At seven months the baby had a brain scan and damage was confirmed. There were signs of spasticity and some doubt as to whether she would ever walk. At about this time Sue and Mick felt that Rosemary was beginning to see a little as she seemed to react to light. The prospective adoptive parents had only been to see Rosemary once during all this time and they now phoned Sue and Mick to say that they really didn't think that they could go through with the adoption — they hadn't, after all, set out to adopt a handicapped baby and they felt that it would be too much for them to cope with. Sue and Mick were very sympathetic and were glad that their own adoption hopes were alive again. Sue told me, with considerable amusement, that after they had adopted Thomas (having already got Sarah and Benjamin) Mick had had a vasectomy as they didn't intend to have any more children! The Lord works in mysterious ways . . .! Adoption was finally granted to Sue and Mick in January 1985, two months before Rosemary's second birthday. It was a real pleasure to me to talk to this young couple. It is quite plain that Rosemary is a very lucky little lady indeed. They have a very down-to-earth non-sentimental attitude to her and will see that her needs are filled to the best of their ability. Sue intends to do as much for Rosemary as she can and when the clinic doctor suggested (three times) that she might like Rosemary to go to a day nursery to 'learn to play with other children' Sue was quick to point out that there were three perfectly adequate playmates for her in her own home! The home liaison teacher calls to have a session every two weeks or so and I was somewhat taken aback when Sue, who thought that all day and every day at three would be too much for Rosemary, was unaware that she could go to school for as few days as Sue wished, provided she stayed all day when she was there (unless, of course, Sue could arrange her own transport). I felt it shouldn't have been me imparting that particular piece of information.

Sue and Mick said that they find the rewards of looking after a child like Rosemary are absolutely tremendous. I asked them if they would still have adopted Rosemary if they had known that she would be profoundly handicapped (no definite prognosis had been given) and they said that even if Rosemary had not progressed beyond the baby stage they considered that it would have been a job well worth doing to have looked after her at home until such time as they could no longer do so. They felt very strongly that even a few years of family life was better than never having known any and I must say that seeing the family life the baby was having, I agreed with them wholeheartedly.

Somehow, one gets a completely different viewpoint of mental handicap when talking to a parent who has actually chosen to have a handicapped child, rather than having it thrust upon them as most of us have. Sue really has a very busy time caring for Rosemary and doesn't seem to suffer from the mental tiredness which seems to come very often to the natural parents of handicapped children. She is quite happy to take Rosemary to a mother and toddler group at the local church but finds it 'heavy' as she put it, as the conversation so often leads round to Rosemary's brain damage; it was obviously a topic of conversation which Sue found non-productive. She agreed, however, that it was very important that mothers of mentally-handicapped children should integrate with the mothers of normal children and thus bring about the integration of the children. All in all, it was a very stimulating experience to go and visit Sue and Mick.

Joyce and Alan were not without their own share of family problems. Their daughter is an epileptic and their son developed rheumatoid arthritis as a child. In spite of these difficulties Joyce had been fostering babies for some years and when she was asked by the local authority if she would look after Patricia while her fate was being decided, it presented no great difficulties. It appears that Patricia had been born perfectly normal but had been severely abused by her young father shortly after she came out of hospital — she would then have been three months old — and the resultant brain damage reduced her hearing, caused a certain amount of loss of sight in her left eye and also caused epilepsy. The reason for the baby having been in hospital for so long after her birth was, in fact, because she had been born three months prematurely.

Joyce and Alan had been looking after Patricia for about six months when she was put on the register for adoption. The family had a conference and it was a unanimous decision that they should try and adopt Patricia. They anticipated some difficulty as it seems to be the policy for the fostering parents not to be allowed to adopt that particular child. However, in this case the adopting commission decided that Joyce had established a bond with Patricia and that adoption could be considered.

Patricia is a very lively baby but there are a lot of question marks hanging over her. Nobody can say for sure whether she will walk or not but she was moving round the floor a lot while I was visiting and seemed very curious about her surroundings. Joyce has quite a hectic week with Patricia and her days are occupied as follows:

Monday	Free.
Tuesday	Toy library. Greenwich District Hospital to see paediatrician.
Wednesday	Physiotherapy (every other) and school liaison teacher (every other).
Thursday	Toy library. Newcomen Centre at Guy's for assessment. Also consults doctor for eyes and ears.
Friday	Hydropool.

One presumes that Joyce fits in her shopping, washing, cooking and cleaning as best she can round all these activities! It is very much to her advantage (and Patricia's) that she is a State Registered Children's Nurse. She is extremely experienced in looking after all types of child, but now she has adopted Patricia she thinks that she will give up further fostering.

Ann and Tom had a different experience again. They too had been fostering for the borough for quite a long time and one day Anne rang up a newspaper on impulse after seeing a picture of a boy who needed a home and who was being cared for by the Thomas Coram Foundation. It turned out that that particular child would have been beyond Ann and Tom's capabilities, in their opinion, and the Foundation suggested that they might like to take a Down's child. Having discovered what Down's was, Tom wasn't that keen and Ann said she'd think about it. Ann and Tom were very taken with the baby when they met her (she is Amy, by the way), but Ann decided against having her as she had no experience. However, as time went by Ann had some encouragement from her aunt in North Wales, who had worked as a mental-handicap nurse, and she decided to give it a try. She phoned the social worker and visited Amy in the foster home in Camden every day for a week to get to know her a little. She also explained to her two daughters what she was intending to do and involved them as much as possible.

Ann, looking back, finds a number of things which should not really have happened. She felt that she was under constant pressure from the Foundation and also resented the fact that they forced on her a meeting with the baby's natural parents; a meeting which Ann didn't want and subsequently found very traumatic. She was very honest with me and said that if she had had more time to think about it she possibly would have backed out. (I've felt like that about my normal children on occasions!) Nonetheless, she is doing everything she can for the baby — who is now three-and-a-half years old — and I think I may have caught her on a bad day. The sort of day, perhaps, when the thought of a bedsitter with just you in it looks very inviting! I have quite a few days like that!

Amy is a Down's child who integrates well with normal children. She started at a playgroup when she was aged two, for three mornings a week, and enjoyed it. Ann thought it was more important for her to go to a normal playgroup than to go full-time to special school. Amy has a certain amount of speech difficulty and is learning Maketon at school but Ann was rather bothered about the fact that she herself has not been offered any instruction in Maketon and also that Amy didn't appear to be attempting to speak the word which matched the sign — an important aspect of sign language. She stated her intention of taking both these points up with the school and, speaking as one who is very familiar with Maze Hill School, I have no doubt that her problems will be satisfactorily dealt with. Incidentally, when I asked Ann what she thought about corrective surgery, which is so much a current issue concerning Down's children, she said, 'Not for my child.' As far as hostel care was concerned, she felt that she might at some time need it for Amy and was realistic enough to see it as a respite for herself as well as instructing Amy in what life away from the family is like.

Whether our children are at home or away many of us do not know what we should be asking for by way of residential care. All too often parents and carers accept standards with which they are not too happy because poor respite care is better than none at all. This is a state of affairs which cannot be allowed to continue. The victims of low standards of care are our children and, for the most part, they are silent sufferers. 'Stamina Paper No. 3' covers residential care for all ages of children and adults but, for myself, it is the adult care which looms large on our particular horizon, as James is approaching the time when steps will be taken to find him a place. The point is, of course, that unless you have a profoundly-handicapped child who is actually living in a hospital situation (like many of the children at Goldie Leigh) or you have a mentally-handicapped child with whom you really cannot cope (and there are parents who find the whole thought of caring for a handicapped child so very unendurable that they have to put the child in some sort of care right from the very beginning), the rest of us could, in fact, close our eyes to sub-standard respite care simply because we know that it is only for one week, or two at the most, and then our handicapped kids will be back in the comfort of their own homes. I wonder how many parents have thought to themselves, 'I won't rock the boat in case they won't have him (or her) back.' I have thought this way myself. In actual fact I would far prefer that James went to a hostel where he had a room to himself and was able to take all his appurtenances (perhaps not the snooker table!) with him. I shall quote this very important paper almost verbatim. Not surprisingly it is MENCAP orientated, but it won't hurt to remind those of you who belong to local MENCAP societies what you should be asking for and I hope it will inspire those of you who don't belong to any particular organization to join a group which will help bring about the changes which are so necessary in order to give our mentally-handicapped children the best in life we can. And it is up to us.

The Paper assumes that parents of mentally-handicapped people (and the mentally-handicapped people themselves as they grow older) have a right to a choice of residential provision. The choice should include the following:

Living at home
Living with foster parents (for the under-sixteens)
Residential nurseries
Hostels
Group homes (with support)
Group homes (unstaffed))
Subnormality hospitals

Independent living
Village community

Statutory responsibility for providing residential care for the mentally handicapped is divided thus:

Local Authority Social Services Departments are responsible for the welfare of all the mentally handicapped *who are able to live in the community* (e.g. in their own home, in hostels, group homes, etc.)

The Area Health Authority is responsible for those who require medical and nursing care.

Finance has been provided by Central Government for the joint planning of certain facilities to be undertaken by local authorities, health authorities and voluntary organizations acting together to meet local needs (DHSS Circular HC 77/17). Regulations governing the establishment of Joint Care Planning Teams provide for the representation of voluntary organizations. Local societies should (in consultation with the Regional Officer) ensure that they are represented on such teams locally. Provision of residential care is, therefore, in the first instance the responsibility of the Director of Social Services who will have a specialist officer responsible for residential services.

The main duties of the social services department of a local authority are outlined in the following legislation:

National Assistance Act 1948
Mental Health Act 1959
The Chronically Sick and Disabled Persons Act 1970

Under the National Assistance Act 1948, it should be the duty of every local authority to provide: (1) Residential accommodation for persons who, by reason of age, infirmity or any other circumstances, are in need of care and attention which is not otherwise available to them; and (2) temporary accommodation for persons who are in urgent need thereof, being need arising in circumstances which could not reasonably have been foreseen or in such other circumstances as the authority may in any particular case determine. (Section 21).

The Mental Health Act 1959 provides as follows:

Part 1   Persons with whom the Act deals.
Part 2   Local authority service.
Part 3   Registration of mental nursing homes and residential homes.
Part 4   Compulsory admission to hospital and guardianship.
Part 5   Admission of patients concerned in criminal proceedings, etc.
Part 6   Removal and return of patients within the United Kingdom, etc.
Part 7   Special hospitals.
Part 8   Management of property and affairs of patients.

Under the Chronically Sick and Disabled Persons Act 1970, the following sections are relevant to parents and carers:

Section I   Information as to need for an existence of welfare services, e.g. family support services.
Section II   Provision of welfare services, e.g. practical assistance; aids; holidays; telephone, etc.

'Stamina Paper No. 3' lists the following minimum standards for mentally-handicapped children under the age of sixteen:

Living at home
For the mentally-handicapped child who lives at home the following services are essential. Check:

1 That there is regular full support from relevant specialist services, e.g. paediatrician, speech therapist, psychologist, psychiatrist, physiotherapist.

2 That there is regular support from specialist social worker and/or health visitor. This should include visits at home at intervals of not more than two months.

3 That visits are covered by regular reports to the appropriate authority and available to parents.

4 That there is continuing counselling and advice, short-term relief, clinics, opportunity classes, etc.

5 That full information regarding statutory benefits and services of all kinds is readily available and is conveyed to

parents by specialist social workers.

6 That priority placement on local-authority housing lists is available to families with a severely mentally-handicapped child.

7 That parent 'workshops', to assist parents with the care of their child, are organized and parents made aware that *support services for families should be provided by the local authority.*

8 That a full laundry service is available.

9 That special equipment (draw-sheets, nappies, suitable wheelchairs, washing machines) is available.

10 That adaptations to the home in the form of ramps to doorways, hoists, etc. are available if required.

11 That home help and other kinds of support for families are available.

12 That local short-term care is available regularly, overnight, for weekends, Mondays to Fridays or in emergencies.

13 That options for short-term care include foster homes and children's homes.

14 That there is a 'day care' programme available throughout all school holidays.

15 That any child, irrespective of how difficult, if managed by the parents, has access to short-term facilities.

16 That local authority social and leisure activities are developed or that financial support is given to voluntary agencies.

Foster homes
All the supporting services listed for the child living at home should also apply to foster homes. Check, in addition:

17 That foster parents receive financial remuneration on an agreed scale together with appropriate supplementary finance for clothing, holidays, etc.

18 That the local authority provides regular supervision and support for foster parents.

19 That foster homes are the subject of a regular visit by a specialist social worker.

20 That links between foster parents and natural parents are maintained where possible.

21 That foster parents are encouraged to join, and made welcome in, the relevant local Society for Mentally Handicapped Children.

Residential care in hostels and homes

22 That all parents have full details of local authority options for residential care, inside or outside their area.

23 That the selection of options and policy on placement is jointly decided. That parents and/or nearest relatives, together with the supervisory staff who will have responsibility for the resident, are always included in such joint decisions.

24 That in each local authority area there is a sufficient number of places in residential homes to meet the needs of all the mentally-handicapped children requiring residential care, including those at present in subnormality hospitals.

25 That all sources of placement have been properly investigated. (Social services departments may use provisions outside their own area until they are themselves able to offer the full range.)

26 That full assessment of educational and social potential and of physical and emotional needs of each entrant for residential placement is made, or is available prior to or immediately after placement.

27 That children with severe behaviour difficulties are provided with suitable hostel accommodation and appropriate therapy.

28 That provision is in ordinary houses, local to the child's home where possible.

29 That, whatever the size of the house, accommodation is so arranged that residents live in groups of not more than five.

30 That hostel accommodation offers a variety of rooms — to be alone or to share.

31 That hostels should contain no more than fifteen children.

32 That hostels are mixed sex.

33 That there is space for recreational and leisure activities.

34 That there is a warm domestic atmosphere.

35 That furniture is of a varied and not 'institutional' nature.

36 That the kitchen and laundry are household in character.

37 That a resident's privacy is respected.

38 That toilets and bathrooms have adequate privacy.

39 That the approach of 'learning through doing' is accepted as the philosophy of the staff.

40 That leisure activities involve relationships outside the hostel.

41 That there is ongoing contact with the family of every resident in a home or hostel.

42 That parents, other relatives and friends, are encouraged to visit.

43 That senior staff in homes or hostels have relevant experience and training.

44 That there is support for the staff from professional specialist workers.

45 That specialist services are available as required (speech therapists, psychologists, etc.).

46 That there is regular monitoring and evaluation at least annually, by the local authority, of the standard provision in local authority homes.

47 That parents and relatives are involved in regular discussions on their son's or daughter's development.

48 That the local Society for Mentally-Handicapped Children keeps in close touch with the staff and residents and that staff are encouraged in this by the local authority.

49 That homes funded by private individuals or voluntary organizations are given the same degree of support.

50 That there is regular contact between the residential home and the special school, especially to exchange information regarding assessments.

51 That these assessments are in writing — (adequate records are essential for new staff and to facilitate transfer to new residences when desirable) — and that all involved in joint consultation and decision-making, including parents, receive copies.

52 That while no residential placement should become a 'dead-end', the child's need for security and continuity of residence is considered.

Well, there is enough there to make those in power go pale with fright — and they would, if we applied enough pressure. In my opinion there is nothing unreasonable in any one of those requirements and I am sure that I speak for all parents and carers of mentally-handicapped children. They are very fond of telling us that the cake can only be cut up into a certain number of portions. Don't they realize that to make the cake larger, you simply have to add more of the essential ingredients? Or perhaps, if ingredients are that short, there are some goodies that they should be cutting down on in order to enlarge the 'cake of care'. So, let's see what should be happening to our mentally-handicapped adults in residential care (and this will, hopefully, include James in the not-too-distant future).

Living at home

For the mentally-handicapped adult who lives at home the following services are essential. Check:

1 That there is regular full support from specialist services, e.g. speech therapist, psychiatrist, psychologist, physiotherapist.

2 That there is regular support from a specialist social worker. This should include visits at home at intervals of not more than two months.

3 That visits are covered by regular reports to the appropriate authority and available to parents.

4 That there is regular counselling and advice, with social work support and short-term relief.

5 That full information regarding statutory benefits of all kinds is readily available and is conveyed to the mentally-handicapped person and to parents by specialist social workers.

6 That priority placement on local authority housing lists is available to families with a severely mentally-handicapped adult son or daughter.

7 That parent 'workshops' are organized to assist parents to adjust to the changing needs of their adult son or daughter.

8 That parents are aware of opportunities for their son or daughter to live independently of the family and *that the individual mentally-handicapped adult is entitled to specialist services provided by the local authority.*

Check, in addition:

9 That full laundry service is available.

10 That special equipment (draw-sheets, incontinent pads/aids, suitable wheelchairs, washing machines) is available on demand.

11 That adaptations to the home in the form of ramps to doorways, hoists, etc. are available if required.

12 That home help and other kinds of support for families are available.

13 That short-term local care is available regularly, overnight, for weekends, Mondays to Fridays or in emergencies.

14 That 'fostering' in private families is a possible short-term option.

15 That any adult son or daughter, irrespective of how difficult, if managed by the parents, has access to short-term facilities.

16 That local authority social and leisure activities are developed or that financial support is given to voluntary agencies.

Residential care in hostels/homes/group homes

17 That full assessment of educational and social potential and of physical and emotional needs of each entrant for residential placement, is made or is available prior to or immediately after placement.

18 That parents and mentally-handicapped adults are provided with full details of local authority options for residential care inside or outside their area.

19 That the selection of options and policy on placement is jointly decided. That the individual adult, parents or nearest relatives together with the supervisory staff, who will have responsibility for the resident, are always included in such joint decisions.

20 That in each local authority area there is a sufficient number of places in residential homes to meet the needs of all the mentally handicapped requiring residential care, including those at present in subnormality hospitals who could live in the community.

21 That mentally-handicapped adults with severe behaviour difficulties are not excluded from residential care in the community.

22 That homes are in ordinary houses, local to the adult mentally-handicapped person's home area where possible.

23 That hostel accommodation offers a variety of rooms — to be alone or to share.

24 That hostels should contain no more than fifteen residents.

25 That hostels are mixed sex.

26 That there is a space for recreational and leisure activities.

27 That there is a warm domestic atmosphere.

28 That furniture is of a varied and not 'institutional' nature.

29 That the kitchen and laundry are 'household' in character and can be used by the residents.

30 That a resident's privacy is respected.

31 That toilets and bathrooms have adequate privacy.

32 That residents take part in decision making.

33 That 'learning through doing' results in residents being involved in the running of their own house.

34 That some leisure activities involve relationships outside the hostel.

35 That there is provision made for holidays (The Chronically Sick and Disabled Persons Act 1970 provides for this).

36 That there is ongoing contact with the family, if any, of every resident in a home or hostel.

37 That parents, other relatives and friends are encouraged to visit.

38 That senior staff in homes or hostels have relevant experience and training.

39 That there is support for the staff from professional specialist workers.

40 That specialist services are available as required (speech therapist, psychologist, etc.).

41 That there is regular evaluation at least annually, by local authorities, of the standards provided in local authority homes.

42 That the resident, parents or relatives are included in discussions on progress.

43 That the local Society for Mentally-Handicapped Children keeps in close touch with the staff and residents

and that staff are encouraged in this by the local authority.

44 That homes run by private individuals or voluntary organizations are given the same degree of support and evaluation by local authorities or health authorities as is provided for statutory services.

45 That there is regular contact between the residential home and the adult training centre to ensure co-ordination of assessment.

46 That each individual in residential care (of whatever category, from special care to minimal support) participates in a regular review of his circumstances.

47 That all assessments are in writing (adequate records are essential for new staff) and that all involved in joint consultation and decision-making receive copies.

48 That while no residential placement should become a 'dead-end', there should be regular reviews of the suitability of each placement in consultation with the resident. Regard must be given to the need for security and continuity of residence, in accordance with the wishes of the individual.

49 That consideration is given to the possibility of the individual living independently and that provision is made on local authority housing lists for this purpose.

50 That social work support is available for those living independently.

Once again, Stamina has provided us with a formidable checklist on which there are few things with which one could argue. I do wonder about the possibility of some mentally-handicapped people with *severe* behaviour problems ever being able to be provided for in the community. I think all the teachers I have spoken to agree that there are a very few who will always need to be kept in a hospital environment, both for their own safety and the peace of mind of the people around them. I don't necessarily mean peace of mind from the personal danger point of view, but if I lived next door (or near) to a house occupied by mentally-handicapped adults, I should be perturbed to think that any of them were having to be locked up. Severe behaviour problem is something which, to date, has not come into my life. What I do think is, and I say this as the parent of a mentally-handicapped person, that while you are considering the needs of the handicapped, the needs of the community in which they are going to live must not be overlooked or ignored.

I am particularly aware of the lack of communication as far as assessments are concerned. No one ever tells me how James gets on when he goes to the hostel for a week — there is absolutely no consultation at all. The same with the training centre. James himself is pretty uncommunicative about what goes on (I suppose it's just his normal routine the same as mine is at home — I don't tell him how many loads of washing I've done on a particular day!). While writing this book, I have taken a long, hard look at myself and I am frankly appalled by what I see. So what if the hostel or the training centre don't consult with me — I've got a tongue in my head, haven't I? I have made a firm purpose of amendment, as we Catholics say! After this year's summer holidays (which are nearly upon us) I shall gird myself to do battle with all the people who can tell me what sort of person James is outside our home. And if I can do it — so can you!

One of the depressing things about the local authority is that it considers an emergency to be either illness or death only — and I always get the feeling that death would really be preferable. Take my experience: about four years ago Neville telephoned me at home one morning to say that he had been asked by his managing director to present a paper at a business meeting which was to be held during a weekend which was being laid on for the successful sales staff — in Majorca. Apparently this sort of thing is not unusual in commercial firms — the weekend was a sort of prize for the salesmen who achieved their targets (this is computer selling, by the way, not exactly small beer!), but they were going to have to do some work as well. Where do you come into all this, Liz, you may ask? Well, the managing director asked Neville to take me along as well — I (the mere chattel) had been invited. Needless to say, I was in transports of delight (no — I mean it, I'd never been to Majorca and as it was February the winter had definitely become very boring), so I began to make arrangements. I asked Neville to see if his sister, Janet, would have Peter for the weekend; she has three boys of her own and, as it turned out, was quite glad to have Peter as he was still of an age when he did what he was told — her's were all teenagers. So, that was Pete settled. Now James. Well, ages ago a social worker had told me that if I wanted hostel care for James I only had to pick up the telephone, so I did precisely that. I knew that there would be a bed for James because, after all, it was the winter time and not half-term or anything. Guess what? Yes, you're quite right — there wasn't a bed in the borough. Of course I didn't know then that there were only six short-stay beds anyway and, in my innocence, when the social worker had told me I only had to pick up the phone I didn't realize that she meant just to have a chat. I thought she meant that there would be hostel care available. Silly me! So there I was with two weeks to go and nowhere for James. We had a family conference (the three middle boys were all going to be at home) and they, bless their hearts, told us that they would look after James. You see, they're not silly — they all know that they can take James to the pub, whereas they would have to stay in for Peter! Anyway, we were very grateful to them and toddled off on the appointed day, knowing that James and Peter were being well taken care of and raspberries to the social services! It helped the boys somewhat to know that my friend and neighbour, Jean, had very kindly offered to give James Sunday lunch and that, together with the money I left for fish and chips on the Friday and the money for the Chinese take-away on the Saturday, meant that they didn't have to do very much in the way of cooking. All this does raise the question of what constitutes an emergency. Isn't it allowed to be something pleasurable? Would that be indulging the parents of mentally-handicapped people to an absurd degree? I couldn't have predicted that weekend happening a year before, otherwise I would have booked James into the hostel. So I suppose a holiday you know about well in advance is all right but one that crops up (and it would have been difficult to refuse) may not be considered an adequate reason for short-term care. I expect a lot of people will think that I'm asking a lot, but it wasn't entirely self-indulgent; it did concern our 'bread and butter'. What quite surprises me is that nobody came up with the old chestnut, 'If we do it for you we'll have everyone asking for it,' in the manner of my first and worst social worker.

9

THE YOUNG ADULT

It was a sad day for me when James left Maze Hill School and went round the corner to the Park Vista Adult Training Centre. Life suddenly seemed to get very gloomy. The building was gloomy (an old house which happened to be available — and not very nice, in my opinion) and the trainees seemed gloomy. I never really discovered what they did all day. I didn't like the centre and never went there if I could help it. A defeatist attitude which did James no good at all. Certainly one wasn't invited there by the staff unless there happened to be a meeting of the Parents–Staff Association and that seemed to consist entirely of money-raising for the eternal minibus. I have a deep-rooted hatred of minibuses shared, I am sure, by parents of ordinary children whose schools are forever trying to raise money for one.

Since James has been at the adult centre, not once have Neville and I been asked to go and talk about James's achievements, his progress or his future. Should parents always be the ones to instigate this? I should have thought that it would have been an important part of the individual programme to keep parents informed as to how things are going. At this point I would have liked to include James's programme so you could have an idea of how he occupies his time at the centre. I wrote to the Manager, requesting a copy of the programme. Nothing. I asked James, over the next couple of weeks, to give them the occasional reminder. Nothing. About ten days before final draft I wrote again, making the same request and pointing out that I had a deadline to meet. Nothing. So, do we conclude that James spends his week doing nothing? No, of course he doesn't. He has a very busy week, I expect. It would just be nice to be let into the secret of his activities. Also, it is difficult for us all to realize our children's potential if we don't know where we are all going.

In the early days they did contract work at Park Vista and this was very frowned upon by the 'new thinkers'. It was considered to be exploitation of the handicapped. (So what if they enjoyed doing it? What's that got to do with anything?) Anyway, the contract work was stopped and we did hope that the time was being used profitably on things like social education, literacy, art and craft and such like. Park Vista was lucky in that it had two plots of land to garden and James certainly enjoyed the time spent preparing the ground, planting seeds, looking after the greenhouse and cutting the grass. They also have a group of people who make cement moulds for plants and shrubs; an activity which has been carried on at the annexe. Park Vista was rented from the Co-operative Society and in 1983 the lease ran out. A lovely, new, purpose-built centre was provided in Eltham, a short distance away, and they all moved there at the end of that year. The annexe previously referred to was an old building, just round the corner from the Park Vista house, and had originally been used as a workshop for blind people. The only windows were in the roof — not that you would have seen much if they had been at eye-level. There is just the garden, surrounded by a wall, and blocks of flats beyond. It has been useful to keep the annexe on after the move as it gives some of the trainees a change of environment and activity. They shop for and cook their own lunch when they are there and it gives James the added stimulation of being a more demanding place to reach. Greenwich, from Mottingham, is not an easy journey, whereas the new centre in Sherard Road is just one fairly short bus ride, and if there was a transport strike, it would be no trouble at all for James to walk it. He'd grumble and grouse, but it wouldn't take him very long to get there! I suppose, like most people, James doesn't mind choosing to walk from point A to point B but resents being made to do it.

Some of his friends (admittedly much younger) have had the advantage of doing two years at college before going into the Adult Training Centres and I deeply regret that this facility was not available to James. MENCAP is very conscious that full-time education in school and/or college should be available up to the age of nineteen and have produced an excellent paper (Stamina, once again) on the subject, which I shall quote more or less in full. If you are not a member of a local MENCAP society, the requirements which the society is laying down as being *minimum* may inspire you to join and lend your voice to those of all the other parents who are fighting for their children's and young adults' rights. This book is not intended as a recruitment drive for MENCAP or any other organization, but it is a fact of life that parents have only achieved what they have got so far by banding together and putting pressure on the appropriate authorities to make changes for the better. When we first joined MENCAP (James was about three years old) there was no formal schooling, as such, and it was because some of us in our local society were personally acquainted with the late Bill Hamling, MP for Woolwich, who took a great interest in the affairs of the local handicapped children and the society that, when his opportunity came to put down a motion in the House of Commons, he asked us what we needed and, to cut a long story short, we now have the 1970 (subsequently superseded by the 1981) Education Act. In fact a large group of us from MENCAP went up to the House of Commons to hear the original debate, and I'm desperately ashamed to say that I fell asleep! However, we were all very fond of Bill (even those who were not of his political persuasion had to acknowledge that he was a very caring person) and we parents of mentally-handicapped children have good reason to remember him always with gratitude. It is my personal hope that all the work which he started is not now going to be completely thrown away.

Stamina Paper No. 2 is concerned with services for people with mental handicap over the age of sixteen, including education, training and day care. It is a checklist to help local societies (and you) ensure that people with mental handicap are receiving at least the *minimum* standards of provision. If the standard established for your child is not acceptable, then use the information as a basis for action. So, this Stamina Paper is about:

(a)   Making sure that full-time education in school and/or college, with appropriate curriculum and resources, is available until an individual is nineteen (see 'Stamina Paper No. 1').

(b) That there are appropriate full-time and part-time courses at local colleges of further/adult education for those over nineteen.

(c) That there is a minimum standard at all adult training centres and/or social education centres and that further/adult education be available in all adult training centres.

(d) That services are available to all, regardless of their age or degree of handicap.

(e) That people with mental handicap, resident in hospital, have the same quality of provision as those in the community.

Checklist

(The references to parents in the following list also, of course, include care staff.)

IT IS ESSENTIAL TO ENSURE:

1 That all young people with mental handicap are able to continue in full-time education until the age of nineteen if they or their parents so wish (see 'Stamina Paper No. 1') and that a thorough review and assessment of continuing educational needs is undertaken about two years before leaving school.

Note: THE LAW SAYS (Section 8 (1)(b) of the Education Act 1944) that local education authorities (LEAs) must ensure that there are enough schools to provide 'full-time education suitable to the requirement of senior pupils, other than such full-time education as may be provided for senior pupils in pursuance of a scheme made under the provisions of this Act relating to further education . . .'. Section 8 (2)(c) stresses that LEAs should have particular regard 'to the need for securing that provision is made for pupils who suffer from any disability of mind or body by providing, either in special schools or otherwise, special educational treatment, that is to say education by special methods appropriate for persons suffering from that disability'. The 1981 Act does not alter this duty. A senior pupil is defined in Section 114 of the Education Act 1944 as 'a person who has attained the age of twelve years but has not attained the age of nineteen years'.

LEGALLY, THEREFORE, although compulsory

schooling ends at sixteen, local education authorities are bound to provide full-time education for all young people who want it until their nineteenth birthday, if this is requested by parents prior to leaving.

2 That this period could also be in a further education establishment.

3 That there are enough places at colleges of further education for full-time day courses for all young people with mental handicap leaving school.

4 That parents and the young person are informed in writing of the reasons for recommending a particular placement after school and are involved in the decision-making process.

5 That the review considers all education possibilities.

6 That the curriculum of full-time courses at colleges of further education includes:

(a) continued reading, writing and numeracy;

(b) continued development of personal and independence skills, including the use of facilities outside the college;

(c) access to classes with other students;

(d) creative arts;

(e) instruction in leisure activities;

(f) appropriate speech and language therapy where required;

(g) access to all departments including those offering courses in industrial, technical and commercial subjects;

(h) orientation to future possible placements.

Note:

The curriculum will vary according to the facilities of the college but should offer elements of choice for all students. Colleges should also provide access to all courses for handicapped students in wheelchairs or with other sensory handicaps.

7 That free transport is provided whenever necessary.

8 That further education should continue to be available throughout adult life for all those who wish to take part.

9 That access to the full range of adult education courses is available regardless of the age of the participants.

10 That integration programmes in normal classes be developed (as per the MENCAP Metropolitan Region Adult

Education Integration Programme).

Other day provisions

There is a mandatory obligation on local social services departments to make day-care provision for mentally-handicapped people (DHSS Circular 1974 and National Health Service Act 1977).

11 That local societies make it a primary duty to ensure that *all* people with mental handicap have appropriate day provision.

I feel that this last item emphasizes my previous point about parents joining together to form a pressure group. Parents of young children of school age are easily lulled into a false sense of security because they have very good provision, but if they take the same attitude when their children reach the age where the provision suddenly becomes rather bad (and don't forget the 1981 Education Act) if they haven't banded together to fight for their older children they might just find that there isn't anyone to help them. All the fighting so far (or nearly all of it) has been done by parents of our generation. James is now twenty-seven and we parents cannot go on for ever — we need the next generation to carry on the struggle. There is still a lot to be done as you will see if you compare the Stamina Papers with what is actually happening in your area.

Adult training centres (ATCs) and social education centres (SECs)

(a) Assessments and programmes

12 That a full report is sent from the previous educational establishment, including a copy of the final assessment.

13 That the programmes of ATCs and/or SECs are based primarily on education and training and are not concerned with production, industrial or otherwise, for its own sake.

14 That individual trainees receive regular full reassessments — educational, social, vocational and physical — at intervals not exceeding one year, and that parents be involved in these assessments and subsequent planning.

15 That instructors/staff are involved in these assessments.

16 That, where possible, trainees are aware of, and agree to, the assessments.

17 That parents are given a copy of the assessments.

18 That individual comprehensive programmes are developed for the trainees, with long- and short-term aims.

19 That all the staff are involved in programme development.

20 That programmes are in writing and are available to staff and parents.

21 That, where possible, trainees are fully aware of, and agree to, the programmes.

22 That parents are fully aware of, and invited to participate in, the programmes.

23 That the programmes are regularly monitored, recorded and updated.

(b) *Personal independence and dignity*

24 That there is a programme for personal hygiene and self-care.

25 That the use of public transport is encouraged and that concessionary fares are available. Assistance should be given in obtaining such concessions. Free transport should be available if public transport is inadequate.

26 That training for independence, aimed at integration in the community, is part of the centre programme and that parents are encouraged to participate.

27 That trainees are involved in decision-making through the formation of student/trainee councils.

28 That 'trainees as volunteers' programmes are developed, enabling trainees to be of service to the community.

29 That parents and trainees are consulted about any proposed research project.

(c) *Manpower and environmental resources*

30 That the centre curriculum is structured on a multi-disciplinary basis involving educators, social workers, craftsmen, therapists and other involved staff and trainees.

31 That teaching/lecturing staff are seconded from the local education authority to implement the specialist aspects of the educational curriculum.

32 That there is a continuous programme of staff development. Untrained staff should be trained to at least the level of a two-year full-time college course; and all staff

should receive regular in-service training.

33 That physiotherapy, speech therapy and non-verbal communication are part of the treatment, training and education.

34 That there are adequate resources for social training, including kitchen, laundry and other domestic equipment.

35 That the centre's equipment is appropriate and adequate.

36 That the centre has adequate transport facilities.

37 That there are recreational and personal enrichment programmes including physical education and sport, using community facilities wherever possible.

(d) *People in hospital*

38 That people resident in hospitals leave the grounds, whenever possible, to attend ATCs and/or SECs.

39 That the standard of day care in hospital is equal to that outlined for ATCs and SECs.

40 That full-time education to nineteen years be provided by the local education authority.

41 That further adult education and leisure facilities are provided by the local education authority or other appropriate committees.

(e) *People with profound retardation and multiple handicap (PRMH)*

The minimum standards outlined for ATCs and/or SECs apply equally to all types of day care for people with PRMH. It is also important to ensure:

42 That day care is provided by the local authority for all people with PRMH.

43 That the day care is provided at, or close to, the ATC and not divorced from other active day centres.

44 That there is a consistent, integrated programme with access to appropriate activities in the centre, in conjunction with other trainees.

45 That staff are suitably qualified, including secondment of appropriate staff from the LEA and the health authority.

46 That there is never less than one member of staff engaged with three clients.

47 That clear goals are established for each person.

48 That programmes and progress are recorded in writing.

49 That parents are involved in the programmes.

50 That there should be a specific teaching area.

51 That each unit is well equipped with appropriate specialist equipment, including micro-technological stimuli.

I expect some of you, after reading that Paper, are either laughing hysterically or weeping buckets. If the parents of the younger children have stayed with me throughout the previous Stamina Paper about ATCs they will, I hope, see that maybe there is more to be done than they thought and that they may not be able to do it on their own. A large number of voices crying in the wilderness makes more noise than just one.

Another subject which I tend to get a bit agitated about is nutrition. Not only from the point of view of training-centre meals, but what the trainees are being taught in their cookery programmes. Convenience food is a fact of modern life, whether we like it or not and if, like James, your handicapped adult has to pass McDonald's on the way to and from work, life can get very worrying, not to say fattening! I am lucky to have someone in our local McDonald's who will 'shop' James, so I can have some idea of the amount of time and money he spends in there. If James is being prepared to lead a reasonably independent life I think he should be taught how to cook real food as well as open tins and heat up bought pies and shown, as far as possible, that the nutritional advantages outweigh the convenience. Many mentally-handicapped people are overweight and I am sure that a little more vigilance on the part of the parents and staff (plus some keep-fit?) would be very much in their interests. In the case of the mentally-handicapped (well, certainly James), fat is definitely not beautiful. I asked James, a few weeks ago, what he had had for lunch at the centre that day. 'Quiche pie,' he said, 'with baked beans and chips.' I nearly died. And if he goes on like that, he'll die. There seems to be a conflict among professionals between providing the best possible life for mentally-handicapped people and infringing their right to choose. I wish they would ask the parents. Parents have rights as well. I think they have a right to lead their lives with their handicapped children in as unstressful a manner as possible. It may be that on occasions the rights of the parents will take priority over the rights of the child or adult. If, in order to maintain the good health of a child or adult, it is necessary to persuade him or her to try and change their eating habits, then this should be done. For instance, you are doing a Down's child with a possible heart defect no favours at all in ignoring his nutritional needs, and this applies to many children and adults who may not have a particular problem but by reason of their handicap lead an inactive life, and becomes obese very easily and quickly. The Down's Children's Association provides a very helpful Information Sheet (No. 1, in fact) which gives the details of those vitamins which are needed by Down's children and adults as a result of the changed structure of the wall of their intestines. This is a 'side effect' of the extra chromosome and in addition to the vitamin advice, the association makes the following dietary recommendations:

> An overweight child leads to an overweight adult with all the attendant health risks. The diet of a Down's Syndrome child should be HIGH IN PROTEIN AND FIBRE and LOW IN CARBOHYDRATES AND FATS. This means:
> Grilling rather than frying.
> Restricted intake of sugar, milk (after weaning), bread, cakes and biscuits (other than wholemeal), butter, other fats.
> Plenty of fruit, green vegetables, meat, fish.
> Glucose as a sweetener.
> All these recommendations should be followed in a common-sense manner and are not designed to make family living a misery or eating out awkward! Although a low serum calcium has been found in Down's Syndrome, it is thought that enough is presented to the bowel for absorption for normal bone formation, etc. It is not recommended that Down's children drink a lot of milk just for the calcium content. Fluoride tablets should be given when recommended by your dentist. (More detailed information for doctors [with references] is available from the Down's Children's Association.)

The obesity problem seems to increase with age (don't we know!) and I guess that this is partly because as a mentally-handicapped person gets older he or she just doesn't move around at the same pace as the young ones do. Also I have noticed that many of them put on weight at puberty so there is perhaps a metabolic change which should be taken into consideration. Therefore, good eating habits should be established in childhood if you want to avoid 'ovoid' adolescents and adults. It is ironic that the parents of mentally-handicapped children and adults probably have more jurisdiction over what they (their offspring) eat than any other section of the population. After all, if they are travelling by local authority transport to school or to the centre, they can only put in their mouths what we parents and/or the staff of the school or centre give them. It is only people who are able to travel by public transport, as James does, who have the freedom and opportunity to eat unsupervised. How essential it is, then, to establish good habits as early as possible and I would urge parents and carers to take their child's diet very seriously indeed and look carefully at the amount of salt and sugar he or she is consuming, to name but two constituents which, taken in excess, are very harmful. A lot of interesting research is going on into the possible connection between food additives and hyperactivity. While on this subject, let me introduce you to HACSG, the Hyperactive Children's Support Group. It was founded in November 1977 in order to help and support hyperactive children and their parents, to conduct research and promote investigation into the incidence of hyperactivity in the UK, its causes and treatments, and to disseminate information concerning this condition. Only those parents who have hyperactive children can really know what a trial it can be to live with and if any of my readers are interested in knowing more about this association the address to write to is HACSG, 59 Meadowside, Angmering, Sussex BN16 4BW. They will keep you in touch with new information on 'safe' foods, research, local activities and meetings and will also supply, for £3 (at the time of writing) a diet booklet. Hyperactive children apart, food additives concern us all and we should all be concerned about them. The 'bible' for those people who want to know what all those mysterious numbers are is undoubtedly *E For Additives* by Maurice Hanssen (Thorsons, 1984) and in case you think that this book has nothing to tell you, do have a look at the side of a packet of instant milk dessert sometime (the type which requires half a pint of milk to be mixed into dry powder). Frankly, I'd rather just drink the milk. There is not nearly enough emphasis in schools on nutrition. How many Home Economics teachers ask the children to bring in low-cholesterol cooking fats and wholemeal flour? I'm not so unrealistic as to believe that they all would, but surely it is better to plant the seeds of good nutrition than to ignore it. I do realize that with many mothers doing full-time jobs the time spent preparing meals sometimes has to be greatly reduced (and let's face it, some people just hate cooking!) and that ready-packaged food is a great time saver, but if you can just inject a little 'whole food' into the family diet where maybe none existed before, then you are doing them nothing but good. I decided a couple of years ago that my family would be better off without full cream milk and since then have been having the semi-skimmed variety. After a few initial complaints they now moan if I have to buy full cream milk because they have got used to the other kind! I would quite like to have the fully skimmed milk but quite honestly I think it tastes awful in tea and coffee so I have effected a compromise. I have absolutely no doubt whatsoever that I have improved James's catarrh by cutting out cereal with milk altogether and changing to the semi-skimmed for drinks. Incidentally, porridge is quite good because you can make it with water and just put a very little milk on it — and not too much sugar! Pauline has had tremendous success in reducing Keith's catarrh in this way and I know would back up my advice to reduce all dairy products — and also milk chocolate.

A subject which parents are becoming increasingly anxious about with their mentally-handicapped youngsters coming through adolescence and into adulthood is, of course, their sexual development. All over the country parents are going sheet-white at the mention of the word 'sex' and I know for a fact that many parents are deliberately (or perhaps subconsciously) blinding themselves to the fact that their child has a problem because they don't know how to go about dealing with it. Well, perhaps you can tackle it in the way that you tackled the sexual problems of your normal children? Yes, me too. I wasn't concerned in their problems — they sorted themselves out in the way that most normal youngsters do without any reference whatever to Mum or Dad. The sexual needs of the handicapped is a very important issue and one which, on the grounds of humanity, cannot be ignored. A few years ago I went to a conference on this subject given by Dr Wendy Greengross, who is one of the leading lights in this field. It was a very frank and outspoken conference — well, as far as the speakers were concerned, it was. One elderly lady in the audience (for whom I felt deep sympathy) got up and rushed out of the room with an apology on her lips as soon as Dr Greengross started talking about masturbation. When the time came to look at the slides she had brought for us to see I glanced quickly (*very* quickly) at each one and then ducked down to my notebook and scribbled frantically in shorthand. I expect all the others had fainted. I do know that I was never able to read back the shorthand! Whenever I show our film to nursing students I make a point of saying to them, 'Hands up those of you who discuss your sex problems with your parents.' In ten years I've had about five or six putting their hands up to the accompaniment of a certain amount of surprise from the fellow students. I mean, one doesn't, does one? However, in the case of mentally-handicapped children and adolescents, parents are being forced to face up to a situation which is not of their making (except that they actually gave birth to the child) and they literally do not have a clue, in general, how to go about it or to whom they should go for advice. I asked Doreen what she would do if Colin was in need of help and she said her first port of call would probably be the adult training centre. My other Doreen said that for Kathrine, who is at college, she would approach the college. Neither of them looked particularly overjoyed at the thought of dealing with the subject. In her booklet *Sex and the Handicapped Child* (National Marriage Guidance Council, 1980) Dr Greengross mentions in her introduction that in a survey of 255 Bristol families with a handicapped child, two out of three of the mothers (*mothers*, you note!) were unaware of the help that could be given to them by the social services department. She assumes from this, therefore, that a large proportion of parents do not receive any help in coping with the sexuality of their disabled children. Hopefully things are changing. In July 1984, the King's Fund Centre in London put out a paper entitled *Personal Relationships and People with Mental Handicap* and I will quote what is written on the first page:

This paper was written by Paul Chamberlain, Senior Clinical Psychologist, Coldeast Hospital, Portsmouth Health District. It was originally produced for care staff working in the Portsmouth and Southampton Areas and is used in the training and induction courses there. It was then felt it would be useful to make this paper available for discussion to a wider audience and Paul Chamberlain would be pleased to receive comments at the above address.

It is a paper of some thirteen or fourteen pages long but I'll just give a few of the points made in it.

'People with mental handicap are people first and have the same needs as any other person and they also have the same human rights as any other citizen.' This is a very important point to get home. I have known people actually voice disgust, if you can believe it, at hearing that people with severe physical or mental handicap have got married or are engaged in a relationship.

'People with mental handicap develop personal relationships just as other people do and have the right to express their feelings within these relationships.' Dr Chamberlain goes on to say that while most of us would agree with these two statements, our response to the needs implied has been restrictive and protective. He points out that this is quite understandable; it is difficult to provide the opportunity for social development and growth of personal relationships (with the possible risks involved) and yet protect people from exploitation. But, he says, there is 'dignity in risk' and learning from experience in a controlled and adequately prepared fashion is something we all value.

The theory which states that the needs and rights of people with mental handicap must be recognized in the services provided to them and their families is called 'normalization'. As I have always thought that this meant trying to make people or situations normal, I .will quote what Dr Chamberlain states:

The principle of normalization is 'simply' stated as follows: 'The use of means which are valued in our society in order to develop and support personal experiences and characteristics which are also valued in our society'.

He recommends *The Principle of Normalisation* by J.O'Brien, A. Tyne, (Pub. CMH.1981) for anyone who wishes to extend their knowledge of this subject.

The experts seem to be agreed on most things; for instance, that parents and care workers (let us not forget that those in care have needs as well) are not receiving enough counselling and reassurance to enable them to deal with the problem. This is, of course, because most parents feel hopelessly inadequate at even beginning to discuss and deal with it. I don't know about you, but there is no way I could ever bring myself to give James advice and counsel on the practicalities of a sexual relationship, or even how to deal with his own frustrations outside a relationship. The experts can go on until they are blue in the face telling parents how to do it (counsel, I mean!) but many of us will always need an uninhibited soul who can deal with the subject in a straightforward and unembarassed way in order to help our adolescents.

I shan't forget in a hurry the day, about three years ago, when the previous Manager of James's centre telephoned me at home one afternoon to say that James had been caught 'in a compromising situation' in the toilets with one of the girls (at least it was a girl). Now, let me just get two points out of the way immediately. No, I didn't ask what they were doing and, no, I don't know whether they were the boys' or the girls' toilets! For some reason I don't understand, schoolchildren and students quite often want to know about the toilets and are doomed to disappointment! I said to the Manager, 'Oh, I see. Well I'll have a word with him when he comes home. Goodbye,' and put the phone down in a sweat! Others may know how I felt. Well, James let himself into the house and went straight up to his room as he usually does in the afternoon. He seems to like a bit of peace and quiet when he gets home from the centre and I usually leave him to it. On this occasion, however, I followed him up very shortly after. I knocked on his bedroom door and went in and he turned round, obviously very surprised to see me. 'Sit down a minute, James, will you?' I said. James gave me a very old-fashioned look indeed and sat down. 'Now,' I said, 'What's all this about you and "Miss X"?' 'I don't wish to discuss it,' he said (he honestly did say that) and I said, 'Well, I do,' — and there was a pause of about four years while I tried to think what to say. To this day I can't remember what I finally said! Incidentally, the Manager had told me that this girl had a real problem (she was very oversexed) and, well, I didn't like to think of my James being involved with someone like that — handicapped or not! Just my maternal instincts making themselves felt. In the end I said to him, 'You know, James, you have to be a bit careful with girls like that — they're not always very clean,' and ran out of the room.

For me, one of the interesting things that comes out of that story is that, from the very first moment I tackled James with the situation, he was embarrassed! How could I, embarrassed myself, possibly give James advice when he was in the same state?

It is the general opinion of the professionals who are taking an interest and researching the subject of the sexual needs of the mentally handicapped that parents and care workers are not receiving enough counselling and reassurance to enable them to deal with the problem. I must just interrupt myself here to say that while Alan Course of Maze Hill School regrets the use of the word 'problem' in connection with sexual education I suppose a 'problem' is a situation you don't know how to deal with and a great many people don't know how to deal with this subject. Dr Greengross refers constantly to the professionals and 'workers' and talks about counsellers; these people seem to be hard to find. Dr Chamberlain talks about 'privacy' and this, of course, is an essential need if a relationship is going to develop to a point where the activities of those involved are such that should not be conducted in the presence of others. People have varying degrees of tolerance — I get embarrassed when I see a couple of teenagers necking at a bus stop but I think we all know what is being suggested. Sexual activities are a private business and group homes, hospitals and hostels should allow for young (and not so young) people to develop their feelings and relationships in private.

Something which I think should be mentioned in connection with any sexual relationship which is being helped to develop is the possibility of a baby appearing on the scene. Dr Chamberlain recommends the local family planning clinic, once the relative merits and disadvantages of contraception have been made clear to the girl and boy. He makes the following point:

Contraception, if used properly, is an effective method of

avoiding unwanted pregnancies and although motives may be well-intentioned, it has been used with mentally-handicapped clients as a means of relieving staff or parental anxieties. However, the clients' needs are the most important consideration and the use of contraception is *not* an acceptable alternative to a well structured educational/counselling programme.

If contraceptive advice is given to clients then it is important that the relative merits and disadvantages are made clear to the client. Local family planning clinics may serve as a useful resource to staff and staff should be acquainted with all such resources.

Any problems associated with a client concerning contraception should be discussed at a care review or multi-disciplinary case conference so that an appropriate programme that protects the staff's rights and meets the client's needs can be decided upon.

I should perhaps just mention again that the document I have just quoted from was prepared for staff who are working with mentally-handicapped people in residential care. It goes without saying that the advice which the family planning clinic can offer is there for parents as well and it is a fact that the sexual needs of the mentally handicapped is a subject in which they have displayed much interest and help.

About pregnancy and parenthood, Dr Chamberlain has this to say:

(a)   People with mental handicap have the same right as any other citizens to be parents. However, these rights have to be balanced with the responsibilities of parenthood. *These responsibilities are the same whether the client is mentally handicapped or not.*

(b)   If clients wish to be parents, then it is imperative that these responsibilities are discussed in depth and the clients' expectations and needs identified.

(c)   *Some* of the areas which need to be explored with the couple who wish to be parents are as follows:

(i)   Does the couple possess sufficient skills to live independently?

(ii) Are there support services available which would enable or facilitate more independent living?

(iii) Does the permanence of the relationship need discussing with the couple?

(iv) Is genetic counselling needed?

(v)   What are the couple's expectations about being parents?

(vi) Can the couple support themselves and a family financially?

(d)   Couples should be encouraged to discuss their plans for parenthood or pregnancy with a suitable member of staff and the staff member's approach to this should be discussed at a care review.

You don't need me to tell you that if this is the sort of thinking that is going on among the people who are looking after our mentally-handicapped offspring in hostels, etc., it is certainly our duty as parents to make quite sure that we are all thinking along the same lines. What I want to know is what happens if a mentally-handicapped couple who are involved in a stable relationship, who have had all the couselling there is, decide they want a baby? Perhaps the counsellors are cleverer than I'm giving them credit for and can, in fact, persuade a couple that it is not a good idea for them to have a baby. I've known many mentally-handicapped people and I can't say I've ever met one who could be a parent without 100 per cent support by the social services or whoever. But then, I'm invariably on the side of the baby. Few of us get everything we want in life and compromise is often necessary. We all have needs which are not going to be met and I would have thought that pointing this out to mentally-handicapped people was an important part of counselling. 'Tough luck, buster,' is a hard phrase but we are all subject to it at some point or other in our lives. Surely 'normalization' includes this, too?

Actually, not all parents feel the way I do about mentally-handicapped people being parents. Don, Kathrine's Dad, loves to envisage a perfect world where his daughter would be able to have her baby and look after it with all the support she needed (and that would be a lot). Don knows that I don't agree with this; we have had many an amicable argument about it, usually in front of a class of fifth-year school kids. It just seems to me that it would be traumatic for a child to have to go to school and say, 'My parents won't be at the open day — they are both mentally subnormal and can't understand the work I do.' I'm sure I shall be told if my readers have other opinions!

When a mentally-handicapped Greenwich girl went

missing for a week, many years ago, she was subsequently found to be 'in a pregnant condition'. The baby was born and brought up by the grandparents — the mother still lived at home — and was adopted by them at the age of eight. I would like to quote to you what 'the baby' said in a magazine article, years later when she had grown up, married and had a family of her own:

I never felt as a child that my home life was any different from others — I knew that most children had fathers but I never questioned why I didn't have one. Nan and Gramps adopted me when I was eight years old and I did try calling them 'Mum' and 'Dad' for a while but it sounded silly! I didn't even question why Mum was 'different' but it was hard when I started school and the other children called her 'barmy'. They even made up a rhyme about her, calling her Ginger the barmy (she has red hair). That did hurt and I could never understand why they said it. I'm sure that it worried Nan, too. She was quite convinced that I would never stay at school as I came home every day in tears.

It seemed natural to me to accept handicapped people without question. As a child, I went to all the parties at Park Vista where Mum must have been one of the longest-serving trainees. In fact I probably preferred their parties to 'normal' ones! It is still a source of wonder to me that it takes one second flat to make a friend of a mentally-handicapped person.

My closest friends have always taken to her readily and still do — in fact their support now is invaluable. When I was in my 'teens I do remember worrying about whether or not I would get married. I was always certain that Mum would live with me and it would happen sooner than if we had been contemporary sisters.

As it turned out, I couldn't have chosen a better husband — David has been marvellous with every obstacle that has come before us. Strangely, we never discussed Mum living with us — apparently he took it for granted and it was just a mutual understanding. He took to her well and she adores him — the sun shines out of his boots!

David and I helped at the Focus Club before we were married, so his concern for and knowledge of the mentally handicapped is not only confined to Mum. We readily recognize that there are so many other families with greater handicaps than we have to cope with, and that helps.

We were married five years ago and because of David's job we moved to Crawley. We hardly saw our house in those first

few months — Nan became ill almost immediately and
deteriorated gradually. I was working in London so I would
travel from work to Eltham one evening during the week to
see them. It was a very difficult time and Mum didn't make it
any easier. I can remember arriving at Nan's one Saturday to
find Mum still in bed at 2.00 p.m. because she had refused to
get up. They simply did not have the strength to cope with her
and Mum took advantage of that.

When Nan and Gramps were taken into hospital we said that
Mum could come and live with us until they came home.
Thanks to the kind help of Mum's social worker in Greenwich
we were able to arrange for Mum to attend the Training Centre
in Horsham (which is the nearest centre to Crawley). It
certainly didn't worry her at first — in fact she was so excited
to be living with us and enjoyed the new centre tremendously.

Nan died two weeks later — then Gramps died two months
after. Mum took both deaths badly and became very insecure.
She would have a tantrum if David and I were to go out in the
evening — which was rare — because she thought we weren't
coming back. We were fortunate to have good friends and
neighbours who 'mother-sat' for us and gradually that situation
improved.

Crawley has a lively society and we became involved in a
small way. We admit it was a temptation to become immersed
when we first took Mum along to the Gateway Club, but David
and I agreed our time alone together was rare and precious, so
we wanted to make the most of it. However, I did become a
member of the society's committee and David used to drive
one of the minibuses whenever the need arose and we joined
in the discos and various functions.

I must say that we contacted the Gateway Club for Mum
only through Michael Mackey (of Greenwich) who gave me the
local name and address of the club leader. We didn't have a
visit from any social worker after Mum came to live with us to
let us know what facilities were available. We had to find
everything for ourselves.

Probably having Mum prompted us to start our family
sooner than we might have done as we were already 'tied
down'. Mark is nearly two years old and Claire is two months
old. Mum loves them both and certainly Mark loves his nannie.
(Claire is a little young to know anyone but Mum and Dad!)

While I was pregnant with Mark I remember a good friend in
Crawley, who was the parent of a twenty-year-old
handicapped girl, showing surprise that we were still going to
keep Mum with us after the baby was born. She felt that the

problems would be enormous. I can now see what she meant.

We have had our fair share of problems with Mum and the children. Mark is at the age where he's into everything and Mum is very possessive about her belongings. I get so frustrated sometimes when she's acting like a spoilt child just because Mark is looking at one of her books. I find myself thinking, 'That's my mother behaving like that.' That is probably the hardest strain of all — I don't make enough allowances for her handicap because she is my mother. It was totally different when we lived with Nan and Gramps — I had all the patience and tolerance in the world with Mum. I used to have shocking arguments with my Nan because I criticized her lack of tolerance and understanding as I saw it. It's so different now, though — I suppose it's because I know I can't absolve myself of the responsibility or walk away when the going gets rough. Yet I feel quite cross with myself sometimes for being so unreasonable with her.

Some people obviously find our relationship hard to accept and understand. Mum is well aware that I am her daughter, despite the fact that she thinks I'm older than she is! We are often confused for sisters — I think people find that easier to cope with. I did have problems when we moved a year ago, though. David changed his job which necessitated our moving to Chalk, near Gravesend. Once again I had to make all plans myself for her move from one centre to another — I was most surprised that no one seemed bothered that Mum was moving.

I contacted the social services in Gravesend over the telephone to enquire about the local facilities. The various people I spoke to kept correcting me when I referred to my mother as being mentally-handicapped. They felt sure that I meant mentally ill because she had had a daughter. Indeed, the social worker who eventually visited us when we moved admitted to more than a slight degree of curiosity about our peculiar situation.

I have had a good deal of help from the social services here — perhaps they realize the pressures on us with two young children. However, the first five weeks we lived here I had Mum at home with me as they were unable to arrange transport to and from the centre — Mum is incapable of travelling by herself. Those few weeks certainly took their toll of me. I was beginning to despair of our entire situation — Mum became really moody because she loves going to 'school' (as she knows it) and it was my fault in her eyes that she wasn't going. Mark was only seven to eight months old then and occupied a lot of my time so she made extra work for me that I could have done without.

While I was enquiring about the centre when we first moved I was actually told by one social worker that these training centres were for 'young people'. Mum is fifty-three years old and anyone who knows her knows what a spritely thing she is! Yet is she always going to be like that? What will happen when the centre cannot or will not take her any more? I honestly can't see how I could cope with another period like those first five weeks. I don't think anyone has spared a thought for the mentally handicapped in their old age.

We have come to learn how vital having a break from Mum is. Before Mark was born we had a two week holiday abroad (our first ever!) alone and David's sister looked after Mum for us. It was heaven! More than anything it made us realize what a difference she had made to our marriage. We love her dearly but it seems as though she is constantly between us. We don't know what privacy is any more and I'm only thankful that our marriage is such a good one — we certainly have to test it sometimes!

Since then Mum has been on the holidays arranged by her clubs and centres. In fact, the year Mark was born she went to France with the club — we were green with envy! She has recently come back from a week at Butlin's (looking very healthy — where did she find the sun!) and although we enjoyed the break tremendously, had you seen the look on Mark's face when he saw Nannie waiting for us at the centre you would know why she is still a member of our family despite the problems. Mark makes us realize that she is not 'different' — she is just Nannie.

Our social worker has arranged for Mum to go into the hostel next to her centre in September and David intends to take that week as holiday. We are looking forward to that — we hope to indulge in a selfish week with our two lovely children to ourselves. I constantly remind myself what David has given up to have Mum live with us and it is a great deal. I owe it to him and the children to be a normal wife and mother, if only for a short while, instead of having divided loyalties.

Perhaps my biggest regret is my family — surprisingly Mum has two sisters and a brother. When my grandparents died the silence was deafening concerning Mum's future. There was never a discussion on the subject — I expect they all presumed (or should I say hoped) she would live with us. Yet there has never been any offer of help — not even for an occasional weekend break. My youngest aunt has multiple sclerosis and is in a home, so we try hard to keep in contact and visit her. My other aunt does at least remember Mum's birthday and we see her two or three times a year. Despite my uncle living in Eltham we have not heard from, nor seen him, since a great aunt's funeral over two years ago. Sadly, Mum was attached to him and mentions him often. However, we have some marvellous friends who have offered us continual help and support and for that we are grateful.

Mum has been with us for over four years now and as I have said before, Mum's health and vitality cannot last forever. We don't know what will happen in the future — I can't envisage what the problems of old age coupled with a mental handicap will be like. The centre probably will not be able to deal with the two categories, so what then? I only hope there will be a satisfactory solution for all of us.

I make no apologies for quoting Frances's article in full. There must be a great many of you who have never heard or read what it is like to have a severely mentally-subnormal mother. It is a very exceptional story told by, I think, a very exceptional girl. I am sure Frances has enjoyed her life, in spite of the awe-inspiring difficulties she has had to face (and has yet to face) but, speaking for myself, I couldn't let a child of mine bring a baby into the world to live that sort of existence — and this is where I think that some rights have to be denied. I would hasten to say that I am here expressing my personal opinion. I know my own limits, while other people may feel up to the task of coping with this sort of situation. But is it fair? It is possible, I suppose, that our family dwells rather in the world of severe subnormality — I am sure there are parents, out there somewhere, who feel that with the right training their mildly subnormal sons and daughters could become adequate parents, but for my James and for the sons and daughters of most of the parents I know, it is a dream which even they probably don't have.

Things have changed quite a lot since Patsy Tanner's days at the Park Vista Training Centre (Patsy being Frances's mum). With the acknowledgement that subnormality hospitals are no longer the right places for mentally-handicapped people to be, more emphasis has been placed on training for independence and I felt that I should be doing 'my bit'. The 'behaviourisms' the family put up with among themselves may be quite out of order when it comes to residing with friends or even strangers. For instance, James, up until very recently, had a deep aversion to any water other than that contained in a swimming bath or used in the manufacture of lager! I have mentioned this, on numerous occasions, to my nursing students, and each time someone has suggested that it was probably part of his adolescent period and that there were those among them at that very moment who had the same problem! This was usually pointed out to me by the girls and shamefacedly agreed to by the boys! How many other things can be explained away like this? Probably James's other two aversions — shaving and combing his hair (oh — I forgot — cleaning his teeth and wearing new clothes).

Kids all seem to be either one thing or the other, don't they? You either spend all your time telling them that, no, they don't need new trousers, that there is absolutely nothing wrong with those and you aren't having another pair just because Fred down the road (or on the bus) has got some — or you're arguing with them about how, in exactly ten minutes' time, if they don't put on another pair of trousers, they are going to be arrested for indecency!

James has a bit of a problem with his trousers, actually. Well, it's not his problem exactly. More mine. I mean, he scratches himself (I keep saying, 'don't James,' and hearing the late and great Joyce Grenfell!) and he wears the crutch of his trousers into holes. It really isn't a masturbation problem as such; I think it's probably a bit like me biting my nails — and frankly I'd rather have James's habit. At least you can rush out and buy new trousers for social occasions if needed!

We do have words about it, though, from time to time, as buying James trousers is as pleasurable as a wet bank-holiday. He, like many Down's people, is rather badly proportioned and in order to accommodate his backside (to put it politely!) it is necessary to buy trousers which are very large in the waist and very, very long in the leg. We have to cut miles off a 29-inch inside-leg length and James is about five feet two inches tall. Long in the body but short in the legs and arms.

Anyway, with a view to his ultimate departure from the bosom of his family (assuming that there will ever be anywhere for him to go) I decided, all by myself, that I ought to get James ready for the occasion and, in order to keep his potential flat-mates (or whatever) happy, I would start on his apparel. 'James,' I said to him one day (only a couple of months ago at the time of writing), 'for every morning that I find a pair of pants, a pair of socks and a tee-shirt on your bedroom floor for washing, I will give you a pound. We'll start by just doing it from Monday to Friday when you're at work. How much will that be by the end of the week?' 'Five pounds,' he replied, without a second's hesitation!

It grieves me to have to tell you that Peter, when he heard about this scheme, went mildly berserk; to be paid to change your clothes each day was really too much for my poor twelve-year-old! 'It's not fair,' he muttered, but unfortunately didn't say it quietly enough and Christopher pointed out to him, in rather more emphatic terms than I would have used myself, that James was handicapped and if Peter was still earning £5 a week by the time he was twenty-seven, then he could start saying, 'It's not fair,' — and a good deal more along the same lines. While I understood how Pete felt, and wasn't going to take issue on that particular occasion, it did make a change for somebody else to point out the facts of James's life.

The bribery — sorry, I mean incentive — has worked a treat. And he now has a nice MENCAP 'Dirty Stuff' bag to put the laundry in. Oddly enough, I find it more difficult to remember to empty the bag than to pick up the dirty clothes off the floor! Perhaps it's not so odd, really. Even I eventually notice things on the floor.

If anyone feels like trying the same thing, I must warn you about something. You do have to be a bit organized yourself. Perhaps you all are. Perhaps I'm wasting my time saying it, but in case there is anyone out there unfortunate enough to be as organized as I am (like, not very) this training can rebound on you. So, if you have got behind with the washing (it happens, you know — there are four different people using the washing machine in our house), you have to pay up with good grace. I have found that it has helped me to get into much more of a routine. At least with James! It's great, though, how pleased James is to be doing it successfully. I hand over the five pounds each Saturday (and it's *not* like pocket money — that's a very important point) and he buys his Dad a drink at The Porcupine on Sunday. He has been known to forget to take his money to the pub with him — much to Neville's amusement. See what I mean about not being daft!

Now we have got the clothes-changing bit going, I shall have to start on something else. I haven't quite decided what; probably changing his bed.

I had thought it would be a good idea to fill out a large sheet of paper with a programme of things to be done each day (starting off with just a few in order not to frighten him!) and leaving space to add things as we went along. I think bathing at a certain time on certain days will be next (combined with the bed changing). At the moment he baths on impulse, which is unsatisfactory both as far as the hot-water supply is concerned as well as access to the bathroom. Not that he's in there for long! There is no doubt that James is eminently trainable (I hope that doesn't make him sound too much like a performing animal — it isn't meant to). I think incentives are important. James has two; one is money (and I pay him on Saturdays, incidentally, in order to prevent the likelihood of him spending it all in McDonald's on Friday!) and the other is his own future independence.

He understands that we are preparing him to leave home and appears to be quite enthusiastic at the idea. I'm glad one of them is. Everyone tells me how much I'm going to miss my boys when they eventually leave home. I believe them — I'd like to be able to tell them that what they said was absolutely true. I'd like to be able to tell them quite soon, actually, but so far there is no sign of it happening. They are now twenty-seven (James), twenty-five (Chris), twenty-three (Mike), twenty-two (David) and twelve (Peter). I love them dearly but we have been around each other for too long — we all need some space. Still, it would be much worse if we didn't all get on reasonably well together.

They're quite funny, really. (Is my laughter becoming a touch hysterical, I ask myself!). We do get a bit of respite during the summer when David pops off to do the summer season in the kitchen at a holiday camp in Suffolk. It gives me a few months to build up my strength to face the winter with him at home. I wonder if holiday camps in the tropics are open all year round? What a beautiful thought.

The boys are always saying, 'We'd be out of this place like a shot if we could afford it,' which is mildly hurtful (and I daresay other loving parents are listening to the same thing all over the country), but I console myself with the thought that if things were that bad, they'd go anyway. (Yes, I know that that is saying I want them to go but I don't want them to go — it's just that I want the circumstances to be right.) My friends tell me that I feed them too well. I have to confess that I do consider myself to be quite a good cook and the smug grin was completely wiped off my face quite recently by Chris who, as he finished the very nice dinner which David had made that evening (David really is a talented cook) looked up at me and said, 'Why don't you get David to show you how to make a decent casserole sometime?' I pointed out to him, very, very gently (it was a considerable effort) that it possibly hadn't occurred to him, but twenty-eight years of cooking for unappreciative people did, in time, tend to remove the novelty. I think I said 'people' — it might have been something else. My memory!

James has a horrendous appetite. He refuses nothing — well, he sometimes refuses things on the grounds that he is on a diet, but it is usually quite illogical. For instance, he may come home from work with a *Mars Bar* he has bought (to the accompaniment of much grumbling from me) and will refuse a digestive biscuit with his cup of coffee on the 'diet' grounds. Perhaps he just doesn't like digestive biscuits, or didn't at that particular moment — which is much more likely. I think the teens and twenties of a mentally-handicapped youngster need to be approached, if not quite with the same feeling of a time bomb going off in your face as you get with your normal children, at least with a degree of foresight and tolerance. There is a lot written about the problems of adolescence these days (seems to concern mostly sex and relationships — don't they know about the other things — the moods, the grubbiness, etc.?), but you can have a pretty shrewd idea that, however bizarre the personal problems you may have to face with your mentally-handicapped child, you will never have to go and turn him out of your garage where he is puffing pot with his friends! Also, he is unlikely to feature in television newsreels throwing seats across a football ground. I make this point every time I show our film to schoolchildren and nursing students (I stress it with the schoolchildren) and it gives me a considerable amount of perverse pleasure to point out to them how their so-called normal contemporaries behave. I like to think it gives them food for thought — as indeed it might to anyone.

10

A MEMBER OF THE COMMUNITY

While the thought of our handicapped children moving into middle age and having a very hazy future may give parents sleepless nights, their adolescent period — in which we assume they are still learning (and on after that, of course) — can be very long-drawn-out and gives plenty of time to 'work on them' to prepare them for some sort of independence. Whatever sort of accommodation they are ultimately living in, it is agreeable for parents to know that they are able to share in the life of the establishment and this means lending a hand with the chores as well as enjoying the leisure activities.

I think the task of training a handicapped young person has to be approached with the same amount of patience (if you can find it!) that you have to use when toddlers ask to help you. It is so much quicker to wash and wipe the cutlery (for instance) yourself and put it away than to have them hanging around your skirts (or trousers), in danger of being trodden on. Many kitchens these days have tables where the family eats; you could sit your child down at the table, give him or her whatever has been washed up and needs drying and, apart from keeping a weather eye on them, let them get on with it. I could fill a book with examples of this nature, but I am sure that I would be insulting the intelligence of my readers if I attempted to enlarge upon the subject . I think the thing to do is to try and draw them into helping when you aren't in a hurry — if you ever aren't in a hurry! Most handicapped children are clumsy but careful and given enough time and confidence can perform simple tasks as well as any one. Or nearly. James has always been my most willing helper and if he lays the knives and forks on the wrong side at table, we just quietly change them over. It's no big deal — he's hardly likely to be in a position of doing it where it really matters. As G.K. Chesterton is reputed to have said, 'If a thing is worth doing it's worth doing badly,' — a sentiment with which I heartily concur. If we all strived to be perfect in the things we enjoy doing we should lead very miserable lives indeed.

I do think one of the most important things to concentrate on with a mentally-handicapped child is good eating habits — I don't mean *what* they eat (as far as Down's Syndrome people are concerned, that doesn't seem to be any great problem!) but *how* they eat. We have always tried to get James to eat in a civilized manner — for our benefit (and the world at large) as much as for his. We like eating out and it has been important to us that James should be included in as many family functions as possible, so we have worked on him. His manners in general are very good indeed and his table manners I think are excellent. The only thing which forces me to make horrible faces at him across the table is a bone. He cannot resist picking up bones and nibbling them — but then neither can a lot of ordinary people. There are certain advantages, we have discovered, to taking James to restaurants. We are remembered. The first time we went to Limpets Restaurant in Lymington, Hampshire (I highly recommend it — lovely, lovely food), we were treated as just an ordinary family. The second time we went we were greeted by Lynn Grey, the proprietor, like old friends because she remembered James! The rest of us, you realize, are just ordinary boring people! We now go there each time we camp nearby in Brockenhurst and the warm welcome makes us feel very comfortable indeed. So table manners you are not ashamed of are important. Let me say, straightaway, that I am talking about children with uncomplicated handicaps. I know there are handicapped people with difficulties which make eating an ordeal and my remarks are only intended for those parents who know that their child could eat 'nicely' (awful word!) with a bit — or a lot — of encouragement. If your family is anything like mine, you may find that you have a number of people you can work on at the same time!

Something else which I think important is communication. James is an incredibly sloppy speaker and I think I nag him more over clear speech than anything else. I nag the others as well but I do tend to get a bit desperate over James for obvious reasons. I had an interview a couple of years ago with a speech therapist in Greenwich (James has never had speech therapy) who stated quite categorically that James wasn't in need of therapy but agreed with me that what he really needed was elocution lessons! I'm sure that this is right. He lives in London where he picks up all the slovenly ways of speech and this, added to his fairly mild Down's problem, makes him very often unintelligible. Where have all the elocution teachers gone? Come back — all is forgiven! Clear speech is important and those teachers (yes, *teachers*) I have spoken to who can't see that it matters (I assume that because of the way they speak themselves) might not be so quick to take that attitude if they had a child with a severe speech defect. I shall never forget the day that one of the older boys' friends called at the front door; when I opened it and greeted him he said something to me and I didn't understand a word he said. And he isn't handicapped! Of course it's important. Youngsters these days seem to think that there is something either snobby or 'pooffey' about speaking properly and I'm not talking about accents (which we can't help and which shouldn't be eradicated anyway) but the actual pronunciation of words. You'd sometimes think that t's and h's had never been invented. So if your child has a speech problem that no one seems to think needs anything done about it and you do, go and make a noise at someone — starting, I suggest, with the school.

While on the subject of communication, I must touch on a subject of concern to those parents whose children are able to have quite a high degree of freedom — like James, who comes and goes to his appointed places without transport having to be specially provided for him. He may, at some time, come into contact with the police. He may be lost; if he was living away from home he could be burgled or he may, which God forbid, break the law. You cannot ignore the fact that shops these days positively implore the the morally and/or intellectually weak to steal from them, the way their goods are displayed and MENCAP have put out a helpful leaflet about the mentally handicapped and the police which makes the following points:

(a) Contrary to popular belief, mentally-handicapped people are no more predisposed towards crime than anybody else. When they do run up against the law it is likely to be a crime of a minor nature, often resulting from ignorance or lack of understanding of what is considered to be 'normal' behaviour.

(b) Because mentally-handicapped people have problems of communication and because they are slow learners, they are a particularly vulnerable group when coming into contact with the police. The dangers facing mentally-handicapped people will arise from an inability to understand the full implications of what is happening around them, the nature of the caution which is given and the rights to which they are entitled. By being easily open to suggestion, they can easily be led astray or be persuaded to accept responsibility for something which they haven't done.

(c) The police, on the other hand, receive no formal training in mental handicap. They may, therefore, not fully appreciate the problems faced by mentally-handicapped people. They may accept at face value an admission of guilt obtained under the stress of being in a seemingly hostile environment, or as a result of a simple desire to please and be able to 'escape'.

(d) Difficulties will arise when a mentally-handicapped person fails to understand the police and the police, in turn, fail to recognize mental handicap and its implications.

   This is not to say that all policemen know nothing about the problems of mentally-handicapped people. Some might be aware of a local Gateway Club (leisure organization for the mentally handicapped supported by MENCAP) or of a group home on a council estate. So if they do question someone who is mentally handicapped they will be careful in accepting the reliability of answers.

The 'reliability of answers' is a phrase which means a great deal to me. If the KGB ever had to interrogate James they'd end up shooting *themselves*! Let me relate to you the story of 'James and the missing table-tennis bat'.

Well, as the title indicates, the bat went missing. James first of all thought that he'd left it in somebody's car but a telephone call proved that that was not so. Then he suggested, on enquiry where else it might be, that it could be at Eltham Hill School where he had had an unscheduled table-tennis class. Nothing doing — he went and asked the caretakers (his pals, of course, who talk to him while he's waiting for me on Thursdays). So, where now? Haimo Road? Further phone calls, to no avail. Then we discover that his front-door key has also gone missing. He's obviously going through an unusually careless patch, we think, but we also suspect that the key is buried somewhere in his bedroom. After several days of James hanging about outside waiting for me to come home or (as on one occasion) asking himself into Jean's house for a drink while he waited (the cheek of it!), Neville decided the time had come for some strong action. 'I'll take you to Club when you've been upstairs and found your key,' he said. James went up with much muttering and mumbling, to come down almost immediately to announce that the missing front-door key was zipped inside the table-tennis bat cover. I'm sure I don't need to tell you that the table-tennis bat cover had James's name and address written very plainly inside! As far as I was concerned that was the signal for instant panic! We had only recently (well, the previous year) changed our front and back doors for horrendously expensive double-glazed varieties with several locking points and the thought of having to change the locks on the front door was giving me palpitations! I hate to think what it was doing to Neville. So into action I went. I phoned all the local education offices which James had ever been likely to set foot in; none of them had seen the bat but sympathized with my dilemma. I promised St Anthony a pound. After the various people I hadn't been able to speak to at the time had phoned me back with no news of the missing bat and key, I upped the ante to St Anthony to a fiver. The next day, while checking what keys actually were around, I found James's missing key in a canvas bag in the caravan which we keep on our front path! The bat will gladly be replaced! The money you promise St Anthony for finding things should go to the poor. I shall send a cheque to CAFOD. He was quite right to wait until I offered £5. It would have cost much more than that to change the locks on the front door!

The MENCAP 'Police' Leaflet does suggest various ways in which good relations can be fostered. Gateway Clubs can help by:

1   Inviting local police officers to visit Gateway Clubs so that they can learn to recognize the characteristics of mental handicap and understand the resulting problems. Mentally-handicapped people have difficulty in explaining their needs and understanding signs and social conventions.
2   Ensuring that members carry their Gateway membership cards. This card is recognized by the police as entitling the bearer to special understanding.
3   Ensuring that the Force Order Book, which is to be found in every police station, includes a procedure for dealing with mentally-handicapped people and, in particular, contains the address and meeting times of the nearest Gateway Club and a description of the membership card.
4   Providing a programme of social training for those members who are most at risk so that they can cope with or avoid situations which make them appear to be acting suspiciously, or actually bring them into conflict with the law.

Parents could ensure that their mentally-handicapped children carry on them at all times:

(a)   The name and address of their adult training centre or special school — this will indicate to a policeman that he is dealing with someone who is handicapped, and
(b)   the name, address and telephone number of their parents or guardian.

The police can help by following the procedures laid down for dealing with mentally-handicapped people:

1   If a police officer thinks someone has a mental handicap he should take special care in putting questions and

accepting the reliability of answers. Furthermore, where practicable, a mentally-handicapped adult (whether suspected of a crime or not) should be interviewed only in the presence of a parent or other person in whose care, custody or control he is; for example, a social worker. Any statement arising from the interview should also be signed by the third party. This is a procedure laid down by a Home Office Circular in 1976 and issued to all police forces.

2   The procedure for dealing with mentally-handicapped young persons under the age of seventeen is the same as for any young person under that age. Whether suspected of a crime or not, he/she should only be interviewed in the presence of a parent or guardian, or, in their absence, some person who is not a police officer and is of the same sex as the child. A child or young person should neither be arrested nor interviewed at school if such action can possibly be avoided. Where it is essential to conduct an interview at school, this should be done only with the consent of, and in the presence of, the headteacher or his/her nominee.

(The above procedures are not, unfortunately, legally enforceable. They are guidelines to the policy issued by the Home Office and attached to the 'Judges' Rules'.)

Now, let us not ignore the rest of the family. I give below some of the rights which the ordinary citizen has in cases where they come up against the police:

1   If you are questioned by the police you have the right to remain silent. In some cases (for example, if you are driving a car or are suspected of carrying an offensive weapon) you must give the police your name and address.

2   The police should not compel you to sign any statement, hold out any promises (e.g. bail), or make any threats in order to get a statement. Nor should they force you to have your fingerprints taken without first obtaining a court order.

3   If you go voluntarily to the police station and are not charged, you are free to leave when you want to.

4 Beware of any inducement or threat. Pleading guilty in return for an offer of bail can harm your case.

5 Do not plead guilty until you have talked to a lawyer. In general, don't make any statement until you have taken legal advice.

6 If you are arrested, go quietly and remain polite and reasonable. If you have been wrongly arrested or deprived of your rights you may be able to sue for false imprisonment or make a complaint against the police at a later stage.

7 Anyone can apply for legal aid. It is free if you are receiving supplementary benefit or family income supplement. Application forms are available from any magistrates' court office. If you have trouble filling in the form, ask a probation officer or a solicitor to help.

This is by no means a full list of your rights. Further details are available from the National Council for Civil Liberties, 186 Kings Cross Road, London WC1X 9DE (Tel: 01-278 4575).

That last part of the leaflet I've thrown in for good measure. I really don't believe that all my readers are incipient villains! We have had our brushes with the law in our family — mostly motoring offences — and with five boys it would be surprising (or surprisingly lucky) if we hadn't, so forewarned is forearmed. David, on one occasion at home, was quite casual about the fact that the pocket of his jeans had been ripped by a police officer — I was absolutely horrified, mostly, I think, by David's 'it happens all the time — so what?' attitude. I think many parents of youngsters have had their share of disillusion with the upholders of law and order. I know we have.

Leaving aside all the problems of having a mentally-handicapped child at home, for the parents of all these children the future looms large and somewhat darkly. There is nothing cut and dried about the provision for them and we have to take what we can when we can. We all hope that things will change before it gets to our turn, but the atmosphere among parents definitely is not one of hope. We would all like to know that our respective boroughs are aware of our child's existence and are busy making provision for each individual, but unfortunately this is not so. When I contacted our local social services department, the social worker who came to see me nodded and smiled at my request that provision should be made for James in the not-too-distant future but offered me nothing definite. I was very emphatic in my request for a placement for James with a considerable amount of supervision. Care in the community is a concept with which we cannot disagree but community care on the cheap is worse than being in a large hospital and even those indispensable people who have worked and are working in subnormality hospitals I'm sure will agree with that. They probably know, also, that for some of their charges there is no realistic alternative to hospital care. Wherever the mentally handicapped are living, the operative word is *care* — and it should not be skimped.

It seems to me that people forget that we are dealing with a section of the community which was, not so many years ago, deemed 'ineducable'. Well, we have given the lie to that, but I am anxious that the 'providers' don't go over the top in what they are expecting our children to be able to do for themselves. Real life isn't like a training programme. It is not so neat and orderly and things crop up that you haven't expected. (And how!) It must be the same for mentally-handicapped people who are living in group homes or flats. They may be burgled. Flat-mates may become very ill very suddenly. The frying pan may catch fire, the washing machine may break down. There may be a power cut. Are all these eventualities catered for in training programmes? I have named a few of the perfectly normal things which occur to jolt all of us out of our complacency. There are many more and I think I would be cruel to James if I assumed that he would ever be able to cope with life and its crises on a completely independent basis. He is going to need a considerable amount of supervision. I would like to see more of the type of housing complex which you see around for the elderly. A little group of about six flatlets with one of them occupied by a warden. Many parents I have spoken to find this an attractive proposition.

When I asked Doff and John what sort of future they envisaged for Gavin they talked in terms of him being away from the borough of Greenwich and perhaps living under the auspices of the Home Farm Trust (of which more later).

Most of the parents I talked to liked to think of their handicapped children remaining in Greenwich, probably because they didn't see themselves leaving the borough. Ron, Ian and Jenny's father, wanted much the same accommodation for Ian as I want for James and guessed that Jenny could continue in residential care as she is now. He was very satisfied that Jenny was being well looked after in Goldie Leigh, but was much more uncertain about Ian's future.

Joan and Jim, Penny and Cathy's parents, have a slightly different problem. They want to get the girls settled in a hostel or residential home of some sort in order to avoid Alison, their youngest daughter, taking the burden of looking after Penny and Cathy upon herself. She has expressed a willingness to do this and Joan and Jim would much rather have the girls settled now than come up against a problem later on. All is not well with accommodation for the mentally-handicapped people of Greenwich. We have one handicapped married couple who live a very seedy life indeed in a flat with very little supervision. The society welfare worker called upon them and was absolutely horrified at the state of the place — 'flies everywhere', she said. It appears that the couple had been allotted a home help who hadn't been for ages for reasons of illness (or whatever), no one had been sent in her place and the couple themselves hadn't notified anyone that they needed 'cleaning up'. In fact they probably hadn't noticed that they needed cleaning up. It's all very well for people to say that if they want to live like that they should be allowed to, but do they understand the health hazard? I very much doubt it. I get very concerned about the fact that James could find himself in this 'left to get on with it' situation. It seems to me to be a contradiction for him to go to the training centre every day to work in conditions specially formulated for someone with his mentality, and then expect him to carry on his life in a 'normal' way when he's not there.

Accommodation for our mentally-handicapped adults is only one aspect of their life. Parents also have to think about the services which are going to be available once our handicapped adults have retired from the training centres. What are they going to do with themselves all day? Will there be classes for them to go to? Will there be Pop-In Parlours where they can socialize during the day? What do retired people do and will our handicapped adults be able to do the same?

As usual, MENCAP have researched this problem and have come up with yet another excellent Stamina Paper: Stamina Paper No. 61-1 *Elderly People with Mental Handicap — as age increases:*

Introduction

It is essential to recognize that people who are mentally handicapped are PEOPLE FIRST and have individual needs and some may have special needs.

The increasing need for services for ageing mentally-handicapped people has not yet been generally or adequately recognized. This especially applies to those who missed out on educational or training opportunities. Unless action is taken with some urgency, we can expect a large gap in the near future between the demand for services and those available. Many younger people are achieving a degree of independence and competence in living not expected from the previous generations of people with mental handicap. These mentally and physically more active people will need, as they grow older, new kinds of service; and several alternatives for accommodation and care will need to be developed.

It must be remembered that there are mentally-handicapped people who are unknown to statutory services or other agencies. Since it is the duty of Local Authorities under the Chronically Sick and Disabled Persons Act 1970 to compile a register of all who are in need and to search out those who are unknown to them, it will be necessary to solicit the help of family doctors through the Family Practitioners Committee and other professionals who may be in contact with them, e.g. health visitors, social workers, district or community nurses.

The change in age structure of the general population is already recognized as a major challenge. What needs to be recognized is that ageing mentally-handicapped people have the same rights to a satisfactory quality of life as the rest of the ageing population.

Preparing for retirement

Local societies should conduct a survey of mentally-handicapped people to assess future service needs in order to prepare a policy statement. This policy should be prepared and agreed by the statutory and voluntary agencies.

It is important to ensure that mentally-handicapped individuals are helped to express their own feeling and wishes about future retirement.

It is essential to ensure that any proposal to change services or residential placement for a mentally-handicapped person provides an *improved quality of life*.

Check:

1 That there is a recognized policy to help elderly people who are mentally handicapped to prepare for retirement.

2 That elderly people who are mentally handicapped have access to and are given support to take advantage of the normal statutory and voluntary services available to other people.

3 That the Community Mental Handicap Team (CMHT) is reviewing the special needs of elderly people who are mentally handicapped.

4 That services are developed by the relevant authorities to meet their individual needs, e.g. day occupation; leisure; transport; therapeutic and health needs; holidays, etc.

5 That there is an annual review and discussion with mentally-handicapped people to assess their future requirements.

6 That there is a named person appointed by and responsible to the CMHT to ensure that each person's needs are appropriately met.

7 That the named person gives particular attention to:

(a) quality of life;

(b) health and happiness, living conditions and needs;

(c) activities and interests, e.g. leisure, holidays;

(d) claiming of statutory benefits;

(e) counselling in the event of bereavement.

Supporting elderly mentally-handicapped people at home with relatives or on their own

People who are mentally handicapped should not be segregated from the rest of the community. General resources available to the rest of the community should be used as far as possible.

Check:

1 That they are receiving the state benefits to which they may be entitled, e.g. Retirement Pension, Supplementary Benefit (heating, laundry, etc.), Severe Disablement Allowance, Mobility Allowance, Attendance Allowance, Rate Relief, Housing Benefit.

2 That they are receiving the appropriate Health Service support and aids, e.g. ophthalmology, chiropody, orthopaedics, dentistry, etc.

3 That the 'named person' ensures that someone is appointed to escort them to attend hospital, clinic, or doctor's appointments, Social Security, Social Services visits, etc.

4 That the Health or Personal Social Services visit with sufficient frequency to ensure that they are at all times aware of the situation, i.e. social worker or health visitor.

5 That the 'named person' ensures that the Social Services department assesses the needs of the individual and that these needs are met (Chronically Sick and Disabled Persons Act 1970).

6 That people who are mentally handicapped are encouraged to participate in the day provision of services for elderly people, i.e. recreational activities, outings and holidays.

The needs of relatives caring for elderly mentally-handicapped people

Check:

1 That the relatives are given support and practical help to care for elderly mentally-handicapped people living with them.

2 That advice and information is given to the relatives to enable them to take full advantage of the cash benefits, practical help and services available.

3 That advice and information is given to parents about

leaving money and/or property for the benefit of their son or daughter, e.g. drawing up a Will; forming a Trust. Further help is available from MENCAP's Welfare, Legal and Counselling Services.

4 That the 'named person' ensures that relatives receive the appropriate services, aids, appliances and benefits to which they are entitled.

5 That professional support is given to help in any management problems which may arise.

6 That the relatives are offered regular respite from the care of their elderly mentally-handicapped dependant.

Elderly mentally-handicapped people in residential care

Most of the special needs of elderly mentally-handicapped people in residential care are included in the Stamina Paper No. 3 (quoted earlier in this book) and the Stamina Paper No. 4 which deals with hospitals for mentally-handicapped people and which I haven't included as I didn't think it appropriate. The Paper is readily available from the MENCAP Bookshop at Golden Lane, London EC1. However, it is important to recognize additional problems and needs which may arise. For example, those responsible for the placement of an elderly mentally-handicapped person who has lived at home with relatives or other family members should realize that he or she may find it extremely difficult to adjust to strange surroundings and people they do not know. The change of environment or new situations may prove extremely traumatic, especially if it is associated with bereavement and the loss of familiar faces, together with the change into a completely different kind of environment.

The Community Mental Handicap Team should have a register of all mentally-handicapped people and they have the essential role to ensure that all the information from the various agencies is brought together and available when a mentally-handicapped person has to be moved into a new situation. The personal details and records which will help the new carers to understand and be better informed about a new resident will overcome many of the unnecessary problems which often arise.

It is vitally important to be sensitive to their individual

feelings and wishes; accepting that they have likes and dislikes and other emotional reactions the same as other people. They should have some say in the decisions which have to be made and a choice in the kind of accommodation to be provided for them. If an elderly mentally-handicapped person has no living relatives or close friends to support them, an advocate from the local MENCAP society should be sought to speak on their behalf. Their wishes should be sympathetically ascertained and everything possible done to ensure they are respected. In addition to the guidance given in Stamina Papers Nos. 3 and 4, the following should be particularly checked:

Check:

1 That the elderly mentally-handicapped person has the help, support and counselling to enable them to understand their situation, e.g. illness of parent or relative, death of caring relative, etc.

2 That they do not have to face a dramatic change of life style.

3 That they have personal possessions with them, e.g. photographs; small items of furniture like 'their chair' or 'reading lamp'; records, games, etc.

4 That they have personal choice in their lifestyle and are able to continue their familiar pattern of routine, e.g. cups of tea; going for a walk or going to clubs, etc.

5 That the 'named person' ensures all the options are fully investigated and discussed with the elderly mentally-handicapped person.

6 That the MENCAP local society is informed.

Responsibilities of the local MENCAP society

An increasing number of MENCAP local societies are recognizing their responsibilities towards mentally-handicapped people. It is hoped this trend will continue and be developed throughout the country. MENCAP's role is to work in partnership with the statutory authorities to achieve the best services and quality of life for all mentally-handicapped people. Undoubtedly as we grow older, greater support, help and guidance is needed. Often it is found in the informal and natural process of friendship; someone visiting regularly, showing they care and you are not forgotten. Also, the security that is found by the fact that it is someone from outside the statutorily provided services, someone who is a special friend, can make all the difference.

Another and important part of the caring and befriending role of the local society is to provide an independent and vital 'monitoring' of the services. If changes are necessary, representation and co-operation with the authorities to improve the situation will best be achieved from the practical experience and information gained from the befriending service.

When the parents of a mentally-handicapped person die, the local society may be the best source of immediate help and support. Every effort should be made to inform elderly parents and the professionals who are responsible for the various services that the local MENCAP society is willing to provide a support role and if necessary provide an emergency care service until more permanent arrangements can be made.

Many parents are not aware of the national services available to help them provide for the future and local societies should do everything possible to communicate details about them regularly. Particular emphasis should be placed upon the MENCAP Trustee Visitors Service and the services of the Welfare, Legal and Counselling Group of MENCAP which offers help and advice on the preparation of Wills and Trusts.

In some cases the elderly mentally-handicapped person may not be receiving services or benefits to which he or she is entitled. The local MENCAP society can play an important role in this area by befriending, regularly visiting and acting as a personal advocate for them.

Local MENCAP societies should examine how best they can help mentally-handicapped people who are bereaved and how best they can support them in the weeks and months which follow the loss of relatives and to adjust to their new situation.

Check:
1 That the local society has a service of support and friendship to offer mentally-handicapped people who are orphaned.

2 That parents and professionals know about the support service which is available and who to contact.

3 That parents and relatives are informed about the national services available from the Royal Society, e.g. MENCAP Trustee Visitors Service and legal advice on Wills and Trusts.

4 That the local statutory authorities have a recognized and known procedure to deal with the emergency situations when parents die.

5 That there are regular reviews of the needs of the elderly mentally-handicapped people in residential care.

6 That an annual report, providing important details about each elderly mentally-handicapped person, is compiled by the local MENCAP society in co-operation with the statutory authorities.

7 That they are receiving the benefits and services to which they are entitled.

8 That the local society ensures they are not forgotten — especially birthdays and Christmas.

'We hope that more and more elderly people who are mentally handicapped will have recourse to normal provisions and services.' (The Jay Report, 1979, p.52)

References

1971 *Better Services for the Mentally Handicapped* (HMSO Comnd. 4683)

1979 *Committee of Enquiry into Mental Handicap Nursing and Care* (The Jay Report) (HMSO Comnd. 7568-1)

1980 *Mental Handicap: Progress, Problems and Priorities* (DHSS)

1981 *Care in Action* (HMSO)

1982 *Care in Community* (DHSS Consultation Paper)

1982 *Elements of a Comprehensive Local Service for People with Mental Handicap* (Independent Development Council) (IDC)

1982 *The Age Concern Handbook*

1982 *People First — Developing Services in the Community for People with Mental Handicap* (King's Fund Centre)

1984 *Next Steps* (IDC)

Of all the papers which I have quoted in this book this last one should bring home to us as parents the importance of affiliating ourselves to an organization which is loud in its demands for better services for the mentally handicapped. I said that this book was not intended as a recruitment drive for MENCAP, but I think it will be seen that there is a great deal of thought and care going into the work of this particular organization — which, of course, one might expect from the oldest established organization. It is the latter part of our children's lives which will be entirely in other people's hands in many cases, and Stamina Paper No. 6 will give many people a great deal to think about. In the main, these papers have been written by the real experts — parents. Experts on their own children, that is. When James was young and we had our awful days, I used to say that the only advice I would accept would be from somebody who had four small children under five, the eldest of whom was a Down's! I have modified my opinions a trifle as I've got older, but I suppose what I was trying to say was that you had to have a mentally-handicapped child to know what it was really like looking after one. Even people who foster or adopt don't know what goes on inside your mind. Second-hand trauma just isn't the same!

11

SOURCES OF HELP

With the increase of care in the community and everyone secretly suspecting that we will be left to get on with it with as little help from the social services as they can decently give, where should we parents be looking? Let me tell you in list form:

The social services
Yes, I know I've just been rude about them but are we going to let them get away with it? We are entitled to their care and help and if we make enough noise we'll get it — if only to make us go away. It is one of the grimmer facts of life that if you want something, you may have to make a nuisance of yourself to get it.

The district health authority
Clinics for children under sixteen come under this department. Your health visitor is your early contact; if she's good hang on to her. If she isn't you may find one of your local voluntary organizations can point you in the right direction for your particular need.

The Department of Education and Science
Your child's school can be a source of information if not actual help. There will probably be a social worker attached to the school and there should also be speech therapists and physiotherapists.

If you require any information on benefits, etc. the best contact should be the social worker from the social services department. Should your personal contact fail you, phone the Director of Social Services and complain that your social worker doesn't know his or her stuff! After all, it's part of their job to know. The subject is far too complex for the likes of me and maybe even you. If you do have a complaint I would always recommend going straight to the top — don't mess with the minions!

The next organization on the list of help agencies is not exactly government and not exactly voluntary:

The Family Fund

This came into being in 1973 following upon the thalidomide tragedy. It brought handicap before the gaze of the general public in a way which had never been known before and it became necessary to find some way of administering the money which had been allotted to these children. Sir Keith Joseph (then Secretary of State for Social Services) became very concerned about the fact that there were many other families with equally handicapped children who had no access to any funds for even essentials — let alone the highly desirable goods which compensation made possible. As a result Sir Keith and Anthony Barber, then Chancellor of the Exchequer, set aside £3m, not for compensation but to fill the gaps between each individual family's needs and the resources available through the more usual agencies. The Joseph Rowntree Memorial Trust was asked to administer this fund and it has done so ever since. What started as a three-year project has extended into a permanent fund which is reviewed half-yearly.

The fund is available to help severely handicapped children (or their families) under the age of sixteen and it must be borne in mind that the social and economic circumstances of the family must justify help from the fund and that their needs can be met within its terms of reference.

The type of things that the Family Fund will help with are washing machines, tumble dryers, holidays, outings, transport expenses, driving lessons, telephones, clothing, bedding, recreational items, fridge/freezers and a variety of other things which help to solve the special problems faced by a family with a severely-handicapped child.

The Family Fund pamphlet includes an application form which may be completed by a parent (or someone on behalf of the parent and with their consent) and if the application is quite straightforward they will arrange for one of their visiting social workers to call on the family. Provided there are no hitches (sometimes parents give inadequate information and further enquiries have to be made) a grant should be made within a month or six weeks of writing to them. The booklet *The Family Fund and How It Helps* is well worth the price of the stamp needed to write and request it — there are some interesting hints and tips in it.

The Family Fund also offers advice on how to cope with an overactive or hyperactive child and I am sure that this could be of interest to many parents.

If your child is over sixteen then you would be well advised to send for their booklet *After 16 — What Next?* It is full of helpful information.

Of the voluntary organizations — and there are many — I will give you the basic information on the main ones, starting with:

The Royal Society for Mentally-Handicapped Children and Adults (MENCAP)

Who hasn't heard of MENCAP? The Leader in the field of parent societies for the mentally handicapped, it has been around now since 1946 when it started life as the Association of Parents of Backward Children. It became the National Society for Mentally-Handicapped Children in 1955 and in 1981 it became 'Royal'. A constantly expanding range of services is provided through twelve regional offices and 500 local societies, so there is a very good chance of there being a local society near you, wherever you live. There are, incidentally, 55,000 members of MENCAP, most of them being parents and friends of mentally-handicapped people. The primary object of the society is to create a sympathetic climate of public opinion towards mentally-handicapped people, to increase public awareness and understanding of their problems and to secure the provisions that they need. This last objective, I'm sure you will agree, is emphasized in no small way by the Stamina Papers quoted in previous chapters. So, what do they do with the funds? First of all, there are two residential homes, one in Horndean, Hants, and one in Winterton, Norfolk, each housing 24 severely handicapped school-age children. There are two houses in Folkestone which provide family-type accommodation and four training establishments in various parts of the country.

The Homes Foundation is being created with the aim of providing residential accommodation for mentally-handicapped adults and to relieve the anxiety of parents on the future of mentally-handicapped members of their families when they themselves become too old to care for them. This is a very sensitive area which comes to all parents and carers (they may be brothers and sisters or other relatives) as they see old age looming up before them. These homes may be acquired in a variety of ways: through local authority or housing association allocations; joint funding projects or by gifts and bequests.

The Pathway Employment Service provides a job placement service to meet the needs of mentally-handicapped people. An increasing number of local authorities now recognize this MENCAP service which has the official support and backing of the Manpower Services Commission, the Confederation of British Industry and the Trades Union Council. Pathway employment officers have already found work for many mentally-handicapped people and provide an advisory service to parents and professionals on the assessment and training of mentally-handicapped people of all ages. Considering how little access mentally-handicapped youngsters seem to have to careers personnel generally, this seems to me to be a very important service.

To me, as an ageing parent (not yet an 'Aged Parent'!), one of the most valuable services provided by this organization is the *Trustee Visitors Service*. It provides a visitor for mentally-handicapped people after their parents have died. Each beneficiary is befriended by a visitor who calls at the home, hostel or hospital in which he or she is living. Entry into the scheme is by legacy, by life insurance, or by direct payment of £2,500 (at the time of writing). Real friendships develop between visitors and beneficiaries, and great care is taken in choosing the right people to do this work. There are at present over 2,000 parents who have enrolled their children in the service and 160 mentally-handicapped people are receiving regular visitors. Birthdays and Christmas are remembered and beneficiaries are often taken out on visits to places of interest and to visitors' homes. This can be very reassuring to parents whose handicapped child is either an only child or is isolated from the rest of his or her relatives for whatever reason.

In addition to the previous services, MENCAP also have the following busy departments:

Advisory services. This covers Welfare and Rights, Counselling, the Rural Advisory Service and the Residential Advisory Service. One of the most important functions of the MENCAP advisory service is that of advising parents how they may leave financial provision for their mentally-handicapped child. There is a MENCAP information sheet entitled *Leaving Money to Benefit your Mentally-Handicapped Child* which briefly states some of the ways in which provision can be made. This is a very fraught and complex subject and I strongly recommend this leaflet to parents.

Education. The Education and Training Department provides day-release courses and seminars and will advise parents and professionals on special education provision and problems.

Communications. This department co-ordinates all the information, publications, press and public-relations functions of the society. It prepares policy statements for the media when important issues affecting mentally-handicapped people and their families are before the public and is also responsible for creating good public relations with all sections of society — and that is something with which we can all help. It is this department's job to keep all the society members and affiliated groups informed of matters which are relevant and which affect them. This is done through the MENCAP newsletter and the quarterly magazine *Parents' Voice* which, some years ago, sported a lovely picture of my James on its cover! A proud moment indeed.

Holidays. This has been dealt with comprehensively in the text and I won't repeat it all again.

The Bookshop at Golden Lane (headquarters) carries a large stock of informative and varied reading. You will find publications from other organizations on various aspects of mental handicap as well as their own publications. There are also many inexpensive (bearing in mind how pricey books of any sort can be) pamphlets and leaflets about almost every problem you may come across in the rearing of your mentally-handicapped child. There is also, on sale, a super range of gifts and goods made by mentally-handicapped people and, of course, the Christmas card range at the appropriate season. The phrase 'Christmas cards' tends to be like a knell sounding for many families all round the country. Come September, people start muttering to themselves, looking round the house seeing what can possibly be moved, shoved in the loft, thrown away or, 'Don't you think it's time you left home, dear?' (to the kids, I would hasten to add!). The time has come to accommodate large quantities of cardboard boxes. Ours go into the dining room and from September to December I have to be pretty choosy who we entertain! Close friends, like Doff and John, are OK, because they have the same problem, but the Royals have to wait until after Christmas! Seriously, Christmas cards are a very good way of introducing yourself and your handicapped child to the neighbours. Put a few catalogues through some doors around where you live and the response may surprise you. It can be a very good link with people who have no involvement with handicap and enables them to help a good cause in a painless way, besides possibly alleviating the loneliness of a family which is having to restrict its outings because of the child's handicap.

Appeals. This is always a very busy department in a national charity and it is no less so at MENCAP. There are two sister organizations, The Showbiz Car Club of Great Britain and the BacchUs Organization, helping to raise money and I need hardly add that all offers of help with fund-raising are very warmly welcomed!

The Spastics Society
Well known, of course, as the leading society in the world for the care, treatment, education and training of children and adults who have cerebral palsy. The society was

founded in January 1952 by a group of parents who were concerned about the neglected needs of their disabled children. It covers England and Wales and now has nearly 200 affiliated local groups throughout the country. Since its inception the Spastics Society has established 60 national schools and centres of various kinds to cater for the wide variety of needs among children and adults with cerebral palsy. The society also offers advisory and supportive services to anyone with cerebral palsy who approaches them either directly or through parents or professional contacts. They run the following departments:

Personal social services. This offers information, assessment and counselling services covering all aspects of disability and daily living activities, financial and other benefits, practical services, planning holidays and many other items. Overnight accommodation is available at Fitzroy Square; when I contacted the society to ask if the accommodation was available to cerebral-palsy sufferers who were mentally-handicapped (accompanied by parent or carer) the helpful man in the Information Department said, 'Yes, of course', and went on to describe the accommodation as 'a sort of hotel'. A range of aids and equipment is on display at Fitzroy Square (which houses Advice, Information and the Assessment Centre) and also in the Visiting Aids Centre which travels extensively through England and Wales. There is also a wide variety of opportunities for leisure activities and the Sports and Recreation Officer organizes both national and international activities and develops new leisure outlets.

Education. The Spastics Society runs seven schools for pupils of differing abilities aged five to eighteen. Four of these schools cater for pupils who are intellectually as well as physically disabled. Another specializes in assessing the learning potential of children who are so severely disabled that their level of ability is not so easily ascertained. The two other schools cater for physically-disabled pupils of average intelligence. In addition the society has a unit for physically-disabled children who have severe behaviour problems. The society has set up two further education centres for young people with cerebral palsy who need further time to mature and adjust to the outside world after the sheltered environment of school. It also maintains a college at Wallingford in Berkshire for training personnel of all disciplines who work with children or adults with disabilities.

Training and employment. The society has a sheltered workshop and seven industrial units which provide employment for men and women with cerebral palsy who are not able to compete for ordinary jobs. At its industrial training centre, courses are offered in light engineering, bench work and woodwork.

Accommodation and personal care. The Spastics Society's primary concern is to serve and promote the interests of people with cerebral palsy and their families, in all aspects of their lives. Among the various types of accommodation offered are two Family Help Units, one providing short-term care for children and one for adults, two day centres for young men and women with multiple disabilities, one of which offers weekly residential and some short-term care as well. They also have three seaside hotels for holiday and out-of-season bookings. One of these is specially for children and is run by the Stars Organization for Spastics.

Help at local level. The society's affiliated local groups run a further 100 establishments to help children and adults with cerebral palsy in their own areas. They include schools, day centres, work centres, holiday bungalows and caravans. Local groups also provide welfare services for people with cerebral palsy, such as help with aids and equipment and holidays.

The Down's Children's Association
This is still quite a baby in comparison with the two aforementioned organizations, but it is a very robust baby and is growing fast! It is the leading organization for helping parents and professionals with the care, treatment and training of children with Down's Syndrome. It has a resource centre in London and a research centre in Birmingham, a dozen branches and scores of self-help groups. In Scotland its sister organization is the Scottish Down's Syndrome Association. The association was founded in 1970 as a result of the efforts of Rex

Brinkworth, MBE, BA, DCP, a child psychologist who demonstrated that Down's children are less handicapped if they are given extra stimulation and training from the very earliest age. How does the association help?

(a) By encouraging new parents to embark on a detailed programme of stimulation, exercise and diet to bring the very best out of their child — a potential much greater than used to be thought.

(b) By providing a counselling service for parents at a time of shock and distress.

(c) By setting up local self-help groups so that parents can share their problems and help each other to adopt a positive approach to solving them.

(d) By providing information and advice about education, teenage problems, life after school, leaving home and housing.

(e) By promoting and carrying out research into ways of diminishing the effects of Down's Syndrome.

(f) By creating greater public awareness of the potential of Down's children, a more sympathetic understanding of their needs and greater respect for their right to lead fulfilling and useful lives. The association believes that the mere possession of Down's Syndrome in a new-born baby is not a qualification for it being allowed to die.

The association booklet which is sent out to new parents is very informative and is supplemented by leaflets — two which Maggie Emslie (the Director) gave me were 'Games to Develop Listening Ability' and 'Healthy Eating for your Child', both of which contained helpful information.

ASBAH (Association for Spina Bifida and Hydrocephalus)

While spina bifida is not known as a mentally-handicapping condition, nevertheless 80 per cent of people who suffer from it also develop hydrocephalus, and this, if not controlled in time, can cause some children to have difficulty in seeing in perspective, to lack concentration and to have learning difficulties. Hydrocephalus is a condition which can occur independently from spina bifida.

Early in the 1960s parents came together to form groups

for mutual support and to help handicapped children to lead a full life. There are now more than 80 local associations covering most of England, Wales and Northern Ireland (Scotland has its own association). In each locality meetings are held for the exchange of information and to plan events and projects. Members receive practical and financial help and local associations raise funds for these ends. It was from local associations that the idea for a national organization came and ASBAH was founded in 1966. Its aim is to give every support and help possible to those who, through no one's fault, are born with one or both of these disabilities, to their families and those who care for them.

Support is channelled through social work and welfare grants, and advice covers a variety of topics: the provision of aids and equipment, adaptation to property, accommodation, education, social development and independence training, leisure, occupation and employment. The stress caused by the birth of a severely handicapped child is considerable. There are many hurdles in the lives of such a family, as the handicaps of a spina-bifida child are multiple. The support of a specialist field worker, particularly in areas where the social services are under heavy pressure, does much to help families to cope with the strain. The association has now made over twenty such appointments and further expansion of the scheme is planned. In addition there is now a personal counselling service.

The need to understand the complex conditions is great and families, young adults and professional workers now look more and more to the association for information and advice. In the pressure of a hospital visit many questions remain unanswered. ASBAH provides an information service and publishes a range of books.

Research of a wide-ranging nature is in progress in this country and many parts of the world. Recently there have been encouraging results in the UK from a preliminary study on prevention of neural tube defects using multivitamin supplements. The research programme is of particular importance as abortion is only a very second best to prevention based on knowledge of the causes.

Funding. Support for research is an important part of the work of ASBAH. A large fund is necessary so that money is always available to support (without delay) any important project which might arise. ASBAH has a centre in Yorkshire, Five Oaks, which has been specially adapted to make it suitable for handicapped people. It offers an individual training programme and leisure courses such as fashion, photography, fishing and arts and crafts. Some social independence courses are held at Five Oaks and there is also a specially designed activities centre. Funds for this work are raised locally and nationally to meet increasing demands on the association's services. A grant from the Department of Health and Social Security assists, but 97 per cent of the work of the association is financed voluntarily. The problems are immense and call for support on an increasing scale.

Dr Barnardo's

Surely one of the best-known names among charities. Their history of caring goes back to the 1860s when Thomas Barnardo first pledged himself to help London's destitute, homeless children. There are not many 'orphans' any more, so Dr Barnardo's devotes its energies to children who are mentally, physically or emotionally handicapped. The following is a quote from their literature relating to mental handicap:

Mental handicap is a problem which, each year, affects thousands of families in this country. For them the joy and excitement of the birth of a baby can turn to disbelief when they are told that their young infant is mentally handicapped in some way. Some are so despairing that they totally reject their imperfect baby. In cases of severe handicap children may spend much of their early life in long-stay hospitals, but many parents feel strongly that their handicapped child is as much a part of the family as their other children and they prefer, where possible, to care for him or her in their own home. As a result, eight out of ten mentally-handicapped children in the UK now live at home with their parents.

Barnardo's, a firm believer in the importance of the family, shares the view that in most cases the best place for a handicapped child to be brought up is in the family. At the same time it realizes the enormous stress facing parents in this position. To help make it easier for the families to meet this challenge it has schemes which help them in various ways, from finding volunteers who will 'baby-sit' while parents have a much needed break, to making sure they know all about benefits to which they may be entitled.

In London, for instance, our recently established Southwark Project has now reached the stage where it can help to provide various services for families with handicapped children. These include an early counselling service which is offered when parents first learn that their baby is mentally handicapped; a toy library offering a range of specially selected toys which parents can borrow; an advice service and a scheme which puts parents in touch with other local families in which there are mentally-handicapped children. In the north-west, mentally-handicapped children have been helped in another way, thanks to a growing band of people who work with us as professional foster parents. We have been able to find foster homes in that area for eight more children who previously were living in children's homes or hostels. The north-west has also seen the official opening of the new premises being used by our Chorley Project. This is one of three Barnardo schemes in that part of the country which provide support services for mentally-handicapped children and their families. Between them, these three projects alone are helping a total of 270 families.

I am sure that many people will be as surprised as I was that this organization has become so involved in mental handicap. Just a brief word on their funding. Whilst they receive some funds from the Government for special schemes, Dr Barnardo's receives no money from the Government or other official bodies for running costs except contributions which local authorities make when they ask them to accept a child or youth into their care. They are dependent upon voluntary funds. For example, 70 per cent of the cost of most of their family support services — like educational toy libraries or play-buses which tour deprived areas — comes from individual donations from the public.

The Home Farm Trust
This charity believes that the handicapped should have the chance to grow up, leave home and enjoy independent lives. In its home, the trust has established a way of life in which they live and work together in large families,

lovingly cared for by professional staff. In this environment, many respond to new challenges and progress well beyond their original capacities. I will quote the *Aims and Objectives* from their own information pack:

In accepting that the quality of care is dependent on the collective commitment of all members of the 'caring team', whether members of the home staff or not:

1 To provide a flexible home-like environment which facilitates development to maximum potential and affords residents choice and options on the various life styles that are available.

2 To preserve the identity and personality of residents by respecting personal dignity, individuality and independence, to sustain morale and to safeguard individual right.

3 To recognize the detailed personal and social needs of individual residents and through assessment, monitoring and review of those needs, ensure appropriate levels of care and the formulation of careful, realistic forward plans for their future.

4 To promote and preserve their adult status in co-operation with their families and to educate them in the basic rights of citizenship.

5 To supplement and ultimately replace the warmth of the family home.

6 To raise the self-esteem of residents to a level at which their satisfaction in life is continually enhanced.

7 To foster a community spirit both inside and outside the home.

8 To afford residents the opportunity to live outside the home in the community and if possible to work there with the aid of social support from the trust.

9 To ensure staffing levels are adequate and that staff are afforded support and training in line with internationally accepted standards and that their needs and performance are regularly reviewed in the light of the trust's philosophy.

10 To ensure that the full range of facilities provided by the National Health Service is available to our residents and that the necessary liaison with the primary health-care services functions smoothly and effectively.

A great deal more information about their work is available, which I obviously can't go into — they are more than willing to send literature to anyone who asks for it. I wasn't very surprised to read that they have a waiting list — it all sounded just the sort of place that I would like for James were it a little nearer home. The rural life doesn't suit everyone, of course, but the houses in the booklet all looked delightful and the settings seemed to be very tranquil — which even appeals to a dyed-in-the-wool Londoner like me! (When you've got five sons, four of whom are adult and still living at home, tranquillity can be in short supply!) The address of the Home Farm Trust is given on page 228.

In-Touch

I have to admit that I hadn't come across this charity until I started researching for the 'help' chapter of this book (James's problem being rather run-of-the-mill) and I was absolutely bowled over by it. It is a Mental Handicap Contact and Information Service run by Ann Worthington, presumably from her own house in Sale, Cheshire. The object of the organization is to put parents of children with rare disorders in touch with each other and when I read her newsletter I couldn't believe that there were so many different syndromes from which people could suffer. On a large sheet of paper there were three columns of different syndromes and disorders, listed in alphabetical order. Mrs Worthington gives titles of the latest books on the various subjects of interest to her members, together with information about videos, etc. There is also a section in her letter concerning chronic physical disorders in adults (e.g. irritable bowel syndrome) so help is available to all sorts of people with all sorts of problems, not just parents of children with mental handicap. The organization works in close touch with Contact-a-Family.

USEFUL ADDRESSES

Advocacy Alliance, 2nd Floor, 115 Golden Lane, London
EC1Y 0TJ (01–253 2056)

ASBAH (Association for Spina Bifida and Hydrocephalus),
Tavistock House North, Tavistock Square, London, WC1
9HJ (01–388 1382)

Autistic Society, National, 276 Willesden Lane, London,
NW2 5RB (01–451 3844)

Blind, Royal National Institute for the, 224 Great Portland
Street, London W1N 6AA (01–388 1266)

Campaign for Mentally-Handicapped People 12a Maddox
Street, London W1R 9PL (01–492 0727/8)

Camphill Village Trust, Delrow House, Hillfield Lane,
Aldenham, Watford, WD2 8DJ (092–76–6006)

Care Concern, Ruthin, Clwyd, North Wales (082–42–4343)

Care for the Mentally Handicapped, Central Office, 9 Weir
Road, Kibworth, Leicestershire (053–753–3225)

Cheyne Centre for Spastic Children, 61 Cheyne Walk,
Chelsea, London SW3 (01–352 8434)

Children's Bureau, National, 8 Wakley Street, London,
EC1V (01–278 9441)

Contact-a-Family, 16 Strutton Ground, London SW1
(01–222 2695)

Crossroads Care Attendant Schemes Ltd, Association of, 94a
Coton Road, Rugby, Warwickshire CV21 4LN
(0788–61536)

Deaf Children's Society, National, 45 Hereford Road,
London W2 5AH (01–229 9272)

Deaf, Royal National Institute for the, 105 Gower Street,
London WC1E 6AH (01–387 8033)

Department of Health and Social Security (DHSS),

Alexander Fleming House, Elephant and Castle, London SE1 6BY (01–407 5522)

Dial UK, Dial House, 117 High Street, Clay Cross, Derbyshire (0246–864498)

Disability Alliance, 25 Denmark Street, London WC2 8NJ (01–240 0806)

Disability and Rehabilitation, Royal Association for, (RADAR), 25 Mortimer Street, London W1N 8AB (01–637 5400)

Disabled Living Foundation, 380/384 Harrow Road, London W9 2HU (01–289 6111)

Down's Children's Association, 4 Oxford Street, London W1N 9FL (01–580 0511/2)

Dr Barnardo's, Tanners Lane, Barkingside, Ilford, Essex (01–550 8822)

Elizabeth Fitzroy Homes, Caxton House, Station Approach, Haslemere, Surrey GU27 2PE (0428–52001)

Environment for the Handicapped, Centre of the, 126 Albert Street, London NW1 7NE (01–482 2247)

Epilepsy Association, British, Crowthorne House, New Wokingham Road, Wokingham, Berkshire RG11 3AY (034–46 3122)

Epileptics, National Society for, Chalfont Centre, Chalfont St Peter, Bucks (024–07–3991)

Family Fund, PO Box 50, York YO1 1UY (0904–21115)

Federation of Gateway Clubs, National, 123 Golden Lane, London EC1Y ORT (01–253 9433)

Health Visitors Association, 36 Eccleston Square, London SW1 (01–834 9523)

Home Farm Trust Homes for the Mentally Handicapped, 54 Queen Square, Bristol BS1 4LH (0272 23746)

Institute of Mental Handicap, British, Information and Resource Centre, Wolverhampton Road, Kidderminster, Worcestershire DY10 3PP (0562–850251)

International Cerebral Palsy Society, 5a Netherhall Gardens, London NW3 5RN (01–794 9761)

In-Touch Trust, 10 Norman Road, Sale, Cheshire M33 3DF (061–962–4441)

Kith and Kids, 27 Old Park Ridings, Grange Park, London N21 2EX (01–360 5621)

Leonard Cheshire Foundation, 26–29 Maunsel Street, London SW1P 2QN (01–828 1822)

MacIntyre Communities, Westoning Manor, Westoning, Bedfordshire (0525–713861)

MENCAP, Royal Society for Mentally-Handicapped Children and Adults, 123 Golden Lane, London EC1Y ORT (01–253 9433)

MIND (National Association for Mental Health), 22 Harley Street, London W1N 2ED (01–637 0741)

One-to-One, 123–5 Gloucester Place, London W1H 3PJ (01–486 0074)

Phenylketonuria and Allied Disorders, National Society for, 14 Newfound Drive, Cringleford, Norwich, Norfolk NR4 7RY (0603–54811)

Playboard (Association for Children's Play and Recreation Ltd), Britannic House, 50 Great Charles Street, Queensway, Birmingham B3 2LP (021–233 3399)

Riding for the Disabled Association, Avenue 'R', National Agricultural Centre, Kenilworth, Warwickshire CV8 2LY (0203–56107)

Rudolph Steiner Schools, Anthroposophical Society in Great Britain, 35 Park Road, London NW1 (01–723 4400)

Scottish Society for the Mentally Handicapped, 13 Elm Bank Street, Glasgow G2 4QA (041–226 4541)

SESAME, Christ Church, 27 Blackfriars Road, London SE1 (01–633 9705)

SHAPE, 9 Fitzroy Square, London W1P 6AE (01–388 9622/9744)

Spastics Society, 12 Park Crescent, London W1N 4EQ (01–636 5020)

Special Education, National Council for, 1 Wood Street, Stratford-upon-Avon, Warwickshire (0789–205332)

Speech-Impaired Children, Association for All (AFASIC), 347 Central Markets, London EC1A 9NH (01–236 3632/6487)

SPOD (Sexual and Personal Relationships of the Disabled), 286 Camden Road, London N7 0BJ (01–607 8851/2)

Sports Association for People with Mental Handicap (UK), c/o The Sports Council, 16 Upper Woburn Place, London WC1H 0QP (01–388 1277)

Students, National Bureau for Handicapped, 40 Brunswick Square, London WC1 (01–278 3459/3450)

Toy Libraries Association, Seabrook House, Wyllyotts Manor, Darkes Lane, Potters Bar, Herts (0707–44571)

Voluntary Organizations, National Council of, (NCVO), 26 Bedford Square, London WC1B 3HU (01–636 4066)

Youth Hostels Association (England and Wales), Trevelyan House, St Stephen's Hill, St Albans, Herts AL1 2DY (0727–55215)

The above list is only a selection of general and specialist organizations. Most are national, or at least regional, in their interest and influence. For a more comprehensive list, see the following:

FURTHER READING

The Disability Rights Handbook (published by the Disability Alliance, 25 Denmark Street, London WC2 8NJ and updated annually in November)

Charities Digest (published by the Family Welfare Association, 501–5, Kingsland Road, Dalston, London E8 4AU)

Useful Addresses for Parents With A Handicapped Child (published by 'In-Touch' – address as before)

Parents Information Bulletin (Published by MENCAP)

All the above books are available from the MENCAP Bookshop at 123 Golden Lane, London EC1Y ORT (or you could try your local bookshop, or W.H. Smith).

If you happen to be visiting London, I am reliably informed that there is an excellent Reference Library at the King's Fund Centre, 126 Albert Street, London NW1.

INDEX

NOTE: Handicapped refers to mentally handicapped unless otherwise stated.

benefits, statutory,   82, 156, 160,
  212–13
  for elderly person,   206
bereavement and handicapped
  person,   142–3, 205, 207, 209–10
  see also: death; Financial Provision
    Advisory Service
Bicknell, Professor Joan,   14–17
birth,   19–28
Bliss (language programme),   127
bonding,   76, 151
brain damage,   35, 36
Brinkworth, Rex,   219–20
British Hospital for Mothers and
  Babies (Ma's and Ba's),   23–4, 30,
  53
bronchitis,   61–2
Brook Hospital,   77
brothers and sisters
  attitude to handicapped
    child,   129–30
  guilt feelings,   131
  problems and needs of,   68, 131–2
  role of,   129–31

cardiac sphincter, slack,   80
case conferences (school),   126
catarrh,   59, 177
Cecil Rooms Junior Training
  Centre,   84, 87, 88
  see also: training centre
cerebral palsy,   33–4, 36, 60, 217–19
  see also: Spastics Society
Chamberlain, Paul,   178–9, 181–3
charities,   214–225
  see also: addresses; ASBAH;
    Down's Children's Association;
    Family Fund; Home Farm Trust;
    MENCAP; Spastics Society
Chase, Dr,   53
checklists (Stamina Papers):
  adults at home,   160–1
  adult in hostel/home,   161–3
  after diagnosis,   48–9
  ante-natal services,   27
  child at home,   156–7
  elderly person,   208
  family support services,   67–8
  foster homes,   157–8
  hostels and homes,   158–9
  retirement,   205–6
chest infections,   59, 61, 78
Children and Young Persons Act
  (1963),   111
chiropody,   206
chromosome, additional,   41, 175

Chronically Sick and Disabled Persons
  Act (1970),   111, 112, 113, 155,
  156, 162, 204, 206
clinic
  importance of visits to,   52–3,
    54–5, 56, 64, 71
  reluctance to attend,   57
  as source of advice and
    support,   65–6, 212
clubs
  Focus,   114, 139–40
  Gateway,   22, 119, 139–41, 185,
    199
  and holidays,   114–5
cmv (cytomegalovirus) screening,   27
college of further education,   167,
  169, 170
communication, lack of,   90, 164
communication, non-verbal,   173
community care,   12, 49, 111, 161,
  202
Community Health Council,   127
community, as member of,   194–211
Community Mental Handicap Team
  (CMHT),   66, 67, 68, 69, 205, 207
Community (District) Nurse,   81
Community Service Volunteers,   70
consultants, attitude of,   12–13, 30,
  65, 120–1
contact with similar parents,   55, 57,
  59–60, 63, 70
  see also: In-Touch
Contact-a-Family,   225
contraception for handicapped
  person,   181–3
  see also: sex education
contract work,   167
convulsions,   35
Coram Foundation, Thomas,   152–3
counselling
  advisory services,   216, 218,
    220–3
  by CMHT,   69
  genetic,   27, 51–2, 55, 77–8, 183
  lack of,   30, 31, 55
  need for,   53, 57, 58, 62, 156, 160
  and normalization,   183
  on sexual needs of handicapped
    person,   180–1
Course, Alan,   135–6, 181

day-care centre, provision
  of,   99–100, 157, 171
  and PRMH,   173
death
  of handicapped child,   101–2